FIELD GUIDE
TO THE MAMMALS OF
SOUTHERN AFRICA

FIELD GUIDE TO THE
MAMMALS
OF SOUTHERN AFRICA

CHRIS AND TILDE STUART

RALPH
CURTIS
BOOKS

Cover photographs: (top left) Buffalo (Gerald Cubitt); (top right) Lion (Gerald Cubitt); (bottom left) Cape Fur Seal (Chris and Tilde Stuart); (bottom right) Waterbuck (Gerald Cubitt); (spine) Burchell's Zebra (Daryl Balfour).

Consultant: Professor J.D. Skinner, Director, The Mammal Research Institute, University of Pretoria.

Ralph Curtis Books Publishing
P. O. Box 349
Sanibel Island
Florida, U.S.A.
33957-0349

Library of Congress Catalog Card number: 99-74801

First published 1988
Second Edition 1993
Second U.S. Edition (softcover) 1999

Photoset by CTP Book Printers (Pty) Ltd, Parow
Reproduction by Hirt & Carter Cape (Pty) Ltd, Cape Town
Printed and bound by Kyodo Printing Co (Singapore) Pte Ltd

ISBN 0 88359 047 6

Contents

Acknowledgements

We gratefully acknowledge the help we received from many friends and colleagues. No doubt many more names should appear below, and we ask pardon of those who assisted us in different ways but whose names have unintentionally escaped mention.

Pierre Swanepoel and Lloyd Wingate of the Kaffrarian Museum in King William's Town, Dr. Naas Rautenbach of the Transvaal Museum, and the staff of the South African Museum are thanked for allowing us access to the mammal collections in their care.

Our sincere thanks for information, photographs and other assistance go to the following: Prof. Paul K. Anderson (University of Calgary); Dr. Ric Bernard (Rhodes University); Dr. Hu Berry (Etosha Ecological Institute); Dr. Bill Branch (Port Elizabeth Museum); Dr. John Carlyon; Dr. Alan Channing (University of the Western Cape); Dr. Jeremy David (Sea Fisheries Research Institute); Dr. Nico Dippenaar (Transvaal Museum); Anthony Duckworth and Laura Fielden (University of Natal); Patrick J. Frere (Langata Bird Sanctuary); Mike Griffin (S.W.A. Directorate of Nature Conservation and Recreation Resorts); Dr. Hans Grobler (Natal Parks Board); Dr. Anthony Hall-Martin (National Parks Board); Dr. Graham Hickman (University of Natal); Niels Jacobsen (Transvaal Division of Nature Conservation); Howard Langley (Rondevlei Bird Sanctuary); Malan Lindeque (Etosha Ecological Institute); Ian Manning; Dr. Daan Marais; Penny Meakin; Dr. Gus Mills (National Parks Board); Peter le S. Milstein (Transvaal Division of Nature Conservation); Pam Newby; Harald Nicolay; Guy Palmer (Cape Department of Nature and Environmental Conservation); Professor Mike Perrin (University of Natal); Dr. Naas Rautenbach (Transvaal Museum); Dr. Graham Ross (Port Elizabeth Museum); Judith A. Rudnai; †Dr. Reay Smithers; Dr. Steven Tischhauser; Tony Tomkinson; Dr. H. van Rompaey; Alan Weaving (Albany Museum); Viv Wilson (Chipangali Wildlife Trust); Lloyd R. Wingate (Kaffrarian Museum).

Our special thanks go to Dr. Merlin Tuttle, founder of Bat Conservation International (page 30), for his encouragement and photographs, and to Professor John Skinner and the University of Pretoria for permission to reproduce certain of the spoor drawings from *The Mammals of the Southern African Subregion* by the late Reay H. N. Smithers.

Finally, we should also like to express our appreciation to the staff of Struik Publishers, and in particular to Peter Borchert and Eve Gracie for their support and advice and to John Comrie-Greig for the final editing of the manuscript.

Chris and Tilde Stuart
Greyton, 1988

Photographic credits

All photographs in this book are by the authors except for those listed below. Copyright vests in the individual photographers.

Copyright in the whale and dolphin paintings vests in the artist, David C. Thorpe.

P. K. Anderson: 251 (top left, top right)
Daryl Balfour: 173 (top)
Ric Bernard: 55 (top, bottom left)
Peter Best: 255 (top, centre left)
M. Bester: 255 (centre right, bottom)
W. R. Branch: 73 (bottom)
Tony Bruton: 101 (top left)
John Carlyon: 49 (centre left), 51 (bottom left), 81 (bottom), 83 (centre right), 117 (bottom), 125 (bottom left), 157 (top), 199 (top left)
Thomas Carr: 253 (top)
Alan Channing: 93 (top right)
Gerald Cubitt: 77 (top), 79 (bottom right), 95 (top), 97 (bottom), 155 (top right), 203 (bottom)
W. de Beer (National Parks Board): 163 (top)
N. Dippenaar: 41 (bottom)
P. J. Frere: 169 (top, bottom right)
Mike Griffin: 107 (lower centre), 117 (centre left)
J. H. Grobler: 35 (centre), 133 (top), 155 (centre right), 195 (bottom right), 201 (top left)
Graham C. Hickman: 33 (top, centre), 35 (bottom)
N. H. G. Jacobsen: 43 (centre right), 93 (bottom), 105 (centre left), 111 (bottom)
C. H. Langley: 41 (top), 109 (top right), 219 (top right)
Ian Manning: 191 (top left, top right)
Daan Marais: 141 (bottom), 147 (top), 153 (top right)
W. Massyn (National Parks Board): 39 (top left, centre left), 61 (bottom right), 63 (top right), 65 (centre), 69 (bottom right), 73 (top right, bottom right), 85 (top), 105 (top left), 109 (bottom left)

Penny Meakin: 83 (top, centre left), 199 (top right)
M. Mills: 149 (bottom left)
Peter le S. Milstein: 215 (top left, top right)
E. Moll: 223 (bottom)
Rory Nefdt: 59 (bottom right)
H. Nicolay: 145 (bottom)
U. de V. Pienaar: 135 (top)
I. L. Rautenbach: 43 (bottom left), 51 (centre left), 53 (top, bottom left), 57 (top left), 59 (top right), 63 (bottom left), 65 (top left, top right, bottom right), 67 (top left, top right), 69 (top), 71 (top left, top right), 73 (bottom left)
Sea Fisheries Research Institute: 253 (centre, bottom)
Hazel Smithers: 135 (bottom)
Peter Steyn: 89 (bottom)
Steven Tischhauser: 159 (top)
Tony Tomkinson: 189 (top, bottom)
Transvaal Nature Conservation Division, Pretoria/t.d.: 209 (bottom right)
Merlin Tuttle: 47 (top right, bottom right), 49 (top, bottom right)
J. D. Visser: 35 (top), 57 (bottom) 67 (bottom), 81 (top), 87 (top right) 95 (bottom), 105 (centre right), 119 (top right)
H. von Rompaey: 145 (centre right), 147 (centre left, bottom left, bottom right)
Alan Weaving: 219 (bottom left)
Lloyd Wingate: 49 (bottom left), 51 (top, bottom right), 57 (centre left), 59 (centre right), 63 (bottom right), 71 (bottom right), 107 (upper centre)
E. A. Zaloumis: 129 (bottom), 207 (bottom)

Introduction

Compared with the birds (8 900 species) or the fish (30 000 species) the mammal group is a small one. It contains between 4 000 and 4 500 living species, of which some 337 species are currently known to occur in the Southern African Subregion. Some of these, however, are known from very few, or even single, records. The richest period of mammal diversity was during the late Tertiary, when an estimated three times as many mammal species roamed the earth than do so today. Taxonomists are constantly revising and reassessing the scientific status of many mammals, particularly the smaller species such as bats, shrews and small rodents. This often results in scientific names being changed and, on occasion, new species being described; Juliana's Golden Mole, for example, was described from the Transvaal in 1972 and the Long-tailed Forest Shrew from the southern Cape as recently as 1978. The bats are especially mobile, and it is very likely that additional species from this group will be discovered and added to the faunal complement of southern Africa in due course.

Mammals have a number of common characteristics that set them apart from other vertebrates: they breathe with lungs; they possess a four-chambered heart; they have three delicate bones in the middle ear; females have mammary glands that produce milk for suckling the young; and nearly all species have a covering of body hair.

The Southern African Subregion – defined as that part of the African Continent and its coastal waters south of the Cunene and Zambezi rivers – can be divided into six major biotic zones (see below and map), each differing in climate and vegetation. This does, however, present an oversimplified picture, and each of these zones can be further subdivided into many different habitat and vegetation types.

1. Desert

Desert is characterized by its very low rainfall (usually less than 100 mm per year) and sparse plant growth. Extensive areas may be devoid of any vegetation, being covered by sand-dunes or consisting of flat gravel plains and rugged hill country. Several species of mammal have evolved mechanisms that help them to survive in this harsh environment. In the Southern African Subregion this biotic zone is represented by the Namib Desert of South West Africa/Namibia.

2. Arid zone

Areas classed as 'arid' receive higher rainfall than true desert, but this rarely exceeds 500 mm per year. In southern Africa, rainfall is at its lowest in the west, gradually increasing towards the east. The Kalahari, Karoo, Bushmanland, Namaqualand and Damaraland fall within the arid zone. The southern section, *viz.* Bushmanland, Namaqualand and the Karoo, consists mainly of extensive rocky plains and isolated hills and hill ranges, with a vegetation comprising low, woody shrubs and succulents. Much of the area is veined with river courses which are vegetated along their banks with bushes and low trees. In the northern parts, for example the Kalahari 'Desert' of the northern Cape and Botswana, sandy soils are more prevalent with low (often acacia) trees and bushes, and relatively good grass cover. This zone once supported vast numbers of ungulates, but the free-roaming herds of Springbok, Red Hartebeest, Blue Wildebeest, Eland and Burchell's Zebra have diminished greatly and are now restricted to the more sparsely populated parts of Botswana.

3. Savanna woodland and 4. Savanna grassland

The savanna biome can be divided into two zones, *viz.* savanna woodland mostly in the north, and savanna grassland in the south. Savanna woodland,

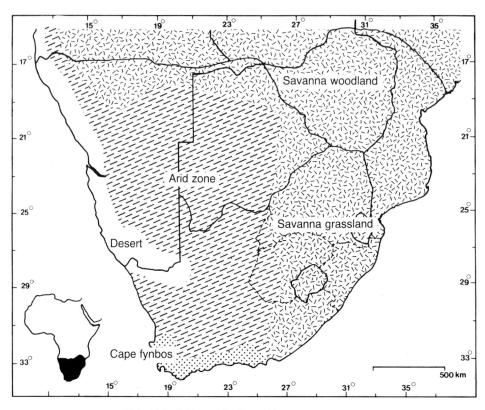

Major biotic divisions of Southern Africa

which extends from the northern Transvaal down the coastal belt of Natal to the eastern Cape, includes mopane woodland, thorn scrub and dense woodland habitats in the east. Grass cover ranges from sparse to good. It is within this zone that many of the subregion's major game reserves are situated. Savanna grassland consists largely of mixed grassland, with tree and shrub growth more or less restricted to the edges of watercourses and to hills and more rugged terrain. Much of the formerly extensive savanna grassland of the southern Transvaal has been destroyed by cultivation or drastically modified by overgrazing.

5. Cape fynbos
This small but significant zone is restricted to the western and southern Cape, and its vegetation can be broadly divided into mountain and lowland fynbos. This very limited area is so rich in plant species that it is classed as one of the world's six 'floral kingdoms' although it covers only 0,04 per cent of the world's land surface area. The vegetation is dominated largely by evergreen shrubs and bushes. The fynbos zone has suffered more than any other in the subregion from agricultural and other human influences, but it is not a mammal-rich region.

6. Indigenous forest
The sixth zone, indigenous forest, is poorly represented in southern Africa. It is restricted, in limited pockets, to the southern and eastern Cape, Natal, the eastern and northern Transvaal, the eastern highlands of Zimbabwe and the

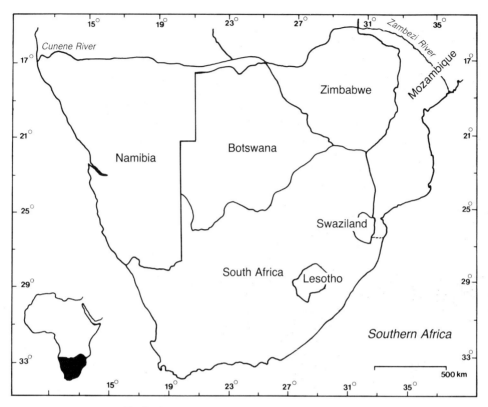

The Southern African Subregion

adjacent areas of Mozambique. Because of its fragmented and widely scattered nature, this zone is not shown on the map. Several mammal species, such as the Giant Golden Mole and the Samango Monkey, are found only in this habitat.

(Although falling within the larger savanna zone, the Okavango and Linyanti swamps deserve separate mention. The Okavango Swamp of north-western Botswana is the largest inland river delta in the world and southern Africa's most important wetland. The Linyanti Swamp is situated in eastern Caprivi. These two areas are home to many species of water-adapted mammal, including Sitatunga, Lechwe and Hippopotamus. Both swamps are under increasing human pressure and there is an urgent need for careful resource and conservation planning).

How to use this field guide

This book covers the area south of the Cunene River in the west and the Zambezi River in the east. The Atlantic Ocean laps the western seaboard, and the southern and eastern shores are bounded by the Indian Ocean.

The main purpose of this field guide is to enable the observer to identify mammals in the wild. One of the difficulties facing the mammal-watcher is that many species are small and secretive, and therefore rarely seen or difficult to find. In addition, many of the smaller species can be identified only by a specialist who has access to comparative study material of skins and skulls, usually in a museum. In the case of the whales and dolphins, the marine environment simply does not lend itself to easy observation. Little difficulty should of course be experienced in identifying to species level the larger, medium-sized and some of the smaller mammals. However, for many species identification will normally be possible only to family and generic level; this applies particularly to the golden moles, shrews, bats and small rodents, where positive identification may require expert examination of the skull, teeth and sometimes even the chromosomes. Where this is the case, it is pointed out in the text. Each species account is divided into sections under subheadings to enable the reader to look up that aspect which he finds of particular interest.

As is the case with bird-watching, the tools of the mammal-watcher are simple: a good pair of binoculars, a notebook and pencil, and a suitable mammal reference book. Care should be taken when identifying juvenile animals as they may differ considerably from the adults. This applies particularly to the antelopes, where subadults of one species may be confused with the adults of another species. Another aspect that should be borne in mind is that a number of species possess one or more subspecies or races that differ from each other in colour, pattern or size. This is mentioned in the species account where applicable.

Description. Descriptions in this field guide concentrate on external features that will assist the reader in species identification. Follow these six steps when identifying a mammal:
1. Decide to which group the mammal belongs. (Is it an antelope, or does it belong to the dog family?)
2. Estimate the shoulder height, total length and tail length if possible. (Is the tail shorter than the head and body? Are the ears long or short?)
3. Look for outstanding features. (Does it have white or black stripes, spots or a bushy tail?)
4. Check the distribution map to ascertain whether the animal occurs in the area.
5. Check the habitat preference of the mammal. (You will not see a klipspringer bounding across open plains, or a black-backed jackal in dense forest.)
6. Make a note of any specific behavioural trait which may aid in identification. (Did you see a large group together, or did an individual busy itself digging a burrow?)

Identification pointers. The main aids to identifying a species are summarized in each species account, and prominent features are highlighted under the heading '*Identification pointers*'. Where one species is similar to or could be confused with another, their distinguishing features are also mentioned (for example, the Side-striped and Black-backed Jackals).

Distribution. A glance at the distribution map will give a quick indication of a species' distribution within southern Africa. It should be remembered that the scale of the maps is such that only general distribution patterns can be given.

For example, although the Rock Dassie is shown to have a continuous distribution, it can clearly only occur where suitable habitat is available. Always consult the notes on a species' habitat preference in conjunction with the distribution map.

Habitat. An indication is given in the text of the habitats favoured by each species. It should be borne in mind, however, that a species may be encountered within other habitats.

Behaviour. Behavioural characteristics which may aid in identification are given preference, but other aspects of interest are also mentioned.

Food and *Reproduction*. The notes under these headings may assist in identifying a mammal, but are usually given for general interest.

As a further aid to identification, a spoor identification chart has been provided. It is not exhaustive, but includes the tracks of those species which are most likely to be encountered, or which are particularly distinctive. The 'reading' of tracks and signs adds a fascinating dimension to mammal-watching; a great deal of information may be gleaned without the animal itself being observed. (See page 256.)

Measurements. The most useful measurement in the field identification of larger and medium-sized mammals is shoulder height. Other measurements are given as an aid to determining whether a mammal is 'small', 'medium-sized' or 'large'. A useful method of learning to judge measurements is to cut pieces of wood into known lengths and place these at different distances. With practice, you should be able to apply these estimates to mammals in the field. All measurements given here are metric, and it is important to note that **average** figures are given for each species. It should always be remembered that these measurements can vary considerably within a species and the figures given in this book should be taken only as a guide. In the case of antelope, two horn measurements are provided: the average length, and the record length as given in *Rowland Ward's Records of Big Game*.

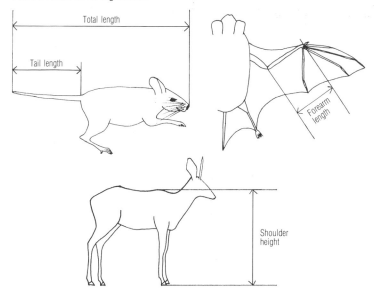

13

Conservation and wildlife management

During the past 2 000 years, approximately 200 species of mammals and birds are believed to have become extinct – one species every ten years. This rate has accelerated, with many of these species having disappeared during the course of this century. In southern Africa, two species of mammals have become extinct in recent times: the Quagga, *Equus quagga*, and the Blue Antelope or Bluebuck, *Hippotragus leucophaeus*. The Quagga once occurred in large herds on the southern and central plain of southern Africa, but was driven to extinction by hunting and competition with domestic stock. The last quagga died in Amsterdam Zoo in 1883. Present thinking is leaning towards the theory that the quagga was simply the southernmost subspecies of the plains or Burchell's Zebra. But even if current research should prove this to be the case, the extinction of this distinctive subspecies is still inexcusable.

The Blue Antelope, on the other hand, was almost certainly a full species. At the time of the arrival of the first European settlers at the Cape of Good Hope, it would appear that this close relative of the Roan and Sable Antelopes was already declining in numbers and range. At that time it was restricted to the area now known as the Overberg in the south-western Cape, although the fossil and sub-fossil record shows that it was at one time more widely spread to the east and west along the coastal plain. It is theorized that the decline of the Blue Antelope, like the Quagga, was a result of its having to compete for grazing with the sheep of the indigenous people of the Cape, and was accelerated with the arrival of the European settlers and their fire-arms. It finally disappeared around 1799-1800, gaining the dubious distinction of being the first mammal recorded to have become extinct on the African continent in historic times.

The Cape Mountain Zebra, the Bontebok, the Black Wildebeest and the Square-lipped Rhinoceros have all come perilously close to the brink of extinction. Fortunately, however, these once numerous species were protected in good time, and their futures now seem secure. Many species have been eradicated from their original ranges, and we will never again see Elephant herds making their way across the sand flats within sight of Cape Town, or hear Lions roaring in the Nuweveld Mountains above Beaufort West. The Hook-lipped Rhinoceros was once to be found throughout southern Africa; today, it occurs only in a handful of sanctuaries in the north and east, with some 60 per cent of the survivors inhabiting the Zambezi Valley of Zimbabwe. Other species, such as Oribi, the Roan and Sable Antelopes, Wild Dog and Riverine Rabbit, are all currently a cause for concern to conservationists.

The development of modern technology in southern Africa has frequently encouraged wasteful and exploitative use of the natural environment. Apart from the direct hunting of wild mammals, probably the single greatest factor that has influenced our wildlife is the uncontrolled manner in which agriculture has modified or completely changed the character of many habitats and vegetation types. Competition with domestic stock for food, cultivation, overgrazing and soil erosion are factors which have contributed to the decline of our wild mammal populations. Predators that include domestic animals in their diet were, and are, trapped or poisoned; because it is impossible to restrict control to the species that has caused the damage, many thousands of non-target animals, including the Bat-eared Fox, small grey mongoose and a variety of harmless rodents, are still killed each year. Problem animal management (or 'vermin control' as it used to be called) is a field that deserves far greater attention in order to reduce the death toll amongst harmless species and to increase selectivity for the real problem animals.

The pivotal problem, of course, is human overpopulation and the resulting demands on the environment. Man creates or encourages pressures on the environment, and as a result the mammal fauna is adversely affected. It is our responsibility to achieve a compromise between development and destruction which will allow man and nature to live in harmony.

Although it is often difficult to balance economics and conservation, there is a growing awareness that wildlife can increasingly help to pay its way. Africa, with its vast – but diminishing – mammal resources, draws tourists and sport-hunters to its many sanctuaries and game-farms. Carefully managed game populations, such as the elephant and buffalo in the Kruger National Park in South Africa and Hwange National Park in Zimbabwe, together with the many game-farms in South Africa, South West Africa/Namibia and Zimbabwe, can provide recreational outlets for city-dwellers and employment for country-dwellers while at the same time producing red meat and other products that generate income. In the case of the privately owned game-farms, landowners have found that this is a profitable form of land use. Many such farms are situated on marginal agricultural land, with low livestock-carrying capacities. Game species, long adapted to these areas, are able to thrive without the costly dipping and dosing programmes associated with sheep, goat and cattle husbandry. In parts of Transvaal and South West Africa/Namibia, this may be the only economically viable form of land use.

Many conservation-orientated people find the commercial aspects of conservation and wildlife utilization objectionable, and believe that man has a moral duty to protect and not to exploit the environment and its biota. Although this is a morally correct standpoint, it is one that is becoming increasingly unrealistic. It would be difficult to convince a farmer to conserve large numbers of springbok and blesbok merely for the sake of conservation; if he cannot be assured of a cash return for his large game herds, he would go back to sheep- and goat-farming. By the same token, the suburban gardener cannot be expected to accept the regular destruction of his potato-patch by molerats with equanimity.

Programmes to conserve the mammals of southern Africa are closely tied to habitat conservation. It is no good conserving a species or group of species if the habitat to which they are adapted is not also protected. But in the last resort mankind must also be convinced of the necessity of managing his own population and keeping it in check.

'Unwittingly for the most part, but right around the world, we are eliminating the panoply of life. We elbow species off the planet, we deny room to entire communities of nature, we domesticate the Earth. With growing energy and ingenuity, we surpass ourselves time and again in our efforts to exert dominion over fowl of the air and fish of the sea.

'We do all this in the name of human advancement. Yet instead of making better use of lands we have already to our use, we proclaim our need to expand into every last corner of the Earth. Our response to natural environments has changed little for thousands of years. We dig them up, we chop them down, we burn them, we drain them, we pave them over, we poison them in order to mould them to our image. We homogenize the globe.

'Eventually we may achieve our aim, by eliminating every 'competitor' for living space on the crowded Earth. When the last creature has been accounted for, we shall have made ourselves masters of all creation. We shall look around, and we shall see nothing but each other. Alone at last.'

Norman Myers.

Family introductions

The following are general accounts of the mammal families and subfamilies occurring in southern Africa.

INSECTIVORES Order Insectivora

Golden Moles Family Chrysochloridae
Fifteen species occur in southern Africa but most are inadequately known as they are difficult to trap and are rarely seen because of their subterranean life-style. Some are known only from very restricted geographical areas. They leave characteristic domed tunnels just below the soil surface and not the mounds or heaps normally pushed up by molerats. All golden moles are small (the largest has a total length of 23 cm), and have no external tail. The head is wedge-shaped, with a horny pad at the tip of the muzzle which is used for burrowing. They are blind and their ears are merely small openings through the fur without pinnae. The hindlegs (with 5 digits each) are less well developed than the forelegs (with 4 digits); the third digit of each forefoot carries a long, heavy claw to facilitate digging. Thirteen species have smooth, dense and glossy fur but the two larger species have longer, coarse hair. Golden moles have been aptly described as 'animated powder-puffs'. They show a marked preference for looser, sandy soils. They are not related to molerats (Family Bathyergidae, page 22).
Key features: Tail, eyes and ears not visible; glossy fur; surface tunnels; do not have pair of large incisors in upper and lower jaw.

Hedgehog Family Erinaceidae
There is only one species in the subregion. It is characterized by its small size (total length 22 cm), and by the short, stiff spines which cover the back and sides. It has a pointed snout and a band of white hair across the forehead. Its tail is not visible. Nocturnal.
Key features: Spine-covered back and sides; usually brownish in colour; curls up if threatened.

Elephant-shrews Family Macroscelididae
Eight species occur in the subregion. All are small (the largest has a head-and-body length of 19 cm) and are characterized by the elongated, constantly twitching, trunk-like snout. The ears are rounded and prominent, and the eyes are large. Hindlegs and -feet are much longer than forelegs and -feet. The tail is about the same length as the head and body and is only sparsely haired. If disturbed, elephant-shrews can move very rapidly.
Key features: Small and mouse-like but with long, mobile trunk-like snout.

Shrews Family Soricidae
Sixteen species have been recorded from the subregion. All are small to very small (largest has head-and-body length of 12 cm) with a long, narrow and wedge-shaped muzzle (not as elongated and mobile as in elephant-shrews). The tail is usually shorter than the head-and-body length and the legs are short. The fur is short, soft, and in most species dark in colour. Most species are associated with damp habitats. Some species are extremely difficult to identify in the field and careful examination of the teeth, skull and even chromosome structure is often required.
Key features: Small and mouse-like; long, wedge-shaped head; tiny eyes.

BATS Order Chiroptera
All bats belong to the order Chiroptera, which is divided into two distinct suborders: the suborder Megachiroptera contains the fruit-eating bats and the suborder Microchiroptera contains the insect-eating bats. At the present time

seven species of fruit-bats and 67 species of insectivorous bats have been recorded as occurring in southern Africa, but it is highly probable that several more bat species will be added to the subregion's faunal list in the future, after more intensive biological surveying.

Bats are the only mammals capable of true flight. The forelimbs with their greatly elongated fingers have evolved into wings, over which the skin of the upper and lower surfaces has fused to form a very thin wing-membrane. This membrane extends along the side of the body to the ankles. When at rest, bats usually hang head downwards, suspended by the claws of the hindfeet and with the wings either folded against the body, or enveloping it. The fruit-eating and insect-eating bats differ in several ways:

Fruit-bat: two wing-claws

Insectivorous bat: one wing-claw

Character	Fruit-bat	Insectivorous Bat
Size	Usually large	Usually small
Wing-claws	2*	1
Tail	Absent or short	Medium to long
Interfemoral (tail) membrane	Poorly developed	Usually well developed
Eyes	Large	Small
Ear tragus	Absent	Usually well developed but absent in horseshoe bats.
Echolocation	Absent, except in *Rousettus aegyptiacus*	Present

(* in southern Africa)

Bats rely to a great extent on their hearing and this is particularly so in the case of the microchiropterans or insect-eating bats which have perfected the art of echolocation. Their ears are extremely well developed and most microchiropteran species, with the exception of the horseshoe bats, have a small lobe, the *tragus*, in front of the ear opening. Whilst in flight insectivorous bats emit high-frequency sound waves through the mouth (*e.g.* the family Vespertilionidae) or nostrils (*e.g.* the family Hipposideridae). These clicks and bleeps are reflected by objects in the immediate vicinity of the bat and are picked up on the rebound by the bats' ears, thus providing information on obstacles and potential prey to the bat. Anyone who has observed bats in flight will appreciate the rapidity with which they analyse and react to these 'messages'. The time between the emission of the call, the reception of the bounced echo and the bat's physical reaction to the stimulus may in fact be as little as one hundredth of a second. Among the fruit-bats only the Egyptian Fruit-bat *Rousettus aegyptiacus* possesses the ability to echolocate; its clicks are made by the tongue, emitted through the mouth and are of a lower frequency than those of insect-eating bats.

Fruit-bats Suborder Megachiroptera Family Pteropodidae
Seven species occur in the subregion but only three are regularly encountered. Dobson's Fruit-bat is known from only a single specimen collected in Botswana, and the validity of the Angolan Epauletted Fruit-bat is not certain. Local bats previously assigned to the Gambian Epauletted Fruit-bat are here regarded as indistinguishable from the Angolan species. All fruit-bats are large in size with pointed, dog-like heads. Their ears are fairly prominent but lack ear extensions or tragi. The tail is very short and the tail (interfemoral) membrane is indistinct (fig 1.1, page 18). Unlike the insectivorous bats, the fruit-bats have two claws on each wing. Two of the commoner species have white tufts at the base of the ears and roost in trees; the Egyptian fruit-bat lacks such white tufts and roosts in caves.
Key features: Large size; dog-like faces.

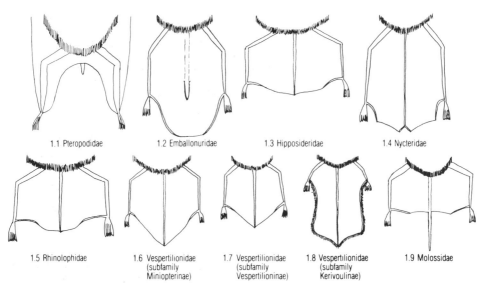

1.1 Pteropodidae   1.2 Emballonuridae   1.3 Hipposideridae   1.4 Nycteridae

1.5 Rhinolophidae   1.6 Vespertilionidae (subfamily Miniopterinae)   1.7 Vespertilionidae (subfamily Vespertilioninae)   1.8 Vespertilionidae (subfamily Kerivoulinae)   1.9 Molossidae

Figure 1: tail conformation in different families of bats (not to scale)

Insectivorous Bats   Suborder Microchiroptera

There are six families and 66 species of insectivorous bats in the subregion. Many species are difficult to separate without detailed examination. Unlike the fruit-bats, insectivorous bats have only one claw on each wing and they are generally much smaller in size. The conformation of the tail and the interfemoral membrane which it helps to support are useful diagnostic features at family level (see fig. 1, above).

Sheath-tailed and Tomb Bats   Family Emballonuridae

Three species occur in southern Africa. They are easily separated from other bats by the distinctive tail conformation: somewhat more than half of the tail is enclosed by the interfemoral membrane, the remainder being free. The tail-tip, however, does not reach the outer edge of the membrane as it does in the free-tailed bats (figs. 1.2 and 1.9). The eyes are larger than those of most insectivorous bats. They roost against a surface and never hang free.
Key features: Tail distinctive – partly free but not projecting beyond outer edge of membrane; simple face with no nose-leaves.

Leaf-nosed and Trident Bats   Family Hipposideridae

Four species occur in the subregion, two leaf-nosed bats and two trident bats (but note that the trident bat *Triaenops persicus* is usually called the Persian Leaf-nosed Bat). They are all similar in general appearance to horseshoe bats but can be separated from the latter by their more simple nose-leaves. Their tail conformation resembles that of horseshoe bats (figs. 1.3 and 1.5). Trident bats have a three-pronged process on the top edge of the nose-leaves. The leaf-nosed bats have large ears and tiny tragi. Commerson's leaf-nosed bat is one of the largest insect-eating bats in southern Africa. All species usually roost in caves.
Key features: Similar to horseshoe bats but nose-leaf structure simpler and less 'horseshoe'-like.

Slit-faced Bats   Family Nycteridae

Six species occur in the subregion, but only one has a wide distribution range. Bats of this family have disproportionately long ears (nearly 4 cm in the case of the Egyptian Slit-faced Bat), which are parallel-sided and are held more or less vertically, unlike, for example, the ears of the long-eared bats (fig. 2.14) which are held out at an angle of 45° to the head. There is a slit in the skin down the middle of the face which, when unfolded, reveals small nose-leaves. The terminal vertebra of the tail is bifurcated, giving a Y-tipped appearance, a feature diagnostic of this family (fig. 1.4). Slit-faced bats tend to roost singly or in small numbers, hanging free rather than adpressed against a vertical surface. All six species in the subregion belong to the genus *Nycteris*.

Key features: Very long, vertically held ears; Y-shaped tail-tip; groove down middle of face.

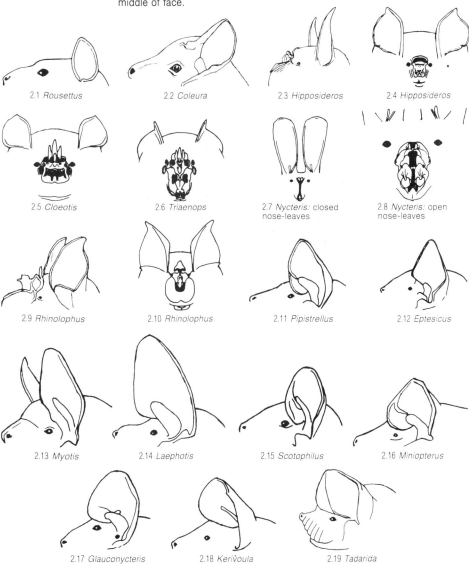

2.1 *Rousettus*

2.2 *Coleura*

2.3 *Hipposideros*

2.4 *Hipposideros*

2.5 *Cloeotis*

2.6 *Triaenops*

2.7 *Nycteris:* closed nose-leaves

2.8 *Nycteris:* open nose-leaves

2.9 *Rhinolophus*

2.10 *Rhinolophus*

2.11 *Pipistrellus*

2.12 *Eptesicus*

2.13 *Myotis*

2.14 *Laephotis*

2.15 *Scotophilus*

2.16 *Miniopterus*

2.17 *Glauconycteris*

2.18 *Kerivoula*

2.19 *Tadarida*

Figure 2: face and ear conformation of different bat groups (not to scale)

Horseshoe Bats Family Rhinolophidae

The ten species of horseshoe bat in the subregion are difficult to separate to species level. All have complex nose-leaves which play an important rôle in echolocation. The plate-like or 'horseshoe'-shaped main nose-leaf above the upper lip varies little in shape between the different species. Above the horseshoe, however, there is a protruding saddle-shaped outgrowth known as the *sella*, and in the region of the forehead is an erect, triangular fold of skin called the *lancet* (see fig. 2.10). It is these outgrowths together with the tooth structure which allow taxonomists to distinguish the different species. The ears are prominent, are widely separated, but have no tragi; the horseshoe bats are in fact the only family of insectivorous bats to lack the tragus. The interfemoral membrane is more or less squared off between feet and tail-tip, as in the leaf-nosed and trident bats (figs. 1.5 and 1.3). Most species are cave- and crevice-roosters and they hang free, not adpressed against the walls of the roost. The wings are short and rounded and when the bat is at rest they envelop the body.

Key features: Horseshoe-shaped nose-leaf with projections; no tragus.

Vesper Bats Family Vespertilionidae

This is by far the largest bat family in the Southern African Subregion with 29 species recorded to date. Nine species are, however, known from very few records. All vesper bats have simple mouse-like muzzles and lack any out-of-the-ordinary facial structures. Their ears are well-developed and carry tragi which vary in shape according to the species. The tail is completely enclosed by the interfemoral membrane which tapers towards the tail-tip and projects backwards in a V-shape (figs. 1.6, 1.7 and 1.8, page 18). The bats of this group are difficult to identify to species level.

Key features: Mouse-like faces; membrane extends to tail-tip in V-shape.

Long-fingered Bats Subfamily Miniopterinae

Three species occur in southern Africa. The members of this subfamily are characterized by the second phalanx of the third digit being about three times as long as the first phalanx; in the other vesper bats it is not specially elongated. At present the three species can only be conclusively identified and separated by examination of various skull features beyond the scope of this book.

Key feature: Second phalanx of third digit greatly elongated.

Various vesper bats Subfamily Vespertilioninae

This subfamily contains eight genera and 24 species. Members of two genera are relatively simple to place but the remainder are generally confusing and variable in appearance even within a single species. Many species occur only marginally in the subregion and are rarely encountered. The Butterfly Bat (page 66) has distinctive reticulated venation on the wings. The long-eared bats (*Laephotis*) are represented in the subregion by three species with very large ears which are held at an angle of 45° to the head (unlike, for example, the long ears of the slit-faced bats which are held vertically). The hairy bats of the genus *Myotis* (page 62) can be separated from other vesper bats by their longer, more pointed muzzles and their soft erect fur. Note, however, that the individual hairs are straight and not curled at the tip like those of the woolly bats.

Key feature: Mouse-like faces.

Woolly Bats Subfamily Kerivoulinae

Two species occur. They are small and are characterized by a long, woolly coat, the individual hairs of which are curled at the tip — unlike that of the hairy bats (page 62). The interfemoral membrane is fringed with short hairs — a feature peculiar to this subfamily (see fig. 1.8).

Key features: Long, woolly hair; fringe of hair around tail membrane.

Free-tailed Bats Family Molossidae
Of the 14 species recorded from the subregion, only four are regularly
encountered. Members of the family are characterized by having the first
third to half of the tail encased in the interfemoral membrane to its end, with
the remainder of the tail projecting beyond the outer edge of the membrane
(fig. 1.9). In the family Emballonuridae (page 50) the end of the tail is also
free, but is shorter than the membrane and projects from the central area of
the membrane at an angle (fig. 1.2). All but one species, the Large-eared
Free-tailed Bat, have shortened faces and this is emphasized by the
relatively large ears. A tragus is present but is small. Many species have
distinctively wrinkled upper lips (and are often called 'bulldog bats; see fig.
2.19). The feet have a fringe of prominent hairs. The fur is short and flattened
and usually dark brown or reddish-brown. Unlike most bats, free-tailed bats
can scuttle around rapidly on walls and on the ground. Several species
commonly roost in houses.
Key features: Partly free tail projecting well beyond end of interfemoral
membrane; wrinkled lips.

PRIMATES Order Primates

Monkeys and Baboons Family Cercopithecidae
Four species occur in southern Africa but one (the Yellow Baboon) is only
found marginally in the subregion on the south side of the Zambezi River in
central Mozambique. Two are long-tailed 'typical' monkeys, the Vervet
Monkey pale in colour and an open woodland dweller, the Samango Monkey
dark in colour and a forest-dweller. Baboons are large in size, have dog-like
muzzles and have a marked kink in the tail about one-third of the way along
its length. They are largely terrestrial but climb readily. All are diurnal.
Key features: Unmistakable monkey-like appearance; diurnal.

Bushbabies Family Lorisidae
Three species occur in the subregion, one of which is apparently restricted to
Mozambique. All are small, slender animals, the largest being the Thick-tailed
Bushbaby with a total length of 75 cm; it has a long bushy tail, dense soft fur
and very large eyes. The ears are large, membranous and mobile. Its harsh
screaming call is often the only indication of its presence. The smaller
species have long but less bushy tails. All three species are nocturnal and
largely arboreal.
Key features: Large eyes and ears; long furry tails; mainly arboreal;
nocturnal.

PANGOLIN Order Pholidota

Pangolin Family Manidae
Only one species occurs in the subregion. It is quite unmistakable with its
upperparts and sides covered entirely in large, hard, plate-like, brown scales.
Key feature: Body covered with large overlapping brown scales.

HARES AND RABBITS Order Lagomorpha

Hares and Rabbits Family Leporidae
Six species occur naturally in the subregion and a seventh, the European
Rabbit, has been introduced to a few offshore islands. All have short, fluffy
tails but the two true hares have white and black tails while the rabbits have
uniform-brown or reddish-brown tails. The true hares have long,
well-developed hindlegs whereas those of the red rock rabbits and the
Riverine Rabbit are less developed. The Riverine Rabbit is very rare and
localized. All species are primarily nocturnal.
Key features: Unmistakable rabbit appearance; short, fluffy tails; long ears.

RODENTS Order Rodentia

Only the rodents have the characteristic large pair of chisel-like incisor teeth at the front of both the upper and lower jaw (the dassies have one pair above and two pairs below – see page 24). Rodents are, however, very varied in size and appearance, from the 20-kg Porcupine to the 6-g Pygmy Mouse. Seventy-eight species, belonging to nine families, occur in the subregion; four of these have been introduced from other countries.

Key features: Two prominent pairs of large incisor teeth, one pair in upper jaw, one pair in lower jaw.

Squirrels Family Sciuridae

Five species of arboreal (tree-dwelling) and two species of partly fossorial (burrowing) squirrels occur in the subregion. They are characterized by having long bushy tails. The arboreal species have soft hair and burrowing species have coarse hair. Sometimes confused with much smaller (similarly bushy-tailed) dormice (page 92). All are diurnal (dormice are nocturnal).

Key features: Bushy tails; tail often held erect or curved forward over back.

Dormice Family Gliridae

Four species have been recorded in the subregion. They are small, grey, mouse-like creatures with bushy, squirrel-like tails. They do not, however, sit erect or with tail raised like squirrels and they are all nocturnal in habit.

Key features: Greyish and mouse-like but with bushy tails; nocturnal.

Springhare Family Pedetidae

This family contains only one species which occurs in two separate populations, one in southern Africa and one in East Africa. It resembles a small kangaroo with its well-developed hindlegs, small forelegs and long bushy tail. Its eyes are large and its ears long. It lives in burrows in sandy soils and is nocturnal in habit.

Key features: Like miniature kangaroo; reddish-fawn colour; nocturnal.

Molerats Family Bathyergidae

Four species of these burrowing rodents occur in the subregion. The largest species is the Cape Dune Molerat which has a mass of up to 750 g. The name 'molerat' is misleading as these animals are neither moles nor rats. The eyes and ear openings are tiny but visible and the tail is very short and flattened. All species have short legs with long digging claws on the forefeet. They have a round, pig-like snout-tip. The fur is soft but not glossy as in golden moles (page 16). All species push mounds or heaps of soil, unlike the golden moles which tend to raise long meandering ridges just under the soil surface.

Key features: Tiny eyes and ears; very short tail; pig-like snout-tip; obvious pair of incisor teeth; push 'mole-hills' in runs.

Porcupine Family Hystricidae

Only one species occurs in southern Africa and it is unmistakable. It is the largest rodent in the subregion with a mass of up to 24 kg. The upperparts of its body are covered with long black-and-white banded, flexible spines and rigid quills. It is nocturnal in habit.

Key features: Long black-and-white quills and spines; large size.

Cane-rats Family Thryonomyidae

Only two species are found in the subregion. They are similar in general appearance with large stocky bodies and short tails. The brown bristly body hair looks a little like short, soft quills. The Greater Cane-rat is widespread in the east where it inhabits reed-beds and other moist, well-vegetated areas; the Lesser will also use drier habitats. Both species are mainly nocturnal.

Key features: Large size; brown bristly, quill-like hair; moist habitats.

Dassie Rat Family Petromuridae
This family contains only one species which is restricted to rocky habitats in the arid west of the subregion, north to Angola. It is somewhat squirrel-like in appearance but its tail is hairy rather than bushy. It is diurnal in habit.
Key features: Brown and squirrel-like, but tail not bushy; rocky habitat.

Rats and Mice Families Muridae and Cricetidae
Both families are usually dealt with together as they can only be separated on the shape of the cheek-teeth. Larger species are usually called rats and the smaller mice but there is no clear-cut distinction between the two terms. Fifty-seven species, in seven subfamilies and 24 genera, occur in the subregion. The majority of species are nocturnal. Three species, the House Rat, Brown Rat and the House Mouse, are alien to the subregion; they are cosmopolitan invaders associated with human settlements.
Key feature: Varied but typically mouse- and rat-like.

CARNIVORES Order Carnivora

Wild Dog, Jackals and Foxes Family Canidae
Five canids occur in the subregion, ranging in size from the Bat-eared Fox to the Wild Dog. All have dog-like features – elongated muzzle, fairly long legs, prominent ears and variably bushy tails. They may have short hair (as in the Wild Dog) or long hair (as in the Bat-eared Fox) and all have non-retractile claws. They are mainly nocturnal in habit except for the Wild Dog.
Key feature: Dog-like features.

Otters, Badger, Weasel and Polecat Family Mustelidae
Five species of mustelid are found in southern Africa. They are small to medium-sized carnivores. The two otter species are associated mainly with aquatic habitats, and have heavy, broad-based, rudder-like tails. Both the Striped Weasel with its short legs and sinuous body and the Striped Polecat have distinctive black-and-white striping along the back while the Honey Badger has silvery-coloured upperparts and black underparts. All species are mainly nocturnal.
Key features: Varied but distinctive group of carnivores: see species accounts.

Mongooses, Civets and Genets Family Viverridae
This family is also varied and has 16 southern African representatives: one civet, one tree civet, two genets and 12 mongooses. They are small to medium-sized carnivores (260 g to 15 kg) with relatively long bodies and muzzles and most species have medium-to-long tails. Most species have well-haired tails. The civets and genets are spotted. The mongooses and Civet are terrestrial but the Tree Civet is mainly arboreal and the genets are at least partly arboreal. Most of the family have nocturnal habits but several mongooses are diurnal.
Key features: Varied but distinctive group of carnivores; long bodies, long muzzles and disproportionately short legs (except for the civet).

Hyaenas and Aardwolf Family Hyaenidae
Two species of hyaena and the Aardwolf occur in the subregion. The hyaenas are moderately large carnivores but the Aardwolf is considerably smaller (and is often, in fact, placed in its own family, the Protelidae). The hindquarters of the Spotted Hyaena in particular are lower than its shoulders and it has a distinctive short, spotted coat and rounded ears. The Aardwolf and Brown Hyaena have long hair, the former with vertical black body stripes. Predominantly nocturnal.
Key feature: Appear higher at the shoulder than at the rump.

Cats Family Felidae

Seven species occur naturally in the subregion and an eighth, the domestic cat, takes readily to the wild. All are highly specialized carnivores with short muzzles and, except in the case of cheetah, have fully retractile claws. They range in size from the 1,5 kg of the Small Spotted Cat to the 225 kg of the Lion. Most smaller species are nocturnal, as is the Leopard, but the Lion is partly diurnal and Cheetah predominantly so.

Key features: All have short muzzles and typically cat-like faces.

AARDVARK Order Tubulidentata

Aardvark Family Orycteropodidae

There is only one species in this order. It cannot be confused with any other mammal, with its large size (up to 65 kg), arched back, long, pig-like snout and very heavy tail and legs. The ears are long and mule-like.

Key features: Large; pig-like; arched back; elongated snout.

ELEPHANT Order Proboscidea

Elephant Family Elephantidae

A single species and the largest land mammal. Unmistakable.

DASSIES Order Hyracoidea

Dassies (Hyraxes) Family Procaviidae

Three rock-dwelling and one tree-living species occur in the subregion. Small (up to 4,6 kg) but stoutly built animals, with short legs, small rounded ears and no tail. The muzzle is pointed and they have well-developed incisors, one pair above and two pairs below. Rodents have one pair above and one pair below. Frequently called 'rock rabbits' but they have no relationship with rabbits.

Key features: Stocky build; tail-less; small patch of different-coloured hair in centre of back.

ODD-TOED UNGULATES Order Perissodactyla

Zebra Family Equidae

Two species occur in the subregion. Both are boldly striped in black and white but where Burchell's zebra has a 'shadow' stripe in the white stripes particularly on its hindquarters, this feature is absent in the mountain zebra. A dewlap on the throat and a 'grid-iron' pattern on the rump also serve to distinguish the mountain zebra from Burchell's.

Key features: Horse-like; striped in black and white.

Rhinoceroses Family Rhinocerotidae

The two species of the subregion are easy to separate on size as well as on the structure of the lips. The Hook-lipped (Black) Rhinoceros is a browser with a hooked, prehensile upper lip, while the Square-lipped (White) Rhinoceros is a grazer with broad, squared-off upper and lower lips. Both carry two horns on the front of the head and are almost hairless.

Key features: Large size; two horns one above the other on front of head.

EVEN-TOED UNGULATES Order Artiodactyla

Pigs Family Suidae

Two species, the Warthog and Bushpig, occur in southern Africa. Both are clearly recognizable as pigs. The head has a typically elongated, mobile snout and the Warthog carries large, curved tusk-like canines. The two species are separated largely by habitat – the Warthog preferring open

woodland savanna and the Bushpig favouring denser cover. The Warthog is diurnal in habit and the Bushpig is nocturnal.
Key feature: Pig-like.

Hippopotamuses Family Hippopotamidae
Only one of the two hippopotamus species occurs in the subregion. It is distinctively large with a massive head and a barrel-shaped body. It usually spends the day in water, emerging after dark to feed.
Key features: Large, barrel-shaped body; aquatic habitat.

Giraffe Family Giraffidae
A single species, with greatly elongated neck and legs.
Key features: Unmistakable; large size and very long neck.

Fallow Deer Family Cervidae
Although several species of deer have been introduced to South Africa, only the Fallow Deer is numerous enough to warrant mention here. It has been widely distributed to game-farms and private estates throughout South Africa. Only the males carry the bony antlers which are shed and regrown annually. While growing, the antlers are covered by skin richly supplied with blood-vessels and are said to be 'in velvet' (see photograph on page 223).
Key features: Males carry branched and palmate antlers for much of the year; females lack antlers; summer coat deep fawn with white spots.

Antelope and Buffalo Family Bovidae
This family is represented in southern Africa by 33 indigenous species and one introduced goat (Himalayan Tahr), the latter with a very limited distribution. All have cloven or centrally split hoofs and the males of all species carry horns as do the females of slightly less than half of the species. Most live in herds of varying size but a number of the smaller species lead more solitary lives. There are 8 subfamilies as shown below.
Key features: Cloven hoofs; all males carry horns.

Buffalo, Eland, Kudu, Sitatunga, Nyala and Bushbuck Subfamily Bovinae
Six species of this subfamily occur in the subregion. The Buffalo is unmistakable, uniformly coloured and cow-like. The other five species, known as tragelaphine antelopes, range from medium to very large in size. There is a crest of long hair, least noticeable in the Eland, along the neck and back. Only male tragelaphines have horns – except for Eland where the females are also horned – and these are always spirally twisted and ridged at front and back; they are never ringed. Body colour varies from grey through to chestnut-brown but all tragelaphines have white stripes or spots to a greater or lesser extent, and thus differ from other antelopes.
Key features: Buffalo uniformly coloured and cow-like; both sexes horned. Only males of tragelaphine antelopes have spirally twisted horns (female Eland is exception); colour variable but white spots or stripes usually present on body – unlike other antelope.

Roan, Sable and Gemsbok Subfamily Hippotraginae
Three species of this subfamily occur in the subregion. They are large antelope with well-developed horns in both sexes. The horns are straight and rapier-like in the Gemsbok and sabre-like and backwardly curving in the other two species; they are distinctly ringed. All three species have a long, tufted tail and distinctive black-and-white facial markings.
Key features: Large size; distinctive horns and black-and-white facial markings.

Waterbuck, Lechwe, Puku and Reedbuck Subfamily Reduncinae
Five species of this subfamily occur in the subregion. They range from

medium to large in size. They are generally heavily built and only the males carry horns. These curve back, up and then forward; they are strongly ringed.
Key features: Horn form of males; association with watery or damp habitats (except in case of Mountain Reedbuck).

Grey Rhebok Subfamily Peleinae
This subfamily has only one member, the Grey Rhebok, and it is entirely restricted to South Africa. It is of medium size and only the male has the short erect horns, ringed for about half their length.
Key features: Grey body; white underparts; straight, erect, short horns.

Wildebeest, Hartebeest, Tsessebe and Bontebok/Blesbok Subfamily Alcelaphinae
Six species of this subfamily occur in the subregion, two wildebeest, two hartebeest, the Tsessebe and the Bontebok/Blesbok. They are medium-to-large antelope, with shoulders higher than the rump and with a long, narrow face. Each species has a distinctive horn structure and both sexes have horns. They are usually found in herds on the open plains or ecotone of woodland and grassland.
Key features: Back slopes down to rump; long faces.

Impala Subfamily Aepycerotinae
This subfamily has only one member, the Impala. It is of medium size and slender build. Only the males carry the slender, well-ringed, lyre-shaped horns. It is the only antelope with a tuft of black hair just above the ankle-joint of each hindleg.
Key features: Medium size; males with lyrate horns; characteristic tuft of black hair on each hindleg above ankle-joint.

Springbok, Dik-dik, Suni, Klipspringer, Oribi, Steenbok and Grysbok Subfamily Antilopinae
Eight species of this subfamily occur in the subregion. The Springbok, whose male and female both carry horns, is placed in a separate tribe from the other seven species, only the males of which possess horns. The Springbok congregates in herds but the other species live singly or in small family parties. The Steenbok, Oribi and Springbok prefer open habitat; the Klipspringer is found only in rocky areas; and the other four species show a preference for well-wooded or bushy habitats.
Key features: Small species except for medium-sized Springbok. Diverse in habit and habitat. See species accounts.

Duikers Subfamily Cephalophinae
Three species of this subfamily occur in the subregion, of which two are forest or dense-bush dwellers while the third prefers more open bush country. The two forest species are small and have arched backs and short, back-pointing horns in both sexes. There is a distinct tuft of hair present between the horns of all species. The Common Duiker has a straight back and is longer in the leg; only the male carries horns. All three species have short tails. All usually occur solitarily or in pairs.
Key features: Small size; skulking habits; tuft of hair between ears.

Himalayan Tahr Subfamily Caprinae
This introduced wild goat is the only member of its subfamily living wild in the subregion. It is only present on the Table Mountain Range, Cape Town. It has a shaggy coat and short, stout, back-curved horns. It cannot be mistaken for any other species.
Key features: Rocky habitat in Table Mountain Range, Cape Town; goat-like.

Blue whale (from side)

Sperm whale (from side)

Humpback whale (from side)

Right whale (from side)

Right whale (from front)

Whale spout
conformation

WHALES AND DOLPHINS Order Cetacea

All of our 38 whales and dolphins – known collectively as cetaceans – fall into one of two suborders, the Odontoceti, which includes the toothed whales and dolphins, and the Mysticeti, or baleen whales. The toothed whales have a single nostril or blow-hole, and the baleen whales have two. Whales and dolphins differ a great deal in shape, size, colouration and markings. In addition, as they are mammals, they must surface periodically to breathe and in the case of the great whales the 'blow' or spout can be used as an aid to identification. The blow is not composed of water as some people think, but is a cloud of vapour produced by condensation when the whale's warm breath – forcibly expelled on surfacing – comes into contact with the cooler air. Although baleen whales have two blow-holes, not all produce a V-shaped spout; the rorquals, for example, tend to produce a single spout. All species have the ability to remain under water for long periods but the Sperm Whale is the master of this art and is able to dive to great depths for up to 90 minutes.

The baleen whales are so named from the great plates of baleen which hang from the roof of the mouth. Baleen is composed of keratin – the horny material of which human hair and fingernails are composed – and grows in long, thin, closely layered plates. The outer edges of the plates are smooth and the inner edges are frayed into interlocking strands. Baleen whales feed on plankton and can be separated into two groups with different feeding behaviour. The 'gulpers' take huge 'bites' of sea-water, then strain out the plankton through the baleen plates by expelling the water through the sides of the mouth; the plankton residue is then licked off by the large tongue. The 'skimmers' swim along with their mouths open, filtering the water until enough plankton has accumulated on the baleen to be scraped off and swallowed. The Sei Whale uses a combination of both methods. The toothed whales take a wide variety of food, which includes squid, fish and crustaceans. The only true flesh-eater is the Killer Whale.

Social behaviour in this interesting group is poorly known but some species are thought to be solitary, others move in small groups or 'pods', while several species may congregate in schools of several hundreds or even thousands. The toothed whales and dolphins in particular have highly developed communication faculties, based on the emission of clicks and whistles, some beyond the limits of human perception. The Humpback Whale has been intensively studied and has an amazingly complex repertoire. The toothed whales also use their calls for echolocation, to locate their fish and squid prey, but this ability has not yet been shown to exist in the baleen whales. There is no doubt that the cetaceans as a group are highly intelligent but the level of their intelligence is still the subject of considerable debate and argument amongst scientists.

Whales and dolphins usually give birth to a single, well-developed young that can immediately follow its mother. Gestation periods are relatively short when one considers the size of the adults, and vary between 9 and 16 months. Young whales do not suckle; the milk is squirted into their mouths. Whales and dolphins are usually only fleetingly seen and it is important to take note of the following points to assist in identification:
1. Size – small, medium or large.
2. Dorsal fin – present or absent; size, shape and position.
3. Blow (air exhalation) – single or double; height.
4. Tail flukes – shape; markings.
5. Patterns or markings.
6. Body shape and general colour.
7. Jumping or breaching – the form it takes.
8. Group size.

Baleen or Whalebone Whales Suborder Mysticeti

Eight species of baleen whales have been recorded off the coasts of southern Africa, ranging in size from the 6-m Pygmy Right Whale to the 33-m Blue Whale – the largest mammal that has ever existed.

Rorquals or Pleated Whales Family Balaenopteridae

Six of the eight baleen whales in southern African waters belong to this family. They are long, slender and streamlined and have flattened heads, pointed flippers and a small, back-curved dorsal fin set far back along the body. They are characterized by a large number of grooves or pleats running longitudinally from the throat and chest to the upper abdomen; these grooves allow for the massive expansions and contractions of the whale's mouth as it first engulfs its prey, then expels the water while sieving out the food organisms through the baleen plates. The two other baleen whales of the family Balaenidae (see below) have smooth ungrooved throats.
Key features: Large size; back-curved dorsal fin; diagnostic longitudinal throat grooves.

Right Whales Family Balaenidae

The right whales, of which two species occur in southern African waters, were so called because they are slow-moving and hence were easily caught by the early whalers; when killed they floated, allowing the whalers to tow the carcasses to land. They were the 'right' whales to hunt. They are characterized by their large heads with arched jaw-line and smooth ungrooved throat. The larger of the two species, the Right Whale, has a smooth back lacking any fin or hump.
Key features: Large size; smooth ungrooved throat; dorsal fin only in smaller of two species.

Toothed Whales and Dolphins Suborder Odontoceti

Thirty species of toothed whales and dolphins have been recorded off the coasts of southern Africa. The smallest of these appears to be Heaviside's Dolphin with a total length of 1,3 m. The largest is the Sperm Whale with a total length of over 15 m. The two nasal cavities of the toothed whales fuse to form a single blow-hole, unlike those of the baleen whales which open separately (although situated together). All toothed whales have teeth, but the number is variable, from two in some of the beaked whales to over 120 in the Long-snouted Dolphin. In the beaked whales, the teeth of the females do not normally erupt through the gums.

Beaked Whales Family Ziphiidae

Eight species of beaked whales have been recorded from southern African waters but most are known from very few specimens and sightings. All members of this family are distinguished by having two grooves on the throat which converge (but do not meet) to form a V-shape, and the males have either one or two pairs of prominent teeth on the lower jaw and none in the upper jaw. The form, position and number of the teeth are important characters in identifying the different species. In all of our 8 species with the exception of Arnoux's Beaked Whale the females are apparently toothless in that the teeth do not erupt from the gums. The flippers are small and the dorsal fin is usually prominent and set well back on the body. The tail-flukes do not have a central notch. All species are also characterized by a more or less developed bulbous swelling on the forehead and head, known as a 'melon'. Most are extremely difficult to identify to species level when seen at sea.
Key features: Between 4 and 9 metres long; prominent 'beak' and bulbous forehead; prominent dorsal fin; one or two pairs of teeth in males only.

Sperm Whales Family Physeteridae

All three species of this family have been recorded from subregion waters. They have distinctly blunt and squared heads. Functional teeth occur on the lower jaw but very rarely on the upper jaw. The head contains the spermaceti organ whose white waxy product is believed to assist in the regulation of buoyancy in deep diving and perhaps also to focus sound used in echolocation. The two smaller species possess a dorsal fin.

Key features: Blunt, square head; dorsal fin present in two smaller species.

Dolphins, Pilot Whales and Killer and False Killer Whales Family Delphinidae

Of the 19 species of this family recorded from the coastal waters of the subregion, only a handful are regularly seen close inshore. Lengths vary from 1,3 m to 8 m. All have long, more or less centrally situated dorsal fins, with the exception of the Southern Right Whale Dolphin which lacks the fin. Members of the family are typically slender and sleek; 9 species have a well-developed beak (mostly the smaller species), 3 have a short beak and 7 have no beak and somewhat globose heads. All have numerous teeth in both jaws except for Risso's Dolphin which lacks teeth in the upper jaw.

Key features: Numerous teeth in both jaws (except Risso's Dolphin); dorsal fin present (except Southern Right Whale Dolphin).

DUGONG Order Sirenia

Dugong Family Dugongidae

One species occurs in the subregion. It is a marine but strictly coastal mammal with a long cigar-shaped body. Its forelimbs are paddle-like flippers and its boneless tail is broad and horizontally flattened. The snout is broad, rounded and well bristled. It could be confused with seals but the head shape is quite different. Less agile than seals.

Key features: Large (3-m) body; large blunt head; bristles around mouth.

SEALS Order Pinnipedia

Fur Seals Family Otariidae

Two species of this family occur in the subregion, one as a resident, the other as a rare vagrant. Their hind flippers can be turned forward under the body when moving on land. They possess small but clearly visible ears.

Key features: Hind flippers can be turned forwards on land; small ears present.

True Seals Family Phocidae

Three species of 'true' seal occur as rare vagrants off the southern African coastline. They lack external ears and their hind flippers cannot bend forward under the body. The Southern Elephant Seal male has a prominent bulbous proboscis.

Key features: Hind flippers cannot be turned forwards under body; no external ears.

Organizations concerned with mammal studies and conservation

1. NON-GOVERNMENT ORGANIZATIONS

Bat Conservation International, P. O. Box 162603, Austin TX 78716, United States of America.
Bat Conservation International was founded in 1982 by Dr. Merlin D. Tuttle. Its purpose is to document and publicize the value and conservation needs of bats, to promote bat conservation projects and to assist with bat management initiatives world-wide. B.C.I. has been instrumental in protecting some of the world's most important bat populations and has members in 40 countries. It welcomes contact with people who have an interest in bats.

Mammal Research Institute, University of Pretoria, 0002 Pretoria, South Africa.
Founded in 1966, this semi-autonomous organization operates within the Department of Zoology at the University of Pretoria. Its highly qualified staff and postgraduate students undertake mammalogical research.

The Wildlife Society of Southern Africa, P. O. Box 44189, 2104 Linden, South Africa.
The Society is concerned with the conservation of southern African wildlife, wild places and natural resources for all the people of the subcontinent.

Endangered Wildlife Trust, P. Bag X11, 2122 Parkview, South Africa.
The Endangered Wildlife Trust has three main aims: to maintain essential ecological processes and life-support systems; to preserve genetic diversity and to ensure that no form of life becomes extinct through ignorance or apathy; and to ensure the sustainable utilization of species and ecosystems.

Worldwide Fund for Nature (South Africa), P.O. Box 456, 7600 Stellenbosch, South Africa.
The South African branch of the Fund raises finance for the conservation of wildlife and the natural environment. Through the support of the South African public, this organisation has been able to create or help develop numerous parks and nature reserves.

African-Arabian Wildlife Research Centre, P.O. Box 6, Loxton 6985, South Africa.
Originally started in 1986 as the African Carnivore Survey, the Centre has been developed to monitor the carnivores and other biota of Africa and, most recently, the Arabian Peninsula. Although its principal aim remains the compilation of available information on mammalian carnivores and promoting their conservation, it now looks at many additional conservation issues.

S.A. Hunters' and Game Conservation Association, P.O. Box 1703, 0001 Pretoria, South Africa.

Chipangali Wildlife Trust, P.O. Box 1057, Bulawayo, Zimbabwe.
The Trust has four basic aims: the conservation of wildlife; conservation education; the stimulation of environmental awareness; and conservation research. The Trust is currently involved in a study of the duikers of Africa.

Kalahari Conservation Society, P.O. Box 859, Gaborone, Botswana.
The aims of the Kalahari Conservation Society are to promote knowledge of Botswana's rich wildlife resource and its environment; to encourage research; and to promote sound conservation policies in that country.

Swaziland National Trust (Nature Conservation Division), P.O. Box 75, Mbabane, Swaziland.

2. GOVERNMENT ORGANISATIONS

Botswana:
Department of Wildlife and National Parks, P.O. Box 131, Gaborone, Botswana.

Namibia:
Ministry of Environment and Tourism, Private Bag 13306, Windhoek, Namibia.

Lesotho:
Lesotho National Parks (Conservation Division), P.O. Box 92, Maseru 100, Lesotho.

Zimbabwe:
Department of National Parks and Wildlife Management, P.O. Box 8365, Causeway, Harare, Zimbabwe.

South Africa:

National Parks Board, P.O. Box 787, Pretoria 0001.

Gauteng: Directorate of Nature Conservation, Private Bag X209, Pretoria 0001.

Northern Province: Department of Environmental Affairs and Tourism, P.O. Box 217, Pietersburg 0700.

Mpumalanga: Department of Environmental Affairs, Private Bag 11233, Nelspruit 1200.

North West Province: Department of Agriculture and Environmental Affairs, Private Bag X6102, Mmabatho 8681.

KwaZulu-Natal: Natal Parks Board, P.O. Box 662, Pietermaritzburg 3200.

Eastern Cape: Eastern Cape Nature Conservation, Private Bag X1126, Port Elizabeth 6000.

Western Cape: Western Cape Nature Conservation, Private Bag X9086, Cape Town 8000.

Northern Cape: Nature Conservation Service, Private Bag X6102, Kimberley 8300.

Free State: Department of Agriculture and Environment Affairs, P.O. Box 517, Bloemfontein 9300.

3. MUSEUMS IN SOUTHERN AFRICA WITH RESIDENT MAMMALOGISTS

Transvaal Museum, P.O. Box 413, 0001 Pretoria, South Africa.
Kaffrarian Museum, P.O. Box 1434, 5600 King William's Town, South Africa.
National Museum, P.O. Box 266, 9300 Bloemfontein, South Africa.
State Museum, P.O. Box 1203, Windhoek, Namibia.
National Museum, P.O. Box 240, Bulawayo, Zimbabwe.
South African Museum, P.O. Box 61, 8000 Cape Town, South Africa.
Port Elizabeth Museum, P.O. Box 13147, 6013 Humewood, South Africa.

INSECTIVORES Order Insectivora

Golden moles Family Chrysochloridae

The golden moles are endemic to Africa south of the Sahara, with 15 species occurring in southern Africa. Material records for several species are scanty, however, with Van Zyl's Golden Mole and Visagie's Golden Mole each being known from only a single specimen. The biology of all the golden moles is poorly known. They are all basically similar in appearance, with no visible eyes, no external ear pinnae and no external tails. The golden moles are not related to the molerats (page 94). The latter are rodents, and have small but visible eyes, short tails, massively developed incisor teeth on both the upper and lower jaw and 5 claws on each forefoot.

Chrysospalax trevelyani

1. *Chrysospalax villosus*
2. *Cryptochloris wintoni*
3. *Cryptochloris zyli*
4. *Calcochloris obtusirostris*

1. *Chrysochloris asiatica*
2. *Chrysochloris visagiei*

Eremitalpa granti

Giant Golden Mole *Chrysospalax trevelyani*
Total length 23 cm; mass 538 g.
Rough-haired Golden Mole *Chrysospalax villosus*
Total length 15 cm; mass 125 g.
De Winton's Golden Mole *Cryptochloris wintoni*
Total length 9 cm.
Van Zyl's Golden Mole *Cryptochloris zyli*
Total length 8 cm.
Cape Golden Mole *Chrysochloris asiatica*
Total length 11 cm.
Visagie's Golden Mole *Chrysochloris visagiei*
Total length 10,5 cm.
Grant's Golden Mole *Eremitalpa granti*
Total length 7 cm; mass 16–30 g.
Arends's Golden Mole *Chlorotalpa arendsi*
Total length 12 cm; mass 40–76 g.
Duthie's Golden Mole *Chlorotalpa duthieae*
Total length 10 cm.
Sclater's Golden Mole *Chlorotalpa sclateri*
Total length 10 cm.
Yellow Golden Mole *Calcochloris obtusirostris*
Total length 10 cm; mass 20–30 g.
Gunning's Golden Mole *Amblysomus gunningi*
Total length 12 cm.
Hottentot Golden Mole *Amblysomus hottentotus*
Total length 13 cm; mass 75 g.
Juliana's Golden Mole *Amblysomus julianae*
Total length 10 cm; mass 21–23 g.
Zulu Golden Mole *Amblysomus iris*
Total length 10 cm; mass 40–50 g.
Identification pointers: All golden moles lack external tails, and have no visible eyes or external ears. Only two, the Giant and the Rough-haired Golden Moles, have long, coarse hair; the others have soft, silky hair. The forefeet carry four claws, of which the third is particularly well developed. The teeth are small and pointed, unlike the heavy chisel-like teeth of the molerats. The snouts are tipped with a leathery pad and unlike the pig-like snout of the molerats. With the exception of a few species the golden moles do not push up heaps or mounds like the molerats, but long, meandering ridges just under the surface.

Description: Only descriptions of the more widespread or distinctive species are given below:
Giant Golden Mole: Long, coarse hair; upperparts dark glossy-brown with paler underparts; small, light-coloured patches at sites of eyes and ears.

Giant Golden Mole

Giant Golden Mole

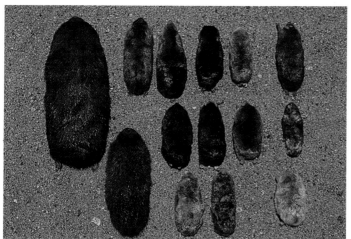

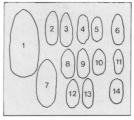

Key to golden mole skins
1. Giant Golden Mole
2. Cape Golden Mole
3. Hottentot Golden Mole
4. Gunning's Golden Mole
5. Zulu Golden Mole
6. Juliana's Golden Mole
7. Rough-haired Golden Mole
8. Arends's Golden Mole
9. Duthie's Golden Mole
10. Sclater's Golden Mole
11. Yellow Golden Mole
12. De Winton's Golden Mole
13. Van Zyl's Golden Mole
14. Grant's Golden Mole

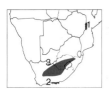

1. *Chlorotalpa arendsi*
2. *Chlorotalpa duthieae*
3. *Chlorotalpa sclateri*

1. *Amblysomus gunningi*
2. *Amblysomus julianae*
3. *Amblysomus iris*

Amblysomus hottentotus

Rough-haired Golden Mole: Long, coarse hair; similar to Giant Golden Mole but has greyer underparts, and the sides of the face and top of the muzzle are pale grey.
De Winton's and Grant's Golden Moles: Both species are similar, their upperparts being pale yellowish to yellow-grey, with paler underparts.
Cape Golden Mole: Upperparts dark brown with changing sheen of purple, green and bronze; paler, duller underparts. Pale eye-spots, with pale-brown line running from each spot to pale-brown chin.
Sclater's Golden Mole: A rich glossy red-brown to dark brown above, with dull grey underparts with a reddish tinge; chin paler than rest of body.
Duthie's Golden Mole: Very dark, almost black, with distinct green sheen; pale, triangular cheek-patches. Could be confused with Zulu Golden Mole where ranges overlap.
Hottentot Golden Mole: Usually rich reddish-brown upperparts with bronze sheen; underparts lighter with grey tinge; cheeks very pale; top of muzzle greyish-brown.
Wherever possible a specimen should be submitted to a natural history museum for confirmation of an identification. However, the use of the distribution maps will assist in narrowing down the number of species involved in any particular area.
Distribution: Consult the distribution maps as most species have very restricted distributions. For example, De Winton's Golden Mole is only known from Port Nolloth on the west coast of South Africa; Van Zyl's Golden Mole has also only been collected at one site on the west coast; Visagie's Golden Mole is known from a solitary specimen taken in the western Karoo. There is some doubt as to the validity of several of these species. Grant's Golden Mole is restricted to a narrow belt of sand-dunes in the Namib Desert. Both Gunning's Golden Mole and Juliana's Golden Mole also have extremely restricted distribution ranges.
Habitat: The Giant Golden Mole has a very patchy and limited distribution as it occurs only in the relict areas of indigenous high forest in the eastern Cape. Gunning's Golden Mole is also associated with forested areas. By far the vast majority of species are associated with sandy soils, although the Hottentot Golden Mole, as well as a few other species, may also utilize clay or loamy soils. Duthie's Golden Mole has a broad habitat range, extending into montane areas. None of the species are able to cope with heavy clay soils.
Behaviour: All of the golden moles are subterranean dwellers, although foraging on the surface may be commoner than is generally believed. Certainly Grant's Golden Mole spends much of its nocturnal foraging time moving about above ground. Because of this habit many fall prey to owls and other predators. As far as is known all species have deeper-running, permanent tunnels, with the surface tunnels being purely for foraging. The Giant Golden Mole pushes mounds with soil removed from newly excavated burrows, in much the same way as the molerats. The Rough-haired Golden Mole creates both surface tunnels and loose mounds, the latter always having an opening. Although some species may be nocturnal, at least several actively forage during the day. Where they occur in gardens they are usually considered a nuisance because of the soil disturbance but they are valuable allies as they eat large quantities of potentially harmful insects and other invertebrates. Virtually nothing is known about their social structure or general behaviour.
Food: All species feed on insects and other invertebrates. The Giant Golden Mole apparently feeds mainly on giant earthworms (*Microchaetus* spp.). Several (if not all) species also eat small reptiles, particularly legless lizards and worm-snakes that share their underground habitat.
Reproduction: From the meagre records it would seem that litters consist of either one or two young, born naked and helpless. Young are probably born during the rainy season when food is most abundant.

Cape Golden Mole

Sclater's Golden Mole

Hottentot Golden Mole

Hedgehogs Family Erinaceidae

Southern African Hedgehog *Atelerix frontalis*
Total length 20 cm; tail 2 cm; mass 400 g.
Identification pointers: Small size; covered in short spines; pointed face; white stripe from ear to ear across forehead.

Description: The Hedgehog's upperparts are covered with short but strong sharp spines. These spines extend from the forehead and the area just in front of the ears over the back to the rump. Although there is some variation the spines are usually white at the base and tip with a dark-brown or black band in between. The face, legs and tail are covered in dark to grey-brown hair. The underparts vary widely in colour from off-white to black. A prominent white band of hair extends across the forehead down beyond each ear. Contrary to popular belief, Hedgehogs have quite long legs but this is only revealed when they move rapidly.
Distribution: The Hedgehog occurs in two separate populations in southern Africa, one in South West Africa/Namibia and the other extending from the eastern part of the Cape Province north into Zimbabwe and eastern Botswana. It is possible that the two populations are linked. Outside the area covered by this field guide, the Southern African Hedgehog occurs only in south-west Angola in a continuation of the South West Africa/Namibia population.
Habitat: The Southern African Hedgehog occurs in a wide variety of habitats but is absent from desert and high-rainfall areas. To date it has not been recorded from regions receiving more than 800 mm of rain per year. Its habitat must provide suitable dry cover for lying up during the day.
Behaviour: Mainly nocturnal, although they are known to emerge during the day at the start of the rainy season. During the day they rest amongst dry vegetation or in the burrows of other species. Fixed resting-places are only used by females with young and by hibernating animals. At other times they use different sites. Hedgehogs hibernate chiefly between the winter months of May to July with peak activity occurring during the warmer, wetter months. They are nearly always solitary, only coming together to mate, or when a female is accompanied by young. The hedgehog has an excellent sense of smell, as well as good hearing but its eyesight is poor. When disturbed or threatened it curls itself into a tight ball with the spines protecting the vulnerable head and underparts.
Food: The hedgehog eats a wide variety of foods, including insects, millipedes, earthworms, mice, lizards, fungi and certain fruits. It eats approximately 30 per cent of its body weight in one night of feeding.
Reproduction: The young, weighing 9–11 g, are born during the summer months after a gestation period of about 35 days. New-born hedgehogs are blind and only the tips of the infant spines are visible. At about six weeks they have replaced the infant spines with a full covering of adult spines and it is at this time that they start to go foraging with the mother. Litters may contain 1-9 young, with an average of 4.
General: Although the coat of spines is adequate protection against many predators – including the Lion – the Hedgehog is a favourite prey of the Giant (or Milky) Eagle Owl (*Bubo lacteus*). Predation by humans for food or for the alleged medicinal properties of the skin and spines takes place in some districts. In some areas there seems to have been a decline in hedgehog numbers in recent years; this is due to a number of factors, including road mortality, predation by humans, capture for pets, detrimental agricultural practices and possibly climatic factors such as extended droughts.

Southern African Hedgehog

Southern African Hedgehog showing detail of spine colouration

Petrodromus tetradactylus

Macroscelides proboscideus

Elephantulus fuscus

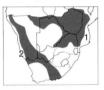

1. *Elephantulus brachyrhynchus*
2. *Elephantulus rupestris*

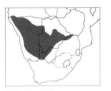

Elephantulus intufi

Elephantulus myurus

Elephant-shrews Family Macroscelididae

Elephant-shrews derive their name from their elongated, trunk-like snout. The hindlegs and feet are considerably larger than the forelegs and -feet and rapid locomotion is achieved by a series of hops.

Four-toed Elephant-shrew *Petrodromus tetradactylus*
Total length 35 cm; tail 16 cm; mass 160–280 g.
Round-eared Elephant-shrew *Macroscelides proboscideus*
Total length 23 cm; tail 12 cm; mass 31–47 g.
Peters's Short-snouted Elephant-shrew *Elephantulus fuscus*
Total length 21 cm.
Short-snouted Elephant-shrew *Elephantulus brachyrhynchus*
Total length 21 cm; tail 10 cm; mass 44 g.
Smith's Rock Elephant-shrew *Elephantulus rupestris*
Total length 28 cm; tail 15 cm; mass 65 g.
Bushveld Elephant-shrew *Elephantulus intufi*
Total length 24 cm; tail 12 cm; mass 50 g.
Rock Elephant-shrew *Elephantulus myurus*
Total length 26 cm; tail 14 cm; mass 60 g.
Cape Rock Elephant-shrew *Elephantulus edwardii*
Total length 25 cm; tail 13 cm; mass 50 g.
Identification pointers: Elongated, highly mobile snout – nostrils at tip; large thin ears; tail fairly long and sparsely haired; large eyes. Apart from Four-toed Elephant-shrew and Round-eared Elephant-shrew, the other species are generally difficult to tell apart in the field. Use distribution maps; note habitat preferences.

Description: Four-Toed Elephant-shrew easily distinguished by its large size. From head to base of tail the back is reddish-brown; sides are grey to grey-brown; white ring around eye; white patch at each ear base; underparts are white. Round-eared Elephant-shrew is one of smallest; variable in colour, but most commonly brownish-grey above, paler below; sometimes whitish-grey in colour; no white eye-ring. All other species have white or greyish-white rings around eyes. The three rock elephant-shrews, the two short-snouted elephant-shrews, and Bushveld Elephant-shrew have reddish-brown to brown patches at base of ears. Colour of upperparts, however, varies considerably in all species. Underparts are always paler than the upperparts.
Distribution: See maps.
Habitat: Habitat preferences taken together with geographical locality are of considerable help in the identification of members of this group. The Four-toed Elephant-shrew is a forest species, associated with fairly dense undergrowth, usually in high-rainfall areas. Three species, the Rock Elephant-shrew, the Cape Rock Elephant-shrew and Smith's Rock Elephant-shrew, as their names imply, are restricted to rocky environments and their distributions do not overlap. The Short-snouted Elephant-shrew, Peters's Short-snouted Elephant-shrew and the Bushveld Elephant-shrew occur in areas with sandy soils. Although the Rock Elephant-shrew and the Short-snouted Elephant-shrew occur in the same geographical areas they are clearly separated by their habitat requirements.
Behaviour: All of the elephant-shrews are almost entirely diurnal, although at least the Round-eared Elephant-shrew may be partly nocturnal. They are all terrestrial and usually solitary but in areas of high density several animals may be observed in close proximity to each other. The rock-dwelling species keep to the shade of overhanging rocks and boulders during the hot midday hours, making occasional dashes to seize an insect. Those species relying more on bush or grass cover generally have regularly used pathways between shelters. The pathways tend to consist of regularly spaced,

Four-toed Elephant-shrew

Round-eared Elephant-shrew

Short-snouted Elephant-shrew

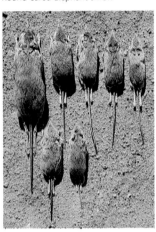

Bushveld Elephant-shrew

Key to elephant-shrew skins
(above l. to r.)
1. Four-toed
   Elephant-shrew
2. Rock Elephant-shrew
3. Smith's Rock
   Elephant-shrew
4. Cape Rock
   Elephant-shrew
5. Bushveld Elephant-shrew
(below l. to r.)
1. Round-eared
   Elephant-shrew
2. Short-snouted Elephant-
   shrew (see overleaf for
   Rock Elephant-shrew)

Elephantulus edwardii

well-worn patches, a result of their rapid, hopping gait. Those species associated with sandy soil usually live in burrows.

Food: All elephant-shrews eat insects and other invertebrates, with a marked preference for ants and termites. In captivity several species readily eat seed and other vegetable matter and it is possible that these items are included in their natural diet.

Reproduction: The young of all species are born fully haired with their eyes open and are able to move around shortly after birth. Litter of 1–2 young born during or just before the rainy season.

Shrews Family Soricidae

Small, short-legged, mouse-like mammals, with long wedge-shaped snouts and very small eyes. Four genera, *Myosorex*, *Suncus*, *Crocidura* and *Sylvisorex*, with 16 species, are presently recognized as occurring in the subregion.

FOREST SHREWS Genus *Myosorex*
Three species of forest shrew occur in southern Africa:

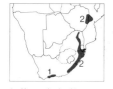

1. *Myosorex longicaudatus*
2. *Myosorex cafer*

Long-tailed Forest Shrew *Myosorex longicaudatus*
Total length 15 cm; tail 6 cm.
Dark-footed Forest Shrew *Myosorex cafer*
Total length 12 cm; tail 4 cm; mass 9–16 g.
Forest Shrew *Myosorex varius*
Total length 12 cm; tail 4 cm; mass 12–16 g.
Identification pointers: Long-tailed Forest Shrew restricted to small area of southern Cape Province; overlaps with Forest Shrew but has longer tail. Area of overlap of the two shorter-tailed species is limited to eastern coastal belt and the eastern escarpment of the Transvaal.

Myosorex varius

Description: Long-tailed Forest Shrew is dark brown to black in colour, with slightly paler underparts. Main distinguishing character is long tail which is black-brown above and slightly paler below. Forest Shrew and Dark-footed Forest Shrew are similar but it is possible to distinguish them where their ranges overlap in the eastern Cape: there the Forest Shrew has more greyish underparts and the under-surface of its tail is paler than the upper-surface, while the Dark-footed Forest Shrew has browner underparts and a uniformly coloured tail. Although hairy, the short tail of the forest shrews lacks the long hairs or vibrissae found in the musk shrews and dwarf shrews.

Distribution: See 'Identification pointers' and maps.

Habitat: All species are associated with well-vegetated and moist areas, with the Long-tailed Forest Shrew found mainly in the transition zone between forest and fynbos. Although named 'forest shrews', they are found in a wide range of other habitats.

Behaviour: Virtually nothing known about behaviour of Long-tailed Forest Shrew. As with all the other shrew species occurring in southern Africa, however, members of the genus *Myosorex* may be active at any time during the night or day. The Forest Shrew is an active digger, excavating shallow burrows, but it will also use holes dug by other species.

Food: All three species are insectivorous but will take other invertebrates such as earthworms and small vertebrates, *e.g.* lizards and frogs.

Reproduction: The Forest Shrew and Dark-footed Forest Shrew give birth during the summer months to litters of 2–4 naked and helpless young.

Rock Elephant-shrew

Forest Shrew

Long-tailed Forest Shrew

1. *Crocidura occidentalis*
2. *Crocidura flavescens*

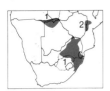

1. *Crocidura mariquensis*
2. *Crocidura luna*

Crocidura fuscomurina

Crocidura cyanea

Crocidura silacea

Crocidura hirta

MUSK SHREWS Genus *Crocidura*

Nine species of musk shrew occur in southern Africa. They are difficult to distinguish from one another and, apart from the two largest species, the only certain way to separate them is by detailed examination of skull structure, dentition and chromosome composition.

Giant Musk Shrew *Crocidura occidentalis*
Total length 20 cm; tail 8 cm; mass 31–37 g.
Swamp Musk Shrew *Crocidura mariquensis*
Total length 13 cm; tail 5 cm; mass 10 g.
Tiny Musk Shrew *Crocidura fuscomurina*
Total length 10 cm; tail 4 cm; mass 6 g.
Maquassie Musk Shrew *Crocidura maquassiensis*
Total length 10 cm; tail 4 cm; mass 6 g.
Reddish-grey Musk Shrew *Crocidura cyanea*
Total length 13 cm; tail 5 cm; mass 9 g.
Lesser Grey-brown Musk Shrew *Crocidura silacea*
Total length 12 cm; tail 5 cm.
Greater Musk Shrew *Crocidura flavescens*
Total length 16 cm; tail 6 cm; mass 39 g.
Greater Grey-brown Musk Shrew *Crocidura luna*
Total length 14,5 cm; tail 5,5 cm.
Lesser Red Musk Shrew *Crocidura hirta*
Total length 13 cm; tail 4,5 cm; mass 15 g.
Identification pointers: Typical shrew appearance; prominent vibrissae on tail. Occupy wide range of habitats and identification will be aided by consulting the distribution maps and habitat descriptions. Positive identification requires that specimen(s) be examined by an expert.

Description: Musk shrews vary considerably in pelage colour. Colour ranges from blackish-brown to greyish-fawn above and dark brown to pale grey below. The most widespread species, the Reddish-grey Musk Shrew, is greyish-red to reddish-brown on the upperparts depending on whether the specimen comes from the western or eastern area of southern Africa; the upper-surfaces of the feet are paler than the rest of the body. The Swamp Musk Shrew is very dark brown to blackish-brown all over, including the tail and upper-surface of the feet. The Giant and Greater Musk Shrews are distinguishable by their comparatively large size and pale-fawn to reddish-brown upperparts, with fawn-grey to off-white underparts. The Lesser Red Musk Shrew is similar in appearance but smaller. The tails of the musk shrews are sparsely covered with fairly long vibrissae; this is a feature shared with the dwarf shrews, but not with the Climbing Shrew or the forest shrews.

Distribution: Greater Grey-brown Musk Shrew is restricted to the Eastern Highlands of Zimbabwe and adjacent areas of Mozambique. Maquassie Musk Shrew only known from a few localities in Transvaal and Zimbabwe. Most widespread species is Reddish-grey Musk Shrew.

Habitat: Most of the musk shrews are found in association with moist habitats, although the Reddish-grey Musk Shrew is also found in very dry areas. The Lesser Red Musk Shrew also extends into drier areas. All species show a preference for dense, matted vegetation.

Behaviour: Musk shrews have alternating activity and rest periods throughout the 24-hour period. Foraging is probably a solitary activity in all species. They actively defend territories within fixed home ranges.

Food: Insects, other invertebrates and possibly small vertebrates.

Reproduction: Most species have their litters of 2–6 naked and helpless young in the warm, wet summer months. Nothing is known about the reproduction of the Maquassie, Lesser Grey-brown or Greater Grey-brown musk shrews. Gestation period of Lesser Red Musk Shrew is 18 days.

Reddish-grey Musk Shrew

Reddish-grey Musk Shrew; note vibrissae on snout

Tiny Musk Shrew

Lesser Red Musk Shrew

Swamp Musk Shrew

DWARF SHREWS Genus *Suncus*

Three species of dwarf shrew occur in southern Africa:

Suncus lixus

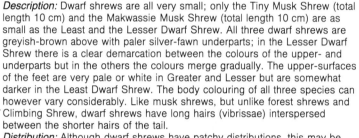

Greater Dwarf Shrew *Suncus lixus*
Total length 11 cm; tail 4,5 cm; mass 8 g.
Lesser Dwarf Shrew *Suncus varilla*
Total length 9 cm; tail 3,3 cm; mass 6,5 g.
Least Dwarf Shrew *Suncus infinitesimus*
Total length 8 cm; tail 3 cm; mass 3,5 g.
Identification pointers: Very small size; could be confused with the Tiny Musk Shrew where ranges overlap.

Suncus varilla

Description: Dwarf shrews are all very small; only the Tiny Musk Shrew (total length 10 cm) and the Makwassie Musk Shrew (total length 10 cm) are as small as the Least and the Lesser Dwarf Shrew. All three dwarf shrews are greyish-brown above with paler silver-fawn underparts; in the Lesser Dwarf Shrew there is a clear demarcation between the colours of the upper- and underparts but in the others the colours merge gradually. The upper-surfaces of the feet are very pale or white in Greater and Lesser but are somewhat darker in the Least Dwarf Shrew. The body colouring of all three species can however vary considerably. Like musk shrews, but unlike forest shrews and Climbing Shrew, dwarf shrews have long hairs (vibrissae) interspersed between the shorter hairs of the tail.

Suncus infinitesimus

Distribution: Although dwarf shrews have patchy distributions, this may be apparent rather than real as they are difficult to catch; they may be more common and widespread than present records indicate. The Lesser Dwarf Shrew is certainly widespread in South Africa, whereas the other two species appear to have more limited distribution ranges. They are absent from South West Africa/Namibia. All three extend into East Africa, with the Least Dwarf Shrew being widely distributed through sub-Saharan Africa.

Habitat: The dwarf shrews occur in a broad range of habitats, particularly the Greater Dwarf Shrew. The Least and the Lesser Dwarf Shrew are commonly found in association with termite-mounds, which provide shelter and probably also food.

Behaviour: Unknown.

Food: These shrews eat insects and probably other small invertebrates. In captivity the Greater Dwarf Shrew will readily attack grasshoppers equalling its own size.

Reproduction: Unknown.

CLIMBING SHREW Genus *Sylvisorex*

Sylvisorex megalura

Climbing Shrew *Sylvisorex megalura*
Total length 16 cm; tail 8,5 cm; mass 5–7 g.
Identification pointers: Thin tail longer than head and body; in southern Africa it is restricted to the eastern half of Zimbabwe.

Description: This is the only southern African shrew with a tail length greater than the length of the head and body. The upperparts are grey with a brownish tinge and the underparts may be pale brown to off-white. The tail is long and thin, dark above and pale below.

Distribution: Only so far recorded from eastern Zimbabwe, but elsewhere in Africa occurs widely south of the Sahara.

Habitat: High-rainfall areas with dense scrub and grass cover.

Behaviour: Unknown.

Food: Unknown.

Reproduction: Unknown.

Lesser Dwarf Shrew

Least Dwarf Shrew

BATS Order Chiroptera

Fruit-eating bats Suborder Megachiroptera Family Pteropodidae

Seven species of fruit-bat have been recorded from southern Africa.
They may be divided into two groups based on the presence or absence
of tufts of white hair at the base of the ears.

Eidolon helvum

Straw-coloured Fruit-bat *Eidolon helvum*
Total length 19 cm; forearm 11 cm; wingspan 75 cm; mass 300 g.
Identification pointers: Large size; dog-like face; no white tufts of hair at
base of ears and no other obvious markings; black wings. Considerably
larger than Egyptian Fruit-bat and with yellowish body fur, particularly on
the shoulders and back.

Description: The Straw-coloured Fruit-bat is the largest bat in the subregion.
Like other fruit-bats it has a dog-like face. Wings long and tapered and are
dark brown to black. General body colour is variable and may be dull
yellow-brown to rich yellowish-brown. The underparts are always paler. The
hindquarters and limbs are usually darker than the rest of the body. The tail
is very short.
Distribution: This large bat is a migrant from the tropics, from Guinea in West
Africa through Zaïre to Uganda, Kenya and Tanzania in East Africa.
Habitat: Typically a species of tropical forest but in southern Africa it even
penetrates into Namib Desert along wooded watercourses in search of ripe
fruit.
Behaviour: In southern Africa it is usually encountered singly or in small
groups, although in the tropics colonies may number well in excess of
100 000 individuals. Normally they hang in clusters of 10 to 50 animals in
trees.
Food: It eats a wide range of both wild and cultivated fruit.
Reproduction: Does not breed in southern Africa.

Rousettus aegyptiacus

Egyptian Fruit-bat *Rousettus aegyptiacus*
Total length 15 cm; forearm 9,0-10,5 cm; wingspan 60 cm; mass 130 g.
Bocage's Fruit-bat *Rousettus angolensis*
Total length 12 cm; forearm 8,1-8,5 cm; wingspan 40 cm; mass 100 g.
Identification pointers: Neither species possesses white tufts at the
base of the ears. Both species are large. Uniformly coloured upper- and
underparts, but underparts always lighter in colour. Male of Bocage's
has collar of stiff, orange-coloured hair on throat and side of neck;
female's throat and neck are sparsely haired.

Rousettus angolensis

Description: Egyptian Fruit-bat plain-coloured without distinctive markings.
Upperparts vary from dark brown to greyish-brown in colour, and underparts
are grey. A paler, usually yellowish collar is present on the neck and the
throat may have a brownish tinge. Round-tipped wings are dark brown or
nearly black and tail is short. Bocage's is similar but is smaller and
upperparts are usually richer brown. Male has distinctive brown-orange collar
of stiff hairs on throat and sides of neck not found in male Egyptian Fruit-bat.
Distribution: Egyptian Fruit-bat occurs from Cape Town eastwards through
Natal into Mozambique and inland to eastern Transvaal and Zimbabwe.
Occurs widely through sub-Saharan Africa and north-eastwards to Egypt.
Within subregion Bocage's Fruit-bat is only known from eastern Zimbabwe
and the adjacent parts of Mozambique.
Habitat: Forested areas or savanna and riverine woodland with plentiful
supply of ripe fruit. A second essential prerequisite is the presence of caves
or old mine-shafts to provide roosts.

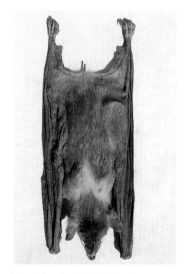

Skin of Egyptian Fruit-bat showing short tail and narrow interfemoral membrane typical of fruit-bats

Some Straw-coloured Fruit-bats have an orange 'collar'

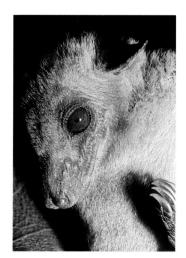

Head of Egyptian Fruit-bat

Fruit-bats differ from insectivorous bats by having two claws on each wing

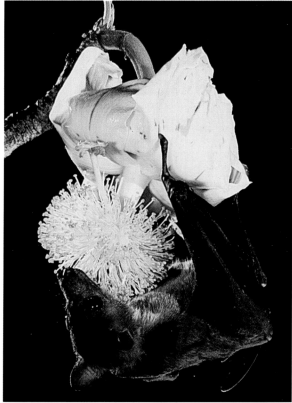

Egyptian Fruit-bats also serve as pollinators

Behaviour: Both species roost in caves during the day but the Egyptian Fruit-bat, being the only fruit-bat to echolocate, utilizes the darkest areas; it does, however, have good eyesight. Bocage's Fruit-bat is reliant on sight for orientation and will roost in the lighter areas of a cave; it also roosts in hollow trees. The Egyptian Fruit-bat may form colonies several thousands strong; Bocage's Fruit-bat colonies are small. Suitable roosting-caves may be several kilometres from feeding-grounds and caves may be vacated at certain times of the year when the bats need to travel too far in search of food.
Food: A wide range of soft fruit is eaten.
Reproduction: The single young of the Egyptian Fruit-bat is born after a gestation period of about 105 days from late winter (in north) to early summer (in south). Nothing is known about the reproduction of Bocage's Fruit-bat in southern Africa.

Wahlberg's Epauletted Fruit-bat *Epomophorus wahlbergi*
Males: total length 14 cm; forearm 8,4 cm; wingspan 50 cm; mass 70–110 g.
Peters's Epauletted Fruit-bat *Epomophorus crypturus*
Males: total length 15 cm; forearm 8,3 cm; wingspan 56 cm; mass 80–140 g.
Angolan Epauletted Fruit-bat *Epomophorus angolensis*
Males: total length 16 cm; forearm 8,9 cm; wingspan 50 cm.
Dobson's Fruit-bat *Epomops dobsonii*
Males: total length 16 cm; forearm 8,5 cm;
Identification pointers: Large size; white hair tufts at ear bases; white or yellowish epaulettes on shoulders of males; uniformly coloured fur in various shades of brown, but lighter underparts. Dog-like faces.

Epomophorus wahlbergi

Epomophorus crypturus

Epomophorus angolensis

Epomops dobsonii

Description: Distinguished by tufts of white hair at the base of the brown ears in both sexes, and by males having a glandular pouch on each shoulder covered in long white hair (or yellowish in the case of Dobson's Fruit-bat); when the pouch is spread, the light hair forms a prominent 'epaulette' – hence the group-name. Tails either absent or extremely short. Overall body colour of all four species is buff to brown with paler underparts, but colour can vary; Peters's Epauletted Fruit-bat, for example, can be yellowish-cream above and off-white below while Wahlberg's tends to be darker brown on average. Wahlberg's and Peters's are quite common in our region (see maps) and often associate together. They are, however, difficult to separate in the field. The only certain way of distinguishing between the species of epauletted fruit-bats is by examining the number and situation of the transverse ridges on the palate.
Distribution: Wahlberg's largely restricted to the eastern coastal belt. It extends inland along watercourses in the Transvaal and Zimbabwe. Peters's Epauletted Fruit-bat is largely restricted to the north-eastern part of subregion, with isolated records from the south-eastern coastal area. The Angolan Fruit-bat is restricted to south-western Angola and north-western South West Africa/Namibia. Dobson's Fruit-bat is known in our region from only one specimen from Chobe River in north-eastern Botswana.
Habitat: Forest and riverine woodland. May occasionally forage and roost away from the preferred woodland habitat, particularly in the case of the two commoner species – Wahlberg's, for example, commonly roosts in trees in parks and along busy streets in Mozambique's coastal cities.
Behaviour: Tree-roosters, with two commoner species coming together in noisy colonies with from a few to several hundred individuals.
Food: Most soft fruits, but possibly all species also feed from flowers.
Reproduction: Most young probably born in the early summer months.

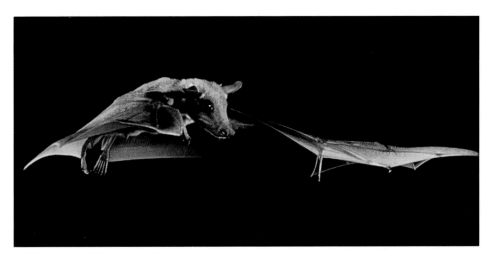

Wahlberg's Epauletted Fruit-bat in flight

Epauletted fruit-bats are free-roosters; note white ear-bases

Peter's Epauletted Fruit-bat

Wahlberg's Epauletted Fruit-bat

Insectivorous bats Suborder Microchiroptera

Sheath-tailed and tomb bats Family Emballonuridae

Bats of this family can be distinguished by the form of the tail, about one half of which is enclosed by the interfemoral membrane, the remainder not being attached to the membrane but not extending beyond it (fig 1.2, page 18). They have simple faces without any projections or nose-leaves. The ears are triangular with rounded tips and each species has a different-shaped tragus.

Coleura afra

Sheath-tailed Bat *Coleura afra*
Total length 7 cm; wingspan 24 cm.
Mauritian Tomb Bat *Taphozous mauritianus*
Total length 10 cm; forearm 6 cm; wingspan 34 cm; mass 28 g.
Egyptian Tomb Bat *Taphozous perforatus*
Total length 10 cm; forearm 6 cm; wingspan 34 cm.
Identification pointers: Tail partly enclosed by membrane, with remainder free but not projecting beyond membrane (see fig. 1.2, page 18 and compare with free-tailed bats, fig. 1.9). Much smaller size of Sheath-tailed Bat; Mauritian Tomb Bat with white underparts and wings; Egyptian Tomb Bat only outer two-thirds of wings white, remainder very dark; underparts light brown to grey with some white hairs on lower belly, but not all white as in Mauritian Tomb Bat.

Taphozous mauritianus

Taphozous perforatus

Description: Tail as described above (see fig. 1.2, page 18). Sheath-tailed Bat uniform brown but slightly paler below and on wings. Mauritian Tomb Bat has grey upperparts, pure-white underparts and greyish-white wing-membranes. Males have a deep glandular sac in the throat; females have only shallow fold. Egyptian Tomb Bat has dark-brown upperparts and slightly paler underparts, although belly is usually off-white; only outer two-thirds of the wing-membranes white, inner third almost black. No throat gland.
Distribution: Sheath-tailed Bat occurs only in extreme north-east of subregion. Mauritian Tomb Bat restricted to southern and eastern coastal belt but extends inland into the Transvaal and Zimbabwe, and to north of Botswana and the Caprivi Strip. Egyptian Tomb Bat only known from scattered localities in northern Botswana and Zimbabwe.
Habitat: Open woodland. The Mauritian Tomb Bat frequently roosts in more exposed positions, such as outer walls of buildings and on tree-trunks; Egyptian Tomb Bat hides in dark cracks and crevices in caves or buildings.
Behaviour: Mauritian Tomb Bat usually roosts singly or in pairs and Egyptian Tomb Bat in clusters of 6 to 10. Roost with belly flat against surface and if disturbed scuttle around a corner. Can detect movement from some distance away indicating that they have good eyesight in contrast to most other insect-eating bats. Sometimes hunt by day.
Food: Insects.
Reproduction: Tomb bats give birth to a single young during summer. Sheath-tailed Bat probably similar.

Trident and leaf-nosed bats Family Hipposideridae

This distinctive group of bats consists of three genera and four species in southern Africa of which two have a single nose-leaf and two have three spear-shaped leaves mounted at the back of the main nose-leaf.

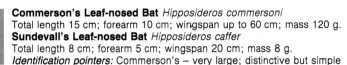

Hipposideros commersoni

Commerson's Leaf-nosed Bat *Hipposideros commersoni*
Total length 15 cm; forearm 10 cm; wingspan up to 60 cm; mass 120 g.
Sundevall's Leaf-nosed Bat *Hipposideros caffer*
Total length 8 cm; forearm 5 cm; wingspan 20 cm; mass 8 g.
Identification pointers: Commerson's – very large; distinctive but simple

Mauritian Tomb Bat

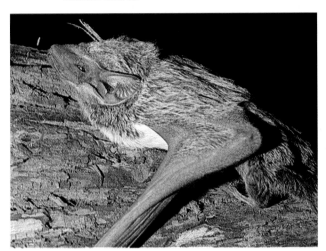

Mauritian Tomb Bat

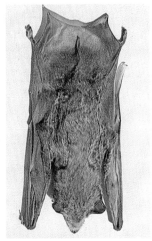

Tomb bat skin showing tail conformation

Commerson's Leaf-nosed Bat

Sundevall's Leaf-nosed Bat

Hipposideros caffer

nose-leaf which lacks the triangular pointed process pointing backwards over the head typical of the horseshoe bats; short hair with overall pale-fawn appearance; males with white shoulder tufts; black feet. Sundevall's – small size; similar nose-leaf; colour variable; long woolly hair. Should not be confused with other bats (but see horseshoe bats and also tail structure diagrams on page 18).

Description: The two species can be easily separated by size difference. Have well-developed nose-leaves and are related to horseshoe bats; unlike the latter, however, they do not have the prominent triangular posterior nose-leaf processes. Ears are large, pointed and leaf-like. Commerson's has short hair, sandy-brown upperparts, but paler neck and head. Underparts also paler, with white, sparsely haired flanks; males have white tufts on sides of shoulders. Sundevall's is much smaller and its dorsal hair is long and woolly. Variable in colour, with some individuals being almost white (especially from South West Africa/Namibia) and others deep yellow-brown or dark grey-brown. Tail structure like horse-shoe bats (fig. 1.3, page 18).
Distribution: Commerson's only occurs in north of subregion. Sundevall's has similar range but extends further south and over much of Transvaal.
Habitat: Savanna woodland; roost in caves, mine-shafts, buildings.
Behaviour: Both species roost in colonies of hundreds of individuals, but Sundevall's sometimes in small groups of 2–3. Hang free at the roosts in clusters but not in contact with neighbours. Slow but agile fliers.
Food: Insects.
Reproduction: Sundevall's gives birth to a single young in summer.

Cloeotis percivali

Short-eared Trident Bat *Cloeotis percivali*
Total length 7 cm; forearm 3,5 cm; wingspan 15 cm; mass 5 g.
Identification pointers: Three-pointed process at top of nose-leaf – a feature shared only with the Persian Leaf-nosed Bat. Similar to the Persian Leaf-nosed Bat but total length only 7 cm to the latter's 14 cm.

Description: Distinctive three-pronged trident-like process at back of nose-leaf between the eyes. Upperparts usually pale grey, while underparts are grey-white to greyish-yellow; wings are dark. Face is whitish-yellow and ears are small and almost hidden by long fur.
Distribution: Patchy distribution in north-east of subregion.
Habitat: Unknown. Roosts in caves and mine-shafts.
Behaviour: Colonies of several hundreds but also small groups. Roosts in darkest areas of caves or mines, hanging in tight clusters from roof.
Food: Insects.
Reproduction: A single young is born in the early summer.

Triaenops persicus

Persian Leaf-nosed (or Trident) Bat *Triaenops persicus*
Total length 14 cm; forearm 5 cm; wingspan 35 cm; mass 12 g.
Identification pointers: Much larger than Short-eared Trident Bat. Three spear-shaped leaves at top of nose-leaf. Only known from extreme north-eastern corner of southern African subregion.

Description: Nose-leaf pitted with small cavities and folds; 3 large spear-shaped leaves mounted at back of nose-leaf. Ears are small, pointed and sharply notched on outer edge. Upperparts from light brown to reddish-brown; underparts paler and sides of face yellowish. Wings dark brown.
Distribution: Eastern Highlands of Zimbabwe and neighbouring Mozambique.
Habitat: Little known. Roosts in caves or old mines.
Behaviour: Usually forms large colonies. In roosting-caves hang from ceiling in clusters, but not touching one another. Have a slow, flapping flight.
Food: Insects.
Reproduction: Unknown.

Short-eared Trident Bat

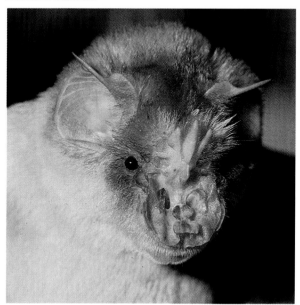

Persian Leaf-nosed (or Trident) Bat

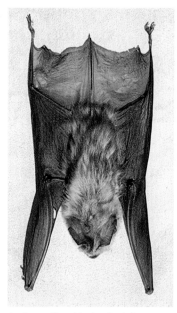

Leaf-nosed bat skin showing tail conformation

Slit-faced bats Family Nycteridae

Immediately recognizable by the long, lobed slit that runs down the centre of the face; when this slit is opened nose-leaves can be seen. Possess ear tragi and have large, more or less straight- and parallel-sided ears. The wings are broad and rounded at the tips.

Nycteris hispida

Nycteris grandis

Nycteris woodi

1. *Nycteris macrotis*
2. *Nycteris vinsoni*

Nycteris thebaica

Hairy Slit-faced Bat *Nycteris hispida*
Total length 9 cm; forearm 4 cm; wingspan 28 cm; ear length 2,2 cm.
Large Slit-faced Bat *Nycteris grandis*
Total length 16 cm; forearm 6,5 cm; wingspan 35 cm; ear length 3,1 cm; mass 40 g.
Wood's Slit-faced Bat *Nycteris woodi*
Total length 9 cm; forearm 3,8 cm; ear length 3,2 cm.
Greater Slit-faced Bat *Nycteris macrotis*
Total length 11 cm; forearm 4,7 cm; ear length 2,9 cm; mass 12 g.
Egyptian Slit-faced Bat *Nycteris thebaica*
Total length 10 cm; forearm 4,7 cm; wingspan 24 cm; ear length 3,4 cm; mass 11 g.
Vinson's Slit-faced Bat *Nycteris vinsoni*
Total length 12,5 cm; forearm 5,1 cm; ear length 2,2 cm.
Identification pointers: Very long, erect ears; facial slit; bifurcated tail-tip. Most likely species to be encountered is the Egyptian Slit-faced Bat. Should not be confused with any other bat, but see long-eared bats of the genus *Laephotis* (page 66).

Description: All slit-faced bats have long, rounded ears, a split running down the length of the face, a long tail bifurcated at the tip and wings rounded at the tip. The Large Slit-faced Bat can be separated by its much larger size. Colour in all species is variable but upperparts are always darker than underparts. Both Large and Greater Slit-faced Bats usually have reddish-brown upperparts and greyer underparts. The Egyptian Slit-faced Bat usually has light-brown upperparts (occasionally reddish-orange) and underparts that range from pale brown to dirty white.
Distribution: Vinson's Slit-faced Bat is known only from a single locality in Mozambique. Greater Slit-faced Bat has only been collected in our subregion in eastern Zambezi Valley in Zimbabwe, but is widespread in equatorial Africa. Hairy Slit-faced Bat has a limited distribution in eastern Zimbabwe and Mozambique but elsewhere occurs widely south of the Sahara. Large Slit-faced Bat has a similar southern African distribution. Wood's Slit-faced Bat is known from two localities in Zimbabwe and south-eastern Zambia. Egyptian Slit-faced Bat has a wide distribution, extending to Europe.
Habitat: Egyptian Slit-faced Bat has wide habitat tolerance, as has the Hairy Slit-faced Bat, although the latter avoids more arid areas. Large and Greater Slit-faced Bats show a preference for riverine woodland. Roosts include caves, buildings and amongst leaves in trees and bushes.
Behaviour: Although most species of slit-faced bat roost in small numbers and are often found roosting alone or in pairs, the Egyptian Slit-faced Bat sometimes forms roosts consisting of several hundred individuals. All are slow but highly efficient fliers. Insect and other prey is taken on the wing and even from the ground and vegetation and then carried to a regularly used perch to feed. Such perches may be recognized by the accumulation of non-edible parts such as moth wings and beetle elytra on the ground below.
Food: Insects and other invertebrates are the usual prey but the Large Slit-faced Bat will also take vertebrate prey, including fish and frogs.
Reproduction: Egyptian Slit-faced Bat: a single young is born during the early summer months and is carried by the mother during feeding forays.

Egyptian Slit-faced bat

Head of Egyptian Slit-faced Bat

Slit-faced bat skin showing bifurcated tail-tip

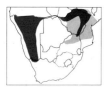

■ *Rhinolophus fumigatus*

▨ *Rhinolophus hildebrandtii*

Rhinolophus clivosus

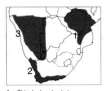

Rhinolophus darlingi

1. *Rhinolophus landeri*
2. *Rhinolophus capensis*
3. *Rhinolophus denti*

▢ *Rhinolophus blasii*

▣ *Rhinolophus swinnyi*

Rhinolophus simulator

Horseshoe bats Family Rhinolophidae

Horseshoe bats are characterized by having elaborate nose-leaves over the face between the mouth and forehead.
Ten species have been recorded as occurring in southern Africa.

Hildebrandt's Horseshoe Bat *Rhinolophus hildebrandtii*
Total length 11 cm; forearm 6,5 cm; wingspan 39 cm; mass 27 g.
Rüppell's Horseshoe Bat *Rhinolophus fumigatus*
Total length 9,2 cm; forearm 5,0 cm; mass 14 g.
Geoffroy's Horseshoe Bat *Rhinolophus clivosus*
Total length 9,7 cm; forearm 5,4 cm; wingspan 32 cm; mass 17 g.
Darling's Horseshoe Bat *Rhinolophus darlingi*
Total length 8,5 cm; forearm 4,5 cm; mass 9 g.
Lander's Horseshoe Bat *Rhinolophus landeri*
Total length 8,0 cm; forearm 4,4 cm; mass 6 g.
Peak-saddle Horseshoe Bat *Rhinolophus blasii*
Total length 7,6 cm; forearm 4,5 cm; mass 4 g.
Cape Horseshoe Bat *Rhinolophus capensis*
Total length 8,5 cm; forearm 4,8 cm; wingspan 30 cm.
Bushveld Horseshoe Bat *Rhinolophus simulator*
Total length 7,0 cm; forearm 4,3 cm; mass 8 g.
Dent's Horseshoe Bat *Rhinolophus denti*
Total length 7,0 cm; forearm 4,2 cm; wingspan 20 cm; mass 6 g.
Swinny's Horseshoe Bat *Rhinolophus swinnyi*
Total length 7,0 cm; forearm 4,3 cm; mass 7,5 g.
Identification pointers: Facial structure characteristic, with main nose-leaf base in form of horseshoe; large ears lacking tragi but with pronounced skin fold at ear-base. When at rest, wings wrap around the body.

Description: For the non-expert this is a very difficult group to identify to species level. Hildebrandt's Horseshoe Bat can be separated on its much larger size. Most species are variable in colour but Dent's Horseshoe Bat is usually pale brown or even cream above with off-white underparts and pale translucent brown wing-membranes edged with white. Swinny's Horseshoe Bat is similar in colour to Dent's Horseshoe Bat but lacks the white edging of the membranes. Another pale-coloured species is Darling's Horseshoe Bat which has dull-grey upper- and pale-grey underparts and pale grey-brown wing-membranes. The Peak-saddle Horseshoe Bat is characterized by having long, woolly hair which is very pale to white, with the palest area being at the back of the neck. The Bushveld Horseshoe Bat is dark brown above with contrasting greyish-white underparts. The other species have brown upperparts and usually lighter underparts. In all cases, however, careful examination of teeth, facial structures and forearm length is necessary for positive identification. Tail form is shown in fig. 1.5, page 18.
Distribution: Consult the distribution maps.
Habitat: Most species are associated with savanna. All species are principally cave roosters but some also make use of dark buildings and Hildebrandt's Horseshoe Bat will also utilize tree hollows.
Behaviour: Rüppell's, Lander's, the Peak-saddle and Swinny's Horseshoe Bats are only found roosting in small numbers, whereas the other species may also roost in much larger colonies. Geoffroy's and Cape Horseshoe Bats are found numbering thousands in some roosts. In such roosts they hang free by the feet singly or in well-spaced groups.
Food: Insects.
Reproduction: The young are born singly in summer.

Lander's Horseshoe Bat

Geoffroy's Horseshoe Bat, orange phase; normally light brown

Bushveld Horseshoe Bat

Rüppell's Horseshoe Bat

Darling's Horseshoe Bat

Cape Horseshoe Bat in flight

(see overleaf for horseshoe bat skin)

Vesper bats Family Vespertilionidae

'Vesper bat' is a group name for the bats of the family Vespertilionidae, and includes the long-fingered, serotine, hairy, pipistrelle, butterfly, long-eared, house and woolly bats. It is by far the largest bat family occurring in the subregion, with three subfamilies, 10 genera and 29 species. Many can only be identified by examination of their dental and cranial characters. All have somewhat mouse-like faces without nose-leaves; the ears are widely separated and usually prominent. Ear tragi are present and are useful in identification. The tails are long and entirely enclosed in the interfemoral membrane (see figs. 1.6, 1.7 and 1.8, page 18). With the exception of the woolly and hairy bats, all have short hair which lies close to the body.

LONG-FINGERED BATS Genus *Miniopterus* (Subfamily Miniopterinae)
Three species, which can only be distinguished on skull size, occur in southern Africa. The Greater Long-fingered Bat is only known from two localities in the subregion, the Lesser is considered to be rare, and only Schreibers's Long-fingered Bat is common and widespread.

Miniopterus inflatus

Miniopterus fraterculus

Miniopterus schreibersii

Greater Long-fingered Bat *Miniopterus inflatus*
Total length 11 cm; tail 5,5 cm; forearm 4,7 cm; mass 15 g.
Lesser Long-fingered Bat *Miniopterus fraterculus*
Total length 10 cm; tail 5,0 cm; forearm 4,2 cm.
Schreibers's Long-fingered Bat *Miniopterus schreibersii*
Total length 11 cm; tail 5,3 cm; forearm 4,5 cm; wingspan 28 cm; mass 10 g.
Identification pointers: All three very similar; all have greatly elongated second phalanx of the third finger which distinguishes them from all other bats of the family Vespertilionidae.

Description: All three species are variable in measurements and in colour; Schreibers's Long-fingered Bat, however, is usually dark brown above and slightly paler below, with almost black wings and interfemoral membrane. The upperparts of the Lesser Long-fingered Bat are usually more reddish-brown, with black wing-membranes and a dark-brown interfemoral membrane. The Greater Long-fingered Bat is similar but chocolate-brown above. In all species the wings are long and pointed and the ears are small and rounded.
Distribution: The Greater Long-fingered Bat has only been recorded in the subregion from eastern Zimbabwe; there are also a few scattered records from East Africa and the west coast of equatorial Africa. With the exception of a record from Malaŵi, the Lesser Long-fingered Bat is entirely restricted to the south and eastern areas of southern Africa; it is rather uncommon. Schreibers's is widespread in the southern, eastern and northern parts of southern Africa and occurs widely in Africa, Europe and Asia.
Habitat: All three species roost in caves or mine-shafts although they will also roost in crevices and holes in trees. The type of surrounding vegetation seems to play no significant rôle in habitat selection.
Behaviour: Schreibers's Long-fingered Bat usually roosts in very large numbers, with over 100 000 individuals not being unusual for a single roost. The other two species are frequently found in close association with Schreibers's Long-fingered Bat but always in much smaller numbers. Females of Schreibers's Long-fingered Bat are subject to seasonal migrations to and from 'maternity' caves. In the roosts they form very dense clusters. Hibernation has been recorded in winter. They are rapid fliers.
Food: Insects.
Reproduction: A single young is born during the summer, particularly in November and December; the gestation period is 8 months. The new-born young only remains clinging to the mother for a few hours and then it is left to hang independently from the rock amongst other juveniles.

Schreibers's Long-fingered Bat

above: skin of horseshoe bat showing squared-off tail

below: skin of long-fingered bat showing triangular tail conformation typical of vesper bats

Horseshoe bats tend to roost singly or in loose clusters

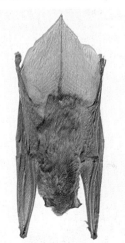

Schreibers's Long-fingered Bat roosts in dense clusters

SEROTINE BATS Genus *Eptesicus* (Subfamily Vespertilioninae)

The serotine bats are all small, short-eared species, usually with brown fur. When examined in profile the front of the skull is almost straight. With the exception of Rendall's and the Somali Serotine Bats it is usually not possible to make a positive identification of the other species in the field. The commonest species are the Cape and Melck's Serotine Bats.

Eptesicus rendalli

Eptesicus hottentotus

Eptesicus melckorum

Eptesicus somalicus

Eptesicus capensis

Rendall's Serotine Bat *Eptesicus rendalli*
Total length 8,5 cm; tail 3,8 cm; forearm 3,6 cm.
Long-tailed Serotine Bat *Eptesicus hottentotus*
Total length 11,5 cm; tail 4,7 cm; forearm 4,7 cm; mass 16,6 g.
Melck's Serotine Bat *Eptesicus melckorum*
Somali Serotine Bat *Eptesicus somalicus*
Total length 8,0 cm; tail 3,5 cm; forearm 3,2 cm; mass 5 g.
Cape Serotine Bat *Eptesicus capensis*
Total length 8,5 cm; forearm 3,3 cm; wingspan 24 cm; mass 6,5 g.
(*Note:* In the past the Somali Serotine Bat was considered to be a subspecies of the Cape Serotine Bat; it is here treated as a full species. The Aloe Serotine Bat, which previously held full species rank as *Eptesicus zuluensis*, is here treated as a subspecies of the Somali Serotine Bat.)
Identification pointers: Small size; relatively short ears; tail entirely enclosed by membrane; straight profile of head. See maps.

Description: With the exception of the Long-tailed Serotine Bat, the serotine bats are quite similar in size, most being 8 cm to 9 cm in total length. Rendall's Serotine Bat is easily recognized by the white wing-membranes, off-white interfemoral (tail) membrane and light-brown ears. The wing-membranes of the rare Somali Serotine Bat are often edged with white. The Long-tailed Serotine Bat can be distinguished by its larger size and in the eastern parts of its range its body fur is almost black. All other species vary considerably, from light brown to dark brown, with slightly lighter underparts and dark brown wing-membranes. It is not possible to separate the Somali, Cape or Melck's Serotine Bats in the field.

Distribution: Within southern Africa Rendall's Serotine Bat is only known from northern Botswana and marginally into Mozambique. It occurs widely in East and West Africa. The Long-tailed Serotine Bat has a disjunct distribution with one population along the west and south coast of the subregion, and another in Zimbabwe and adjacent Mozambique (extending into Malaŵi and eastern Zambia. There is a single record from Taung in Bophuthatswana (formerly the northern Cape). Melck's Serotine Bat is known from the south-west Cape Province but has an apparently separate population in Zambia and eastwards to Tanzania. The Somali Serotine Bat is known from a number of widely scattered localities in the north and east. This species occurs widely in Zambia. Cape Serotine Bats are found virtually throughout Africa.

Habitat: Serotine bats use a wide range of habitats, although Rendall's and the Somali Serotine Bats show a marked preference for open savanna woodland. They roost in a wide range of sites, including under bark and in roofs; Rendall's Serotine Bat also roosts in trees and bushes. The Long-tailed Serotine Bat makes use of caves, old mine-shafts and rock crevices.

Behaviour: The serotines roost in small numbers and depending on the species may be well hidden or hang in exposed clusters. Rendall's Serotine Bat is a low flier, whereas the Cape and Somali Serotine Bats are high fliers. As with most other bats, little is known about their behaviour.

Food: Insects.

Reproduction: Records indicate that some, and probably all, serotines give birth during the summer months. The Cape Serotine Bat may have single young or twins, and occasionally triplets.

Cape Serotine Bat

Long-tailed Serotine Bat roosting in crevice

Somali Serotine Bat

Myotis welwitschii

Myotis seabrai

Myotis lesueuri

Myotis tricolor

Myotis bocagei

HAIRY BATS Genus *Myotis* (Subfamily Vespertilioninae)
The five species of the *Myotis* group in the Southern African Subregion can be separated from other vesper bats by their longer, more pointed muzzles, and their soft, erect fur.

Welwitsch's Hairy Bat *Myotis welwitschii*
Total length 12 cm; tail 6,0 cm; forearm 5,5 cm; mass 14 g.
Angola Hairy Bat *Myotis seabrai*
Forearm 3,2 cm.
Lesueur's Hairy Bat *Myotis lesueuri*
Total length 9 cm; tail 4,3 cm; forearm 3,4 cm.
Temminck's Hairy Bat *Myotis tricolor*
Total length 11 cm; tail 5,0 cm; forearm 5,0 cm; wingspan 28 cm; mass 11 g.
Rufous Hairy Bat *Myotis bocagei*
Total length 10 cm; tail 4,0 cm; forearm 4,0 cm; mass 7,0 g.
Identification pointers: Fairly large ears; elongated muzzle; rich reddish-brown fur on upperparts of all except Lesueur's Hairy Bat; fur stands erect.

Description: Most hairy bats have similarly coloured upperparts of rich reddish-brown, although this can be variable; the Angola Hairy Bat's upperparts may have a yellow tinge while Lesueur's Hairy Bat is honey-yellow. The underparts are usually off-white with a reddish-brown tinge except again for Lesueur's Hairy Bat where they are a light yellow-white. Welwitsch's Hairy Bat has bold red-and-black patterning on the wings and the interfemoral membrane is reddish-brown in colour and speckled with numerous small black spots; its ears are the same colour as the fur on the upperparts but are black around the edges. The wing-membranes of Temminck's Hairy Bat are dark brown and the interfemoral membrane has a covering of reddish-brown hair; its ears are brown. The rare Rufous Hairy Bat has virtually black ears, wing-membranes and interfemoral membrane. The wing- and interfemoral membranes of the Angola and Lesueur's Hairy Bats are dark brown.
Distribution: The Rufous Hairy Bat is only known in the subregion from eastern Zimbabwe, but further north it appears quite common in the equatorial regions from Zaïre to West Africa; there are, however, only a few East African records. Welwitsch's Hairy Bat is recorded from a few localities in the Transvaal and Zimbabwe, and more widely in central Africa. The Angola Hairy Bat is restricted to the far west, from the north-western Cape Province through western South West Africa/Namibia to south-western Angola. Lesueur's Hairy Bat is only known from the western Cape and adjacent parts of the Karoo. Temminck's Hairy Bat is found along the southern and eastern areas of subregion and thence north to East Africa.
Habitat: Welwitsch's, Temminck's and the Rufous Hairy Bats favour open woodland and savanna habitats, whereas the Angola Hairy Bat favours more arid, semi-desert areas. No information is available for Lesueur's Hairy Bat. Temminck's Hairy Bat is principally a cave-roosting species, preferring damp caves, whereas Welwitsch's and the Rufous Hairy Bats prefer to roost in hollow trees and amongst leaves. There is as yet no information on the roosting preferences of Lesueur's or the Angola Hairy Bat.
Behaviour: The hairy bats are slow fliers and they usually hunt within 5 m of the ground. Temminck's Hairy Bats live in small colonies and are subject to some local migration. The Rufous Hairy Bat is found singly or in pairs. Virtually nothing is known about the behavioural characteristics of the bats of this genus within their southern African range.
Food: Insects.
Reproduction: Temminck's Hairy Bat is recorded in the Cape Province as giving birth during October and November.

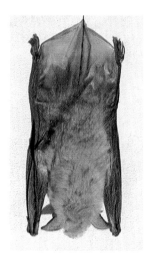

Skin of hairy bat showing tail
conformation

Welwitsch's Hairy Bat

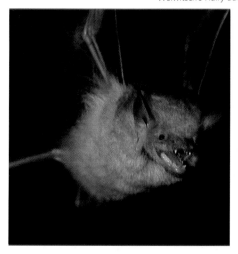

Rufous Hairy Bat

Temminck's Hairy Bat

PIPISTRELLES Genus *Pipistrellus* (Subfamily Vespertilioninae)
Five species of pipistrelle have been recorded from southern Africa. All are small and difficult to describe as they do not have outstanding features. They have tiny heads, the ears are not joined at the base (unlike, for example, some of the free-tailed bats – see page 70) and the forearms in all cases are less than 4 cm in length. Probably the most useful aid to separating the different species is the shape of the tragus but this requires somewhat specialized knowledge.

Pipistrellus kuhlii

Pipistrellus rusticus

Kuhl's Pipistrelle *Pipistrellus kuhlii*
Total length 7,5 cm; tail 3,0 cm; forearm 2,9 cm; mass 5 g.
Rusty Bat *Pipistrellus rusticus*
Total length 7,3 cm; tail 2,7 cm; forearm 2,8 cm; mass 3,5 g.
Banana Bat *Pipistrellus nanus*
Total length 7,5 cm; tail 3,6 cm; forearm 3,2 cm; wingspan 19 cm; mass 4 g.
Rüppell's Bat *Pipistrellus rueppellii*
Total length 10 cm; tail 3,8 cm; forearm 3,4 cm; mass 7 g.
Anchieta's Pipistrelle *Pipistrellus anchietai*
Identification pointers: Small size; Rüppell's Bat has pure-white underparts; tail in all cases completely enclosed by interfemoral membrane; distribution maps should be consulted.

Pipistrellus nanus

Description: Rüppell's Bat is the most easily distinguished of the group because it is the only pipistrelle with pure-white underparts; its ears are dark brown and its upperparts are light brown; its tragus is long, pointed and knife-shaped. Kuhl's and Rusty Bats are very similar, upperparts being fawn to reddish-brown and underparts paler. Kuhl's Bat underparts are sometimes off-white. The wing-membranes of both species are very dark brown to almost black, with a narrow white border around the margins in Kuhl's Bat. The tragus of Kuhl's Bat is knife-shaped and that of the Rusty Bat is sickle-shaped. The upperparts of the Banana Bat vary in colour from light to dark brown, with only slightly paler underparts; its wing-membranes are dark brown and the tragus is hatchet-shaped.

Pipistrellus rüeppellii

Distribution: Anchieta's Bat has so far only been collected from Skukuza in the southern half of the Kruger National Park. Kuhl's Bat is restricted to the south-eastern coastal plain and the eastern parts of southern Africa, with a broad distribution northwards through Africa to Europe and Asia. Rusty Bats are found from the Transvaal and northern Botswana north to Zimbabwe, Zambia and Angola; there is another separate population in Sudan and Ethiopia. The Banana Bat is very widespread in Africa south of the Sahara but in southern Africa is restricted to the eastern and northern regions. Rüppell's Bat is distributed from Mozambique, Zimbabwe and northern Botswana northwards to the Sahel zone and to Egypt along the Nile Valley.

Pipistrellus anchietai

Habitat: Kuhl's Bat has a wide habitat tolerance from oases in desert areas to the fringes of rain-forest. The Rusty Bat shows a preference for savanna woodland and Rüppell's Bat is largely restricted to riverine woodland. In the case of the Banana Bat a preference is shown for moister forested areas, particularly where banana and strelitzia plants are found; this bat often roosts in the curled leaves of these plants. The Banana Bat is also recorded as roosting in roofs. Kuhl's Bat roosts in roofs, under loose bark or in rock crevices.
Behaviour: Both Kuhl's and the Banana Bat roost in small numbers, with the former in groups of up to 10 or 12 and the latter in groups of 2 to 6. All species are slow but acrobatic fliers, emerging at dusk to hunt.
Food: Insects.
Reproduction: The young of Kuhl's Bat and the Banana Bat are born during the summer months, the former having a single young and the latter either one or two.

Rusty Bat

Rüppell's Bat

Kuhl's Pipistrelle

Anchieta's Pipistrelle

Banana Bat

Chalinolobus variegatus

Butterfly Bat *Chalinolobus variegatus* (Subfamily Vespertilioninae)
Total length 11 cm; tail 4,7 cm; forearm 4,5 cm; wingspan 28 cm; mass 13 g.
Identification pointers: Overall pale yellow or fawn appearance; yellowish wing-membranes with numerous black lines forming a reticulated pattern. Resembles no other species.

Description: This is a very pretty bat and should not be mistaken for any other species. Its name derives from the reticulated pattern on the wing-membranes which bears a fanciful resemblance to the veins of a butterfly's wings. The ground colour of the wing-membranes is yellowish-brown, overlaid with black lines. The upperparts range from nearly white to yellowish-fawn and the underparts are paler than the upperparts. The ears are small and similar in colour to the upperparts.
Distribution: In southern Africa it only occurs in the extreme north and north-east, although it does extend down the east coast as far as KwaZulu.
Habitat: Bushveld and open savanna. Roosts amongst leaves in trees and bushes and in the thatch of abandoned huts.
Behaviour: The Butterfly Bat leaves its roost early in the evening to hunt and is a high flier. It roosts in pairs or in very small numbers.
Food: Insects.
Reproduction: Nothing recorded for subregion.

LONG-EARED BATS Genus *Laephotis* (Subfamily Vespertilioninae)
There are three small bats of the genus *Laephotis* in southern Africa. All are extremely rare, and information on their biology is sparse or lacking entirely. The Namib Long-eared Bat is known from only two specimens all told and Winton's Long-eared Bat has only been recorded once in the subregion.

Laephotis namibensis

Laephotis botswanae

Laephotis wintoni

Namib Long-eared Bat *Laephotis namibensis*
Total length 10,5 cm; tail 4,6 cm; ear 2,4 cm; forearm 3,8 cm.
Botswana Long-eared Bat *Laephotis botswanae*
Total length 9,2 cm; tail 4,2 cm; ear 2,1 cm; forearm 3,6 cm; mass 6 g.
Winton's Long-eared Bat *Laephotis wintoni*
Total length 8,5cm; tail 4,5 cm; forearm 3,8 cm.
Identification pointers: Small size; long ears at 45° angle to face are about one-third head-and-body length. May be confused with slit-faced bats (page 54), but the latter hold their ears almost vertically and the slit in the face is prominent.

Description: Long-eared bats have unusually long ears – about one-third of the head-and-body length. The species can be separated on the shape of the tragus. The ears stand out sideways at an angle of 45° to the head and are not held almost vertically as in the larger slit-faced bats (see page 54). All have short faces and lack facial decoration in the form of nose-leaves. General body colour is light to very light brown, with slightly paler underparts. Wing-membranes are light brown.
Distribution: The Namib and Winton's Long-eared Bats are each known only from one locality in the subregion (see map). The Botswana Long-eared Bat has been recorded in the subregion from northern Botswana and Zimbabwe and from Punda Maria in the Transvaal.
Habitat: The two specimens of the Namib Long-eared Bat were taken in the wooded bed of the section of the Kuiseb River which penetrates the Namib Desert. Winton's was taken in a rocky hill area near Algeria Forest Station in the Cape's Cedarberg Mountains in fynbos scrub, and Botswana Long-eared Bat is associated with open woodland in vicinity of rivers.
Behaviour: Unknown.
Food: Insects.
Reproduction: Unknown.

Butterfly Bat

Botswana Long-eared Bat

Winton's Long-eared Bat

Scotoecus albofuscus

 Thomas's House Bat *Scotoecus albofuscus* (Subfamily Vespertilioninae)
Total length 7 cm; forearm 3 cm; mass 4,5 g.

This rare bat is known in the subregion from a single locality in Mozambique. Similar in size to Schlieffen's Bat (see below) but fur is light brown, with paler underparts, white wing-membranes edged with brown, and a brown interfemoral membrane.

Nycticeius schlieffenii

 Schlieffen's Bat *Nycticeius schlieffenii* (Subfamily Vespertilioninae)
Total length 7,5 cm; tail 3 cm; forearm 3 cm; wingspan 18 cm; mass 4,5 g.
Identification pointers: Fawn or reddish-brown upperparts; dark-brown wing-membranes; fairly large, rounded ears; very small.

Description: No outstanding features. Ears are large and rounded, wing-membranes dark brown and fur of upperparts is pale fawn to dark reddish-brown. Underparts lighter than upperparts. Smallest bat in subregion.
Distribution: Restricted to northern and north-eastern areas of subregion.
Habitat: Open woodland. Roosts in crevices in hollow trees and buildings.
Behaviour: Hunts early in evening; flies jerkily. Roosts alone.
Food: Insects.
Reproduction: Births recorded in November.

YELLOW HOUSE BATS Genus *Scotophilus* (Subfamily Vespertilioninae)
Solidly built bats, with bluntish heads and short ears; ear tragus is long and pointed. Fur is woolly and soft with a distinct sheen.

Scotophilus nigrita

Giant Yellow House Bat *Scotophilus nigrita*
Total length 18 cm; tail 7,7 cm; forearm 7,7 cm.
Yellow House Bat *Scotophilus dinganii*
Total length 13 cm; tail 5,3 cm; wingspan 30 cm; mass 27 g.
Lesser Yellow House Bat *Scotophilus borbonicus*
Total length 12 cm; tail 4,6 cm; forearm 4,8 cm; wingspan 28 cm; mass 16 g.
Identification pointers: Variable colouring but usually yellow or yellowish-brown on upperparts and often on underparts.

Scotophilus dinganii

Description: Body colour in this genus is not necessarily yellow. Yellow House Bat, however, usually has distinctive yellowish or orange-yellow underparts although its upperparts are olive-brown to russet-brown. Lesser Yellow House Bat has light or dark yellow-brown upperparts and white to grey-white underparts. Giant Yellow House Bat may be dark red-brown to yellow- or grey-brown above, and pale yellow to white below. In all species wing-membranes are translucent dark brown. Best field criterion to separate Yellow and Lesser Yellow House Bats is smaller size of latter.
Distribution: Giant Yellow House Bat has only been recorded twice from subregion. The other two species are restricted to the northern and north-eastern areas of southern Africa.
Habitat: Savanna woodland, with Lesser Yellow showing preference for riverine vegetation and high-rainfall areas. Yellow often roosts in buildings, as well as hollow trees. Lesser Yellow roosts in hollow trees, changing its roosting location every few days perhaps to avoid predation.

Scotophilus borbonicus

Behaviour: Very little known. The Yellow House Bat roosts in small groups of up to a dozen individuals, although several such groups may utilize the same roost. When roosting they crawl into crevices. They are fast, low fliers.
Food: Insects.
Reproduction: Yellow and Lesser Yellow House Bats give birth in summer to litters of 1–3 young.

Schlieffen's bat with young

Yellow House Bat

Lesser Yellow House Bat

WOOLLY BATS Genus *Kerivoula* (Subfamily Kerivoulinae)
These bats are immediately recognizable by their long, erect, soft, curly-tipped hair. (The long, erect hair of the hairy bats, genus *Myotis*, is straight and not curled at the tips). Also by fringe of hair around interfemoral membrane (fig. 1.8, page 18) There are only two species in southern Africa.

Kerivoula argentata

Damara Woolly Bat *Kerivoula argentata*
Total length 9,5 cm; forearm 3,7 cm; wingspan 25 cm; mass 8 g.
Lesser Woolly Bat *Kerivoula lanosa*
Total length 7,8 cm; tail 3,8 cm; forearm 3,4 cm; mass 7 g.
Identification pointers: Woolly, erect hair; noticeable fringe of short hair around margin of interfemoral membrane (fig. 1.8, page 18).

Kerivoula lanosa

Description: Easily recognized by erect curly hair and characteristic fringe of hair along edge of interfemoral membrane. Ears are funnel-shaped with long pointed tragus. Upperparts of Damara Woolly Bat are rich brown in colour and grey-flecked, and the underparts are greyish-brown. Upperparts of Lesser Woolly Bat are lighter brown but also have a grizzled appearance; underparts are very pale. In both species the wing-membranes are brown.
Distribution: Damara Woolly Bat is only known in the subregion from the northern and eastern areas. The less abundant Lesser Woolly Bat is known from a few records in southern and central Africa.
Habitat: Well-watered savanna woodland. Roost in clusters of dead leaves, under bark, under roofs and in deserted weaver-bird nests.
Behaviour: Roost singly, in pairs or in small groups. Damara Woolly Bat is a late-emerging species, with low, slow and erratic flight.
Food: Insects.
Reproduction: Nothing is known from the subregion for either species.

Free-tailed bats Family Molossidae

These bats are also called mastiff or wrinkle-lipped bats, in reference to their mastiff-like faces and heavily wrinkled upper lip. Distinctive family characteristic is the tail, of which only half or less is enclosed by the interfemoral membrane, the remainder projecting beyond the membrane (fig. 1.9, page 18). Ears are large, have a small tragus and are approximately equal in length and width. Hair is short, smooth and lies close to body. Most species are dark-brown to reddish-brown. Of the 14 species in subregion, 10 are known from very few specimens or are considered to be rare.

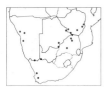

⊡]*Otomops martiensseni*
⊡]*Mormopterus acetabulosus*
⊡]*Tadarida ansorgei*

Sauromys petrophilus

Large-eared Free-tailed Bat *Otomops martiensseni*
Total length 14 cm; tail 4,5 cm; forearm 7,0 cm; mass 33 g.
Flat-headed Free-tailed Bat *Sauromys petrophilus*
Total length 11 cm; tail 4,0 cm; forearm 4,5 cm; wingspan 26 cm; mass 13 g.
Natal Free-tailed Bat *Mormopterus acetabulosus*
Egyptian Free-tailed Bat *Tadarida aegyptiaca*
Total length 11 cm; tail 3,8 cm; forearm 4,8 cm; wingspan 30 cm; mass 15 g.
Ansorge's Free-tailed Bat *Tadarida ansorgei*
Total length 10 cm; tail 3,6 cm; forearm 4,3 cm.
Spotted Free-tailed Bat *Tadarida bivittata*
Total length 11 cm; tail 3,7 cm; forearm 4,7 cm; mass 15 g.
Pale Free-tailed Bat *Tadarida chapini*
Total length 15 cm; tail 3,1 cm; forearm 3,6 cm.
Angola Free-tailed Bat *Tadarida condylura*
Total length 12 cm; tail 4,0 cm; forearm 5,0 cm; mass 22 g.
Madagascar Free-tailed Bat *Tadarida fulminans*
Total length 14 cm; tail 5,5 cm; forearm 6,0 cm; mass 32 g.

Tadarida aegyptiaca

Lesser Woolly Bat

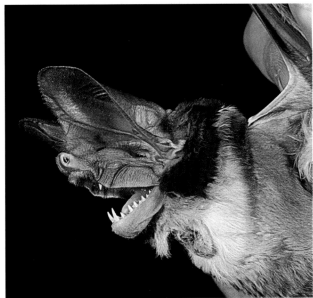

Damara Woolly Bat

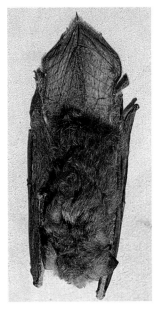

Skin of woolly bat showing long woolly hair and fringe of hair around edge of tail

Large-eared Free-tailed Bat: each extraordinarily enlarged ear has a row of small spines along its forward edge

(see overleaf for other free-tailed bats)

Tadarida fulminans

Tadarida midas

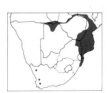

Tadarida pumila

Big-eared Free-tailed Bat *Tadarida lobata*
Forearm 6,3 cm.
Midas Free-tailed Bat *Tadarida midas*
Total length 14 cm; tail 5,0 cm; forearm 6,0 cm; wingspan 45 cm; mass 50 g.
Nigerian Free-tailed Bat *Tadarida nigeriae*
Total length 10 cm; tail 3,5 cm; forearm 4,9 cm.
Little Free-tailed Bat *Tadarida pumila*
Total length 9 cm; tail 3,6 cm; forearm 3,8 cm; wingspan 24 cm; mass 11 g.
Giant African Free-tailed Bat *Tadarida ventralis*
Total length 14 cm; tail 5,5 cm; forearm 6,2 cm.
Identification pointers: All species have part of tail extending beyond limits of the interfemoral membrane (fig. 1.9, page 18). Except for Large-eared Free-tailed Bat (whose long ears extend along face plane), the ears are large and rounded and may or may not be joined by flap of skin across forehead. Most have wrinkled upper lips.

Description: Large-eared Free-tailed Bat is easy to distinguish from other free-tailed bats by very long ears attached along length of face (see photograph); no tragus or antitragus. Upperparts are dark brown with paler band across shoulders; underparts also dark brown. Band of white hair runs along each side of the body from shoulder to knee. Flat-headed Free-tailed Bat is characterized by its flattened head which enables it to crawl into narrow crevices. Largest species is Midas Free-tailed Bat; it has white-flecked dark-brown upperparts and slightly paler underparts. Bands of white hair run from the forearm to the thigh. Angola Free-tailed Bat is typically dark brown above, with tawny throat, grey-brown upper chest, and off-white abdomen. Nigerian and Pale Free-tailed Bats have crests of erectile hair on top of head. The crest of the latter is longer, its wing-membranes are white and interfemoral membrane is dark brown. Tail and wing-membranes of the Nigerian Free-tailed Bat are off-white. Little Free-tailed Bat is smallest and identified by band of white hair on wing-membrane from wing to thigh. Egyptian Free-tailed Bat is common and widespread. It has no outstanding features except that a pale neck yoke, present in most species, is absent. The only certain way of identifying most of the free-tailed bats, however, is by detailed examination of the teeth.
Distribution: See maps.
Habitat: Usually open woodland and riverine associations but Egyptian and Little Free-tailed Bats occur in a wide range of habitats. Most species utilize natural roosts such as rock crevices, caves, hollow trees and crevices behind the loose bark of dead trees. Midas, Little and Egyptian, however, also use man-made structures, *e.g.* brickwork crannies or between overlapping sheets of corrugated-iron roofing.
Behaviour: Usually gregarious: Angola Free-tailed Bat colonies of several hundred individuals, but Flat-headed averages 4 and Spotted averages 6. Unlike other bats they prefer to move into cover when disturbed at the roost, rather than take to wing. They usually roost packed tightly together and the larger colonies can produce a considerable noise. High and rapid fliers.
Food: Insects.
Reproduction: Single young born in summer is thought to be the rule.

Angola Free-tailed Bat

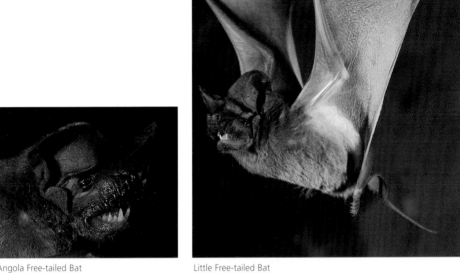

Little Free-tailed Bat

Egyptian Free-tailed Bat

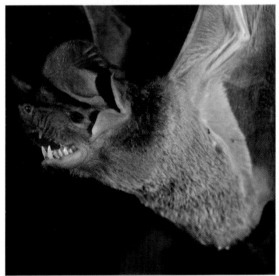

Midas Free-tailed Bat

BABOONS, MONKEYS AND BUSHBABIES Order Primates

Baboons and monkeys Family Cercopithecidae

Chacma Baboon *Papio ursinus*
Male: total length 120–160 cm; tail 60–85 cm; mass 25–45 (average 32) kg.
Female: total length 100–120 cm; tail 50–60 cm; mass 12–20 (average 16) kg.
Identification pointers: Fairly large size; long, dog-like snout in adults; uniform grey to grey-brown colour; males considerably larger than females; apparently 'broken' tail; nearly always in troops – very rarely solitary males.

Description: The largest primate (other than man) in southern Africa. It is relatively slender and lightly built, although adult males have powerfully built shoulders and heads. When the baboon is on all fours the shoulders stand higher than the rump. The long, somewhat dog-like muzzle is particularly pronounced in the males. The body has a covering of coarse hair which may be light grey through to dark grey-brown, but coat colour is variable even within a troop. Only the male has a mane of long blackish hair on the neck and shoulders. The hair on the upper surface of the hands and feet is dark brown to black in colour. Characteristic of the baboon is the posture of the long tail; the first third of the tail is held upwards and the remainder droops downwards, giving it a 'broken' appearance. Males have a single, hard pad of naked grey skin which extends across both buttocks, but the female has one smaller pad on each buttock. During gestation the skin around the female buttock pads is bright scarlet while at the onset of the menstrual cycle the skin distends enormously into rather unsightly swollen red protuberances.
Distribution: Occurs widely in southern Africa in suitable habitat.
Habitat: Wide habitat tolerance but it requires rocky cliffs or tall trees to which to retreat at night or when threatened. Drinking water is essential. It inhabits mountains, hill ranges and riverine woodland.
Behaviour: A highly gregarious and social species which lives in troops of 15 to sometimes 100 or more. Within a baboon troop all adult males are dominant over all females. The adult males have a strict rank order and only the dominant males mate with oestrous or receptive females, although subordinate males do mate with young females and those that are not in oestrus. It is only in their fifth year that the males become dominant over the females. The dominant male determines when the troop will move. The females and infants remain closest to this male, with the non-breeding females staying close to the subordinate males. The youngsters and subadults move around the edges of the troop. Water sources are visited each day. Very vocal and the bark or 'bogom' of the adult male is a common day-time sound of the hills and savanna of southern Africa.
Food: Omnivorous. Digs for roots and bulbs, eats wild fruit, seeds, leaves and flowers, insects and other invertebrates. Raids cultivated crops. Will eat young antelope, hares, mice and birds if encountered. In rocky areas a feeding baboon troop leaves a trail of overturned stones and small rocks.
Reproduction: The birth of the Chacma Baboon's single offspring may take place at any time of the year. When a female comes into oestrus the 'sexual skin' on the buttocks becomes red and considerably swollen. This is completely natural and is not a result of injury or sickness as is often thought. The gestation period is six months. The new-born infant is black with a pink face and for the first few weeks clings to its mother's chest; as it grows older, however, it rides on her back.

A troop of Chacma Baboons

Young Baboons are carried jockey-fashion by their mothers; note swollen red buttock pads typical of adult females, and 'broken' appearance of tail

The Baboon has a dog-like muzzle

Yellow Baboon *Papio cynocephalus*

This baboon apparently only occurs in north-central Mozambique within the Southern African Subregion but its exact southern limits are not known; it is briefly mentioned in this field guide on the grounds that it occurs south of the Zambezi River in the Tete and Gorongoza areas of Mozambique. It is generally lighter in build than the Chacma Baboon and its hair colour is paler and usually yellowish in the adults. Its head is proportionately smaller and its nose slightly upturned. The ears are more pointed than those of the Chacma Baboon. In all other aspects of its biology, however, it is similar to the Chacma Baboon.

Vervet Monkey *Cercopithecus aethiops*

Male: total length 100–130 cm; tail 60–75 cm; mass 4–8 (average 5,5) kg.
Female: total length 95–110 cm; tail 48–65 cm; mass 3,5–5 (average 4,0) kg.
Identification pointers: Typically monkey appearance; grizzled grey hair on head, back and flanks; black face with rim of pale to white hair; long tail; lives in troops. Habitat usually separates this species from the Samango Monkey—see below.

Description: This is a well-known animal with its grizzled grey, fairly long, coarse hair and typical monkey appearance. Its underparts are paler than its upperparts and are frequently white. The face is short-haired and black, with a rim of white hair across the forehead and down the sides of the cheeks. The hands and toes are black. However, there are several subspecies occurring in southern Africa with some variation in colour. The animals from northern South West Africa/Namibia usually have very pale feet and hands while the subspecies in the Tete district of Mozambique has a reddish back. The general hair colour varies from area to area but this monkey is unlikely to be confused with any other species. The adult male has a distinctive bright blue scrotum.

Distribution: The Vervet Monkey is found in the northern and eastern parts of southern Africa, extending along the southern coast to as far west as Mossel Bay. It extends into otherwise inhospitable areas along rivers (including the Orange River as far west as its estuary) and wooded streams deep in the Karoo. It is widespread throughout central and East Africa with the exception of equatorial forest.

Habitat: This is a monkey of savanna and riverine woodland.

Behaviour: Vervet monkeys live in troops of up to 20 or more, but groups are often smaller. The formation of large groups will generally be associated with an abundant food source or water. They are completely diurnal and sleep at night in trees or more rarely on cliffs. A distinct 'pecking order' or hierarchy is well established in each troop. They forage in a well-defined home range, spending much of their time on the ground. They frequently raid crops and gardens and are in consequence heavily persecuted.

Food: Although Vervet Monkeys are mainly vegetarian they also eat a wide range of invertebrates and small vertebrates such as nestling birds. Fruits, flowers, leaves, gum and seeds form the bulk of their food.

Reproduction: A single young, weighing some 300–400 g, is born after a gestation period of about 210 days. Young may be born at any time of the year but in some areas there seems to be a birth peak.

Yellow Baboon engaged in grooming

The male Vervet Monkey has a bright blue scrotum

Characteristic of the Vervet Monkey is the contrast between the black face and the white forehead

Samango Monkey *Cercopithecus mitis*
Male: total length 1,4 m; 80 tail cm; mass 8–10 kg.
Female: total length 1,2 m; tail 70 cm; mass 4–5 kg.
Identification pointers: Typical monkey appearance; much darker than Vervet Monkey, being black on legs, shoulders, and last two-thirds of tail length; long hair on cheeks; brown (not black) face. Forest habitat usually separates it from the more open areas occupied by the Vervet Monkey.

Description: A fairly large forest species with dark-brown face, and white only on lips and throat. Hair on legs and shoulders is dark brown or black, but rest of the back and sides is grizzled grey-brown, browner towards the tail. Long tail is black for the last two-thirds of its length. Long hair stands out on cheeks and forehead. Underparts are paler than upperparts, usually off-white with a suffusion of light brown.
Distribution: Isolated populations in forest and forest pockets from eastern Cape Province to Natal, KwaZulu, eastern Transvaal, and southern slopes of Soutpansberg Mountains; also found in eastern Zimbabwe and Mozambique.
Habitat: High forest, forest margins and riverine gallery forest; may forage in more open woodland but always close to forest.
Behaviour: Lives in troops up to 30 strong, although most are smaller than this. More arboreal than Vervet Monkey. During the hottest hours of the day it rests in deep shade. As with most monkeys, the Samango is a vocal species with a range of different calls. The males have a very loud, far-carrying bark sounding superficially like '*jack*'. Calling and crashing progress through trees is often all that is revealed.
Food: Feeds on a wide range of plants, including fruits, flowers, gum, leaves and seeds. Debarks young trees in softwood plantations and is not popular with foresters. Sometimes eats insects.
Reproduction: Normally single, almost black young born during summer.

Bushbabies Family Lorisidae

Thick-tailed Bushbaby *Otolemur crassicaudatus*
Total length 70–80 cm; tail 35–45 cm; mass 1–1,5 kg.
Identification pointers: Superficially cat-like when seen on the ground and tail usually held erect; uniformly grey to grey-brown; long, fairly bushy tail, same colour as body; large thin ears and large eyes; harrowing and unnerving screaming call made at night; usually seen in trees.

Description: Much larger than Lesser Bushbaby, with which it is sometimes confused. When seen on ground it is superficially cat-like but hindquarters are higher than shoulder region and the long tail is held high off ground, or erect. Hair of upperparts and tail is woolly, fine and grey-brown. Underparts are lighter in colour than upperparts. Characteristic features are the very large, rounded, thin ears and large eyes which shine red in torchlight.
Distribution: Restricted to the far eastern parts of southern Africa, but occur widely in central Africa and East Africa.
Habitat: Forest, woodland (sometimes dry) and wooded riverine margins.
Behaviour: Nocturnal and spends the day sleeping amongst dense vegetation tangles in trees and in self-constructed nests. Rest together in groups numbering 2–6 but usually forage alone at night. A group has a fixed home range of several hectares, within which are a number of resting-sites. Frequently forage on ground. Obvious sign of their presence is the loud screaming call like that of a baby in distress.
Food: Fruit and tree gum, particularly of acacias; also insects, reptiles, birds.
Reproduction: In the south give birth in November (Transvaal); in Zimbabwe and Zambia give birth in August and September. Usually two young are born after a gestation period of about 130 days.

Samango Monkey: note long cheek hair, no white blaze on forehead, and brownish back

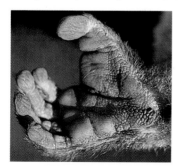

Hand of Thick-tailed Bushbaby showing enlarged and opposable thumb

Thick-tailed Bushbaby

Galago moholi and
Galagoides zanzibaricus

Lesser Bushbaby *Galago moholi*
Total length 30–40 cm; tail 20–25 cm; mass 120–210 (average 150) g.
Identification pointers: Small size with long fluffy tail; large mobile, thin ears; large, forward-facing eyes; prodigious jumping ability and arboreal habitat. Compare with Thick-tailed Bushbaby where distributions overlap.

Description: The Lesser Bushbaby is considerably smaller than the Thick-tailed Bushbaby, with which it is frequently confused. The fine woolly, greyish to grey-brown hair extends on to the fluffy tail, which is slightly longer than the head and body. The ears are large, thin and rounded and extremely mobile. The eyes are very large, forward-pointing and ringed with black, and the head is small and rounded with a short snout.
Distribution: In our subregion this species is restricted to the northern and north-eastern parts. They are widely distributed in woodland areas of central, East and West Africa but are absent from equatorial forests.
Habitat: An animal of woodland savanna, particularly acacia and riverine woodland.
Behaviour: The Lesser Bushbaby is nocturnal and feeds mostly in trees but it does descend to the ground to forage. Family groups of 2 to 8 sleep together but they usually forage alone or in very loose association. Although they construct their own nests of leaves, they will also lie up in dense creeper tangles or in holes. They are territorial and groups occupy home ranges of about 3 ha, but this will vary according to food availability. They jump considerable distances from branch to branch and tree to tree. They are vocal animals with a wide range of calls, from low croaking to chittering and grunts.
Food: The gum or exuding sap of trees, particularly acacias, is very important in their diet but they also eat insects, which they catch with their hands.
Reproduction: After a gestation period of slightly more than 120 days one or two young are born. At birth they weigh about 9 g, the eyes are open and they are well-haired. Females may have two litters a year, in early and late summer. The young are carried by the female when she forages but are left clinging to branches while she moves about in the vicinity.

Zanzibar Lesser Bushbaby *Galagoides zanzibaricus*
Fractionally larger than the Lesser Bushbaby, browner in colour and the call differs to some extent. Within southern Africa they only occur in the extreme north-east, in Mozambique. There is still some confusion as to the true status of this animal. In the field it would be difficult to distinguish between the two species of lesser bushbaby. The map therefore shows their combined ranges.

Lesser Bushbaby

The eyes of the Lesser Bushbaby normally reflect a reddish glow in torchlight

PANGOLINS Order Pholidota Family Manidae

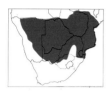

Pangolin *Manis temminckii*
Total length 70–100 cm; tail 30–45 cm; mass 5–15 kg.
Identification pointers: Unmistakable; covered in large brown overlapping scales. Small head, heavy hindquarters and tail; small forelegs.

Description: This scale-covered mammal cannot be mistaken for any other species. Large, brown scales composed of agglutinated hair cover the upperparts, sides and tail. Smaller scales cover outer sides of legs and top of head. Underparts sparsely covered with hair. Head disproportionately small and pointed. It has powerfully built hindlegs, short forelegs and a long, heavy tail. Walks on hindlegs, occasionally using tail and forelegs for balance.
Distribution: Wide distribution in subregion north of Orange River.
Habitat: Habitats range from low to high rainfall areas, including open grassland, woodland and rocky hills, but excluding forest and desert.
Behaviour: Solitary and mainly nocturnal, although occasionally diurnal. May try to run away when threatened but usually curls into ball to protect the head and underparts. May dig own burrows, but readily uses those dug by other species, or simply curls up amongst dense vegetation.
Food: Only eats certain species of ants and termites. Scratches superficially into nests close to the surface, under plant debris and animal dung.
Reproduction: Single young apparently normally born in winter.

HARES, RABBITS Order Lagomorpha Family Leporidae

Two species of hare and four species of rabbit occur naturally in southern Africa. The European Rabbit (*Oryctolagus cuniculus*) occurs on 8 small offshore islands, to which it was introduced by man.

Lepus capensis

Cape Hare *Lepus capensis*
Total length 45–60 cm; tail 7–14 cm; mass 1,4–2,5 kg.
Scrub Hare *Lepus saxatilis*
Total length 45–65 cm; tail 7–17 cm; mass 1,5–4,5 kg.
The Scrub Hare and the Cape Hare vary considerably in size from area to area, although the former is generally larger than the latter.
Identification pointers: Both species have long ears, and hindlegs much longer than forelegs. See distribution maps and habitat requirements. Tail white above, black below.

Lepus saxatilis

Description: Both species of hare have long ears, long, well-developed hindlegs and a short fluffy tail. The body hair is fine and soft.

	Cape Hare	Scrub Hare
Upperparts	Varies; light brown and black-flecked; whitish-grey in north.	Brown-grey to grey; black-flecked.
Underparts	Chest not white; abdomen white; in north may be completely white.	White throughout.
Face	Yellowish on nose and cheeks; pale grey in northern animals.	Lighter (whitish or buff) on sides of face and around eyes.
Nuchal patch (on nape of neck behind ears)	Brownish-pink; pale grey in northern animals.	Reddish-brown.

Pangolin or Scaly Anteater

Pangolin curled up for protection

Scrub Hare

Cape Hare

Most, but not all, Scrub Hares have a white forehead spot

Distribution: Cape Hare has a wide distribution in the western and central areas of southern Africa with isolated populations in the north (Botswana) and east (northern Transvaal and southern Mozambique). Scrub Hare is found throughout southern Africa, with the exception of the Namib Desert.

Habitat: Cape Hare prefers drier, open habitat, while Scrub Hare occurs in woodland and scrub cover where there is grass. Scrub Hare is commonly seen in cultivated areas. Normally the Scrub Hare will not be seen in completely open grassland and the Cape Hare will not be found in dense scrub or woodland; there is some overlap however.

Behaviour: Both species nocturnal but some early morning and late afternoon activity may occur. Both lie up in 'forms' (shallow indentations in the ground made by the body), with those of Scrub Hare being in more substantial cover. They rely on their camouflage when approached, only getting up and running off at the last minute. Normally zigzag, often at high speed.

Food: Predominantly grazers but will feed on other plants.

Reproduction: Young born at any time of the year. Cape Hare may have as many as 4 litters per year. Gestation period about 42 days; 1–3 'leverets' are born fully haired and with open eyes and can move about soon after birth.

RED ROCK RABBITS Genus *Pronolagus*
Three species occur in the subregion.

Pronolagus randensis

Pronolagus crassicaudatus

Jameson's Red Rock Rabbit *Pronolagus randensis*
Total length 48–63 cm; tail 6–13 cm; mass 1,8–3,0 kg.
Natal Red Rock Rabbit *Pronolagus crassicaudatus*
Total length 50–67 cm; tail 3–11 cm; mass 2,4–3,0 kg.
Smith's Red Rock Rabbit *Pronolagus rupestris*
Total length 43–65 cm; tail 5–11 cm; mass 1,3–2,0 kg.
Identification pointers: Different red rock rabbits can usually be identified from distribution maps alone, except where there is possibility of overlap. Apart from habitat they can be separated from the two hare species and the Riverine Rabbit by their much shorter ears.

Description: All rabbit-like and all are similar in appearance. Their distribution ranges only overlap marginally, however, and therefore use of the distribution maps is very important. Colouration can be variable but usually the back and sides are reddish-brown, grizzled with black. Underparts of all species range from pinkish-brown to reddish-brown.

	Jameson's	Natal	Smith's
Rump and back legs	Lighter than back and sides.	Bright red-brown.	Bright red-brown.
Tail	Red-brown; black tip.	Uniform red-brown; **no** black tip.	Dark to red-brown; black tip.
Face and neck.	Head light grey, brown-flecked.	Grey-white band from chin, along lower jaw and to back of neck.	Sides of face greyish.

Pronolagus rupestris

Distribution: See distribution maps.

Habitat: Rocky habitats from isolated outcrops to mountain ranges.

Behaviour: Essentially nocturnal, but may feed on overcast days. Normally rest up in rock crevices or in dense vegetation cover. Usually single.

Food: Predominantly grazers, but Jameson's eats leaves of woody plants.

Reproduction: Young (1–2° per litter) are probably born hairless and helpless in cup-shaped nest lined with soft hair from the female's underparts.

Natal Red Rock Rabbit (also see top of page 87)

'Latrine' sites with heaps of lozenge-shaped pellets are characteristic of areas inhabited by red rock rabbits

Riverine Rabbit *Bunolagus monticularis*
Total length 52 cm; tail 9 cm; mass unknown.
Identification pointers: Similar to red rock rabbits but ears much longer and upperparts drab grey; differs from the two hares in having more or less uniformly coloured grey-brown tail, and not black and white. Dark-brown stripe along lower jaw towards ear base only found in this species; white eye-ring.

Description: Similar to the red rock rabbits but has longer, more hare-like ears. White ring around eye and dark-brown stripe down the side of the lower jaw, extending to ear base. Upperparts grizzled grey; nuchal patch deep red-brown; tail short, fluffy and grey-brown, somewhat darker towards the tip.
Distribution: Calvinia and Victoria West districts of Karoo, Cape Province.
Habitat: Dense riverine bush in arid areas.
Behaviour: Little known but home range is 10–15 ha.
Food: Unknown.
Reproduction: Apparently one 50-g young born in nest in shallow burrow.

RODENTS Order Rodentia

Currently, 78 species of rodent have been recorded from subregion. Four are introduced species. Range in size from the 6-g pygmy mice to 15-kg Porcupine. Rodents are characterized by the pair of large, chisel-like, continuously growing incisors in both jaws.

Squirrels Family Sciuridae

Of the 7 species in the subregion, 5 are arboreal and 2 terrestrial. The Grey Squirrel is an alien introduced from North America *via* Britain.

Ground Squirrel *Xerus inauris*
Total length 40–50 cm; tail 19–25 cm; mass 500–1 000 (average 650) g.
Identification pointers: Terrestrial and lives in burrows; white stripe down each side; long bushy tail; very small ears. Nearly impossible to distinguish from Mountain Ground Squirrel where ranges overlap. Incisors of latter species, however, are orange; those of Ground Squirrel are white. May occasionally be confused with the Suricate (page 142) but the latter species does not have a bushy tail nor side stripes.

Description: Easily identifiable species, being entirely terrestrial yet typically squirrel-like. Upperparts usually cinnamon-brown. Single white stripe runs along each side of body from shoulder to thigh. Underparts are white tinged with light brown in mid-belly. Coarse hair; white incisors.
Distribution: Endemic to the arid areas of southern Africa.
Habitat: Open areas with sparse cover and usually a hard substrate.
Behaviour: This gregarious diurnal species occurs in groups numbering from 5 to 30. It excavates extensive burrow-systems. The females and young remain in close proximity to the burrows but the males move from colony to colony. It frequently stands on its hindlegs to enhance its view of the surrounding area. Its bushy tail is often held over the body and head when the squirrel feeds and acts effectively as a sunshade. Its burrow-systems are often shared with the Suricate and the Yellow Mongoose.
Food: Grass, roots, seeds and bulbs; also insects, particularly termites.
Reproduction: Gestation period probably about 45 days. One to 3, naked and helpless young, each weighing about 20 g, are born in a burrow, from which they first emerge at about 6 weeks of age.

Key to rabbit skins (l. to r.):
1. Riverine Rabbit
2. Jameson's Red Rock Rabbit
3. Natal Red Rock Rabbit
4. Smith's Red Rock Rabbit

Riverine Rabbit

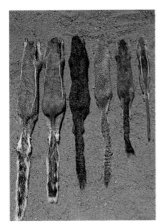

Key to squirrel skins (l. to r.):
1. Mountain Ground Squirrel
2. Ground Squirrel
3. Sun Squirrel
4. Red Squirrel
5. Tree Squirrel
6. Striped Tree Squirrel

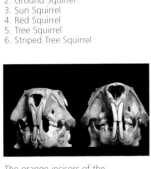

The orange incisors of the
Mountain Ground Squirrel (left)
help to distinguish it from the
Ground Squirrel (right)

The tail of the Ground Squirrel can be used as a sunshade

87

Mountain Ground Squirrel *Xerus princeps*
This species is very similar to the Ground Squirrel and the two are virtually impossible to tell apart in the field. Its incisors are orange and not white as in the Ground Squirrel but other differences require careful examination. It is more closely associated with rocky hills and mountainous country. Although very little is known about this species it is probably very similar in most respects to the Ground Squirrel. In southern Africa it is found only in South West Africa/Namibia but it extends marginally beyond the borders of the subregion into south-western Angola.

Sun Squirrel *Heliosciurus mutabilis*
Total length 40–55 cm; tail 20–30 cm; mass 300–480 g.
Identification pointers: Subregion's largest arboreal squirrel; variable in colour but usually grizzled light brown; bushy, narrowly banded tail. Compare with the Red Squirrel.

Description: This is the largest indigenous, arboreal squirrel occurring in southern Africa. It can vary considerably in colour but the upperparts are usually grizzled light brown. In parts of Zimbabwe, however, it can be black above while in other areas it is reddish. The underparts are pale fawn to white. The tail has a series of narrow, indistinct whitish bands.
Distribution: Restricted in southern Africa to the forests of eastern Zimbabwe and Mozambique. It is widely – if patchily – distributed in East Africa and westwards through the equatorial forest areas into West Africa.
Habitat: Forested areas at both high and low elevations and including riverine forest.
Behaviour: The Sun Squirrel is diurnal and occurs singly or in pairs. Most activity is restricted to the early morning and late afternoon. It is often observed basking in the sun, stretched out on branches. In areas where its distribution overlaps with the Red Squirrel it tends to utilize the higher canopy zone. As is common with most arboreal squirrels it is quite vocal, giving vent to clucking calls accompanied by frequent tail-flicking.
Food: It takes a wide range of plant food but it will also eat insects and possibly smaller vertebrates such as lizards and birds.
Reproduction: All that is known with any certainty is that litters consist of 1 to 4 young and are probably produced in summer.

Red Squirrel *Paraxerus palliatus*
Total length 35–40 cm; tail 17–20 cm; mass 200–380 g.
Identification pointers: Dark-grey to black upperparts; underparts and tail reddish or yellowish. Compare with Sun Squirrel where range overlaps.

Description: The upperparts are grizzled dark grey to black and the underparts, sides of face, feet and tail are usually reddish or yellowish. As the most brightly coloured of all our squirrels it should not be mistaken for any other.
Distribution: It is confined to Mozambique and the extreme eastern parts of Zimbabwe but there are two isolated populations in Natal/KwaZulu. Beyond the subregion it extends into East Africa.
Habitat: Forest habitats, including coastal dune and montane forests.
Behaviour: Diurnal and usually solitary except when a female is accompanied by young. A male, female and small young may be observed in a loose association. It is a very vocal species with a range of different calls. Tail-flicking usually accompanies calling.
Food: It takes a wide range of plant food, including fruits and berries.
Reproduction: One or 2 young, each weighing about 14 g are born after a gestation period of between 60 and 65 days. As with other squirrel species the young are born hairless and blind.

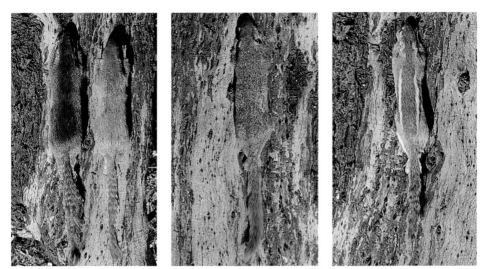

Skins of arboreal tree squirrels on tree-trunk backgrounds (l. to r.): Sun Squirrel (two colour phases), Red Squirrel, Striped Tree Squirrel

The Red Squirrel is an arboreal species

Striped Tree Squirrel *Funisciurus congicus*
Total length 30 cm; tail 16 cm; mass 110 g.
Identification pointers: Small size; white side stripe; only found in northern South West Africa/Namibia. Could be confused with Tree Squirrel but the latter does not have white body stripe.

Description: Smallest squirrel in subregion. Upperparts pale yellow-brown; underparts paler or off-white. Single white stripe runs down side from neck to base of long bushy tail. A darker stripe runs below the white stripe.
Distribution: Restricted to north-western South West Africa/Namibia.
Habitat: Dense woodland, near watercourses and rock outcrops.
Behaviour: Diurnal and arboreal, but descends to the ground to forage. It lives in small family groups. Resting-sites are in tree-holes and its nest or 'drey' is constructed from leaves and twigs in the fork of a branch. Only indigenous squirrel to construct a drey.
Food: A wide range of plant food but also insects.
Reproduction: Two young are born in a tree-hole or drey with most births taking place either at the onset or at the end of the rains.

Tree Squirrel *Paraxerus cepapi*
Total length 35 cm; tail 16 cm; mass 100–260 g.
Identification pointers: Small size; uniformly greyish or yellowish-brown upperparts; no distinctive markings. Most widespread of all our tree squirrels.

Description: Very variable in size and colour. In general animals from western areas are greyer and eastern animals are more yellow-brown. Underparts range from fawn to white. Body has a generally grizzled appearance.
Distribution: It occurs widely in the northern and north-eastern parts of southern Africa.
Habitat: A wide variety of woodland habitats but not true high forest.
Behaviour: Although it is usually seen singly or in mother/young groups, a number of animals live in loose association. The adult male or males in a group will defend a territory against incursions by other squirrels. As with other squirrel species it is very vocal.
Food: A wide variety of plant food and also insects.
Reproduction: After a gestation period of about 55 days, 1–3 young, each weighing about 10 g, are born in a leaf-lined tree-hole, mostly in summer.

Grey Squirrel *Sciurus carolinensis* (Introduced)
Total length 50 cm; tail 22 cm; mass 600 g.
Identification pointers: Restricted to the south-western Cape Province, where it is the only squirrel to occur. Uniform grey-brown or silvery-grey upperparts and white underparts.

Description: This large squirrel has a summer coat that is generally brownish-grey in colour, but after the moult the winter coat is silvery-grey. The underparts are white to off-white. The tail is long and bushy.
Distribution: Native to North America. In subregion it is restricted to alien pine plantations and oak trees in the extreme south-western Cape.
Habitat: Oak woodland, pine plantations and suburban gardens.
Behaviour: Normally solitary or in mother/young family groups, but several may be seen feeding in close proximity. It makes use of tree-holes but also constructs dreys. Although it is arboreal it spends a considerable amount of time on the ground foraging.
Food: Acorns, pine seeds, cultivated fruits, fungi, insects, young birds and birds' eggs.
Reproduction: All year round but birth peaks in August and January. Gestation 45 days; 1–4 young each weigh about 15 g at birth.

Tree Squirrel

Above and left: The Grey Squirrel is an alien introduced from North America via Britain. So far it is confined to the south-west Cape

Dormice Family Gliridae

Four species of dormouse occur in southern Africa, but the Lesser Savanna Dormouse is considered by some authorities to be merely a smaller form of the Woodland Dormouse. Because of their bushy tails they are sometimes mistaken for squirrels but they differ in being much smaller in size and nocturnal in habit.

Graphiurus ocularis

Graphiurus platyops

Graphiurus murinus and
Graphiurus parvus

Spectacled Dormouse *Graphiurus ocularis*
Total length 25 cm; tail 10 cm; mass 80 g.
Rock Dormouse *Graphiurus platyops*
Total length 18 cm; tail 7 cm; mass 45 g.
Woodland Dormouse *Graphiurus murinus*
Total length 16 cm; tail 7 cm; mass 30 g.
Lesser Savanna Dormouse *Graphiurus parvus*
Total length 14 cm; tail 6 cm.
Identification pointers: See distribution maps and habitat descriptions. Distinct black-and-white facial markings and larger size distinguish Spectacled Dormouse; Rock Dormouse distinguished by flattened skull and rocky habitat; the Woodland and Lesser Savanna Dormice smallest in size and most frequently seen. All generally greyish in colour with bushy, squirrel-like tails.

Description: Dormice have bushy, squirrel-like tails, fairly short muzzles, small ears and soft fur. Hair colour is grey to silvery-grey. Spectacled Dormouse is most distinctive, not only because of its relatively large size but also because face is marked with black, white and grey. A dark ring surrounds each eye (the 'spectacles'), and a dark line runs from the sides of the muzzle extending on to the shoulders. Lips, cheeks, underparts and the upper surfaces of the hands and feet are white. Tail is usually rimmed and tipped with white. Rock Dormouse also has a dark facial pattern but this is always much less distinct than in the Spectacled Dormouse. Its bushy pale-grey tail is usually white-tipped. The underparts are grey. An interesting feature of this dormouse is the somewhat flattened skull, an adaptation to living in narrow rock crevices. Although Woodland Dormouse lacks distinctive facial markings, the cheeks, lips and underparts are either white or greyish-white. The tail may or may not be white-tipped. Lesser Savanna Dormouse is very similar to Woodland Dormouse.
Distribution: Spectacled Dormouse is restricted to Cape Province but extends marginally into south-western Transvaal. Rock Dormouse occurs in two widely separated populations, one in the west and the other in the east. Woodland Dormouse has a wide distribution in northern and eastern areas and narrowly along the southern Cape coastal belt; it is difficult to separate from the Lesser Savanna Dormouse (see combined distribution map).
Habitat: Both Spectacled and Rock Dormice are associated with rocky habitats but Spectacled Dormouse also utilizes trees or buildings. Woodland Dormouse is a woodland savanna and bush species but it is also frequently found in association with man-made structures.
Behaviour: All are nocturnal and are agile climbers. Woodland Dormouse may construct substantial nests made up of grass, leaves and lichen and it may become quite tame where it lives in close association with man. Both Spectacled and Rock Dormice appear to be solitary but several Woodland Dormice may share the same nest. In the Northern Hemisphere dormice hibernate in winter; in southern Africa our dormice appear either to hibernate or at least to become more sluggish during cold periods.
Food: Seeds, other plant material and to a large extent insects and other invertebrates. Perhaps geckos, if the opportunity should arise.
Reproduction: Virtually nothing is known about this aspect of dormouse biology. Indications are that the young are born during the summer months.

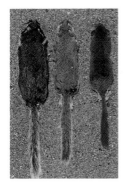

Key to dormouse skins
(l. to r.):
1. Spectacled Dormouse
2. Rock Dormouse
3. Woodland Dormouse

Spectacled Dormouse

Woodland Dormouse

Springhares Family Pedetidae

Springhare *Pedetes capensis*
Total length 75–85 cm; tail 35–45 cm; mass 2,5–3,8 kg.
Identification pointers: Kangaroo-like appearance; long, powerful hindlegs; long well-haired tail with black tip; ears and eyes fairly large. Nocturnal and found in habitats with sandy soils.

Description: A true rodent despite name. Kangaroo-like, with long, powerfully built hindlegs and short, lightly built forelegs. Hindfeet have 3 large nails and forefeet have 5 long, pointed claws for digging. Progresses by hopping and forelegs only used while feeding. Tail long and bushy and black towards tip. Ears long and pointed; eyes large. General colour of upperparts is yellowish or reddish-fawn and underparts are off-white to pale fawn.
Distribution: Widespread, although absent from south-west Cape and South West Africa/Namibian coastal belt, as well as from the extreme north-eastern parts of southern Africa. Absent from the Rift Valley of central Africa and occurs again in East Africa.
Habitat: Compacted sandy soils with short vegetation cover. It will colonize sandy areas along river-banks where these pass through unsuitable habitat.
Behaviour: Nocturnal, terrestrial and apparently not territorial. Although several burrows, housing several individuals, may be situated in close proximity, each burrow is occupied by a single animal or a female with young. Two types of hole are dug: a sloping one which is most frequently used, and a vertical escape-burrow. Burrows may be blocked with sand if the Springhare is in occupation. Its eyes shine brightly in torchlight.
Food: Grass, grass-roots and other plants. Cultivated crops.
Reproduction: A single young, weighing approximately 300 g, may be born at any time of the year. Juvenile emerges 6–7 weeks after birth.

Rodent moles or molerats Family Bathyergidae

Four species of molerat occur in southern Africa, two of which are restricted to the Cape Province of South Africa.

Bathyergus suillus

Bathyergus janetta

Cape Dune Molerat *Bathyergus suillus*
Total length 32 cm; tail 5 cm; mass 550–750 g.
Namaqua Dune Molerat *Bathyergus janetta*
Total length 25 cm; tail 4 cm.
Common Molerat *Cryptomys hottentotus*
Total length 15 cm; tail 2 cm; mass 100–150 g.
Cape Molerat *Georychus capensis*
Total length 20 cm; tail 3 cm; mass 250 g.
Identification pointers: Large size distinguishes Cape Dune Molerat; Namaqua Dune Molerat only large species in north-western Cape Province; small size and uniform colouring of Common Molerat; the Cape Molerat is the only species with distinctive black-and-white markings on the head. Consult the distribution maps.

Description: All have soft fur, short tails, large rounded heads, well-developed and prominent incisors, and tiny eyes and ears. Legs are short and forefeet each carry 4 long claws for digging. Snouts are flattened and somewhat pig-like. Cape Dune Molerat is largest with cinnamon to pale-fawn upperparts tinged with grey, grey underparts and white chin and muzzle. Namaqua Dune Molerat differs from Cape Dune Molerat in having dull- to silvery-grey fur with broad, darker band extending down back from base of neck to rump. There is usually a white ring around the eyes. Tail brown above and white below. Common Molerat variable but usually greyish-fawn to dark brown without any distinguishing markings. Cape

Springhare

Common Molerat

Key to molerat skins (l. to r.):
1. Cape Dune Molerat
2. Namaqua Dune Molerat
3. Cape Molerat
4. Common Molerat

Namaqua Dune Molerat

Cryptomys hottentotus

Georychus capensis

Molerat is easily distinguished from the other species because of black-and-white markings on head; general body colour brown to reddish-brown with greyish underparts.

Distribution: See distribution maps.

Habitat: Sandy soils but Common Molerat also occupies a wide range of other soils excepting heavy clay.

Behaviour: Fossorial, digging extensive underground burrow-systems marked on the surface by mounds of earth (in contrast to the golden moles which by and large do not push mounds). Digging is undertaken by well-developed incisors, then using the feet to shovel earth out of the way. Most digging follows rain. Molerats also move on surface at night, particularly during rains. All our molerats believed to live in small colonies, with several animals sharing a burrow-system.

Food: Vegetarian, eating mostly roots, bulbs and tubers. A nuisance in gardens and agricultural areas.

Reproduction: Very little is known about this aspect of molerat biology. The young of the Cape Dune Molerat are born in the summer months and the usual litter size is 3 or 4. Common Molerats may have as many as 5 young per litter and they are born at any time of the year.

Porcupines Family Hystricidae

Porcupine *Hystrix africaeaustralis*
Total length 75–100 cm; tail 10–15 cm; mass 10–24 kg.
Identification pointers: Unmistakable with body-covering of long quills banded in black-and-white. Confusion sometimes arises between this species and the Southern African Hedgehog but the latter is much smaller, is brown rather than black and white, and has very short spines.

Hystrix africaeaustralis

Description: By far the largest rodent occurring in southern Africa and is unmistakable with its protective covering of long quills banded in black and white. The sides, neck, head and underparts are covered in dark, coarse hair. A crest of long, erectile, coarse hairs extends from the top of the head, down the neck and on to the shoulders. This crest is only raised when the animal is alarmed or angry. The head and snout are broad, with small eyes and short, rounded ears. The legs are short and stout, with heavily clawed feet. Quills are easily detached and are frequently found lying on trails and pathways. The tail is short and carries a number of hollow, open-ended quills which act as warning rattles when vibrated together.

Distribution: Occurs virtually throughout subregion, except Namib.

Habitat: Wide range but preference for more broken country.

Behaviour: Solitary porcupines are most commonly seen but pairs and family parties will also be encountered. It is nocturnal and during the day it lies up in caves, amongst rocks, in burrows (either its own or those of other species) or even amongst dense vegetation. A common feature of well-used porcupine shelters is the accumulation of gnawed bones. It is generally believed that porcupines gnaw these bones both for their mineral content and to sharpen the long incisors. Within its home range a porcupine makes use of regular pathways, along which are numerous shallow excavations exposing plant roots and bulbs. Although several porcupines may share a shelter, foraging is usually a solitary activity.

Food: Roots, bulbs, tubers and the bark of trees, as well as a number of cultivated crops such as potatoes and pumpkins. It has also been recorded as eating from animal carcasses. It is often in fact caught in traps baited with meat originally set to catch carnivores.

Reproduction: Litters from 1 to 4 (usually 1 or 2) young, each weighing from 100 to 300 g are born usually in summer; they are well developed at birth and move around within a few hours.

Cape Dune Molerat

Cape Molerat

Porcupine

Cane-rats Family Thryonomyidae

Two species of cane-rat occur in southern Africa:

Thryonomys swinderianus

Thryonomys gregorianus

Greater Cane-rat *Thryonomys swinderianus*
Total length 65–80 cm; tail 15–20 cm; mass 3,0–5,0 kg.
Lesser Cane-rat *Thryonomys gregorianus*
Total length 40–60 cm; tail 12–18 cm; mass 1,5–2,5 kg.
Identification pointers: Large size; dark-brown speckled hair; short tail; stout appearance. See habitat requirements and distribution maps as Lesser Cane-rat has very limited distribution in southern Africa.

Description: Large, coarse-haired, stockily built rodents with short tails. Two species differ only in size and in positioning of grooves on incisor teeth. Grooves of Greater run close to inner edge of teeth; those of Lesser more evenly spaced over front surface of incisors. Upperparts and sides are generally dark speckled brown and underparts range from off-white to greyish-brown. The body hair falls out readily if an animal is handled. A fleshy pad used in aggressive butting bouts extends beyond the nostrils.
Distribution: Both widely distributed in Africa but in subregion Lesser Cane-rat is restricted to parts of southern Zimbabwe and adjacent areas of Mozambique; Greater Cane-rat occurs in extreme north and east.
Habitat: Reed-beds and other dense vegetation near water but Lesser Cane-rat also utilizes drier habitats.
Behaviour: Predominantly nocturnal although also crepuscular. Tend to forage alone, but they do however live in loosely associated groups. Distinct runs are formed within feeding areas and these are characterized by small piles of cut grass or reed segments along their length. Hunted for their meat and regarded as delicacy.
Food: Feed mostly on roots, leaves, stems and shoots of grasses, reeds and sedges. Greater Cane-rat can be a problem in sugar-cane areas.
Reproduction: Nothing is known about reproduction of Lesser Cane-rat in subregion. Young of the Greater Cane-rat are born between August and December with a litter of 4 (up to 8). Mass at birth 80–190 g.

Dassie rat Family Petromuridae

Dassie Rat *Petromus typicus*
Total length 30 cm; tail 14 cm; mass 200–250 g.
Identification pointers: Squirrel-like appearance; tail very hairy but not bushy; general colour brown; rocky habitat; diurnal.

Description: Somewhat squirrel-like in appearance but although its tail is hairy it is not bushy. Grizzled grey-brown to brown with hindquarters usually being more uniformly brown. Underparts vary from off-white to yellowish-brown. Head is somewhat flattened and ears are small.
Distribution: Largely restricted to the South West Africa/Namibian escarpment but extends southwards into the north-western Cape.
Habitat: Restricted to rocky areas, including isolated rock outcrops.
Behaviour: Pairs or family groups occupy rock crevices. It is active by day although much of its activity is restricted to the early morning and late afternoon; it will however move about in shade even during the hottest part of the day. It is frequently observed basking in the early-morning sun, much like its namesake the dassie. When feeding it usually plucks a leaf or twig and then takes it to shelter to feed. Like the dassies the Dassie Rat urinates at specific sites which become stained yellowish-white.
Food: The Dassie Rat is vegetarian and eats a wide variety of plant food, with a preference for leaves and flowers and to a lesser extent seeds and fruits.
Reproduction: Young born fully haired in rocky crevices in summer.

Greater Cane-rat

Note flat head of Dassie Rat –
an adaptation to allow its use
of narrow rock crevices

The Dassie Rat's tail is hairy, but not bushy

Rats and Mice Families Cricetidae and Muridae

Fifty-seven species of rats and mice, belonging to two families, the Cricetidae and the Muridae, are recorded as occurring in southern Africa. The 4 species below are characterized by having wholly or partially white tails.

Woosnam's Desert Rat Zelotomys woosnami
Total length 24 cm; tail 11 cm; mass 55 g.
Identification pointers: Tail and upper surface of feet white; tail slightly shorter than head-and-body length. Range does not overlap with White-tailed Mouse which is similar but has much shorter tail. Also see Pouched Mouse below.

Description: Easily identifiable with its pale-grey black-flecked upperparts, paler sides and creamy-white underparts. Tail and top of feet are white.
Distribution: North-central and north-western areas of subregion.
Habitat: Arid areas with sandy soil and sparse vegetation.
Behaviour: Nocturnal. Makes own burrows or uses those dug by other species.
Food: Mainly seeds but also insects.
Reproduction: Litters of up to 11 young are born in summer.

White-tailed Mouse Mystromys albicaudatus
Total length 22 cm; tail 6 cm; mass 75–110 g.
Identification pointers: Grey-brown body and short white tail. See Woosnam's Desert Rat above, but latter has proportionately longer tail. Pouched Mouse has short tail but not pure white.

Description: Most characteristic feature is short white tail. Upperparts grey to grey-brown flecked with black; underparts greyish-white. Upper surfaces of feet white.
Distribution: Swaziland and south and east of South Africa.
Habitat: Grassland and heath but also karoo vegetation.
Behaviour: Nocturnal and lives in burrows and cracks in ground.
Food: Seeds, green plant material, and insects.
Reproduction: Litter of 2–5 young. Gestation period 37 days.

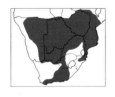

Pouched Mouse Saccostomus campestris
Total length 15–16 cm; tail 5 cm; mass 45 g.
Identification pointers: Dumpy appearance (similar to the domestic hamster); short tail; large cheek-pouches for food transport.

Description: Round, fat body, with soft, silky-grey or greyish-brown fur. Underparts and lower face white. Tail length is much less than head-and-body length. Variable in size and colour.
Distribution: Widespread in southern Africa.
Habitat: Wide habitat tolerance but prefers soft, particularly sandy, soils. Can be found in open or dense vegetation and in rocky areas.
Behaviour: It leads a generally solitary existence, although it may live in loose colonies. It digs its own burrows but also utilizes burrows excavated by other species. Where other shelter is not available it will use termite-mounds, logs and rock piles. One of the principal characteristics of this species is its ability to carry large quantities of food in the cheek-pouches. The food is carried in these pouches to the shelter or burrow, where it can be eaten in relative safety from predators. Compared with most other rodents, it is slow-moving and quite easy to catch by hand. It is nocturnal and terrestrial.
Food: Chiefly seeds, small wild fruits and occasionally insects.
Reproduction: Two to 10 fully haired young, each weighing less than 3 g, are born in the wet summer months, after a gestation period of about 20 days.

Skins of small mice with
white or pale tails (l. to r.):
1. Woosnam's Desert Rat
2. White-tailed Mouse
3. Pouched Mouse

White-tailed Mouse

Pouched Mouse

Giant Rat *Cricetomys gambianus*
Total length 80 cm; tail 42 cm; mass 1–3 kg.
Identification pointers: Large size; long naked tail which is white towards tip; dark ring around eye and long thin ears. The superficially similar Black Rat is smaller and lacks white on the tail.

Description: Largest 'rat-like' rodent in subregion. Distinctive long whip-like tail, white for slightly less than half of its length towards the tip. Upperparts grey to grey-brown; underparts lighter. Hair around eyes is dark. Ears are large, thin and mobile.
Distribution: Extreme north-eastern areas of subregion but isolated populations occur in Soutpansberg and southern Zimbabwe.
Habitat: Forest and woodland but occasionally urban areas.
Behaviour: Mainly nocturnal but if undisturbed can be diurnal. Digs own burrow but also makes use of holes, hollow trees and piles of plant debris. Surplus food is carried in cheek-pouches to store. When a burrow is occupied it is usually closed from the inside. Placid and generally harmless.
Food: Fruits, roots and seeds (including cultivated crops); occasionally insectivorous.
Reproduction: 2–4 young, each weighing about 20 g, are born in summer.

FAT MICE Genus *Steatomys*

Steatomys pratensis

Steatomys parvus

Steatomys krebsii

Fat Mouse *Steatomys pratensis*
Total length 13 cm; tail 5 cm; mass 26 g.
Tiny Fat Mouse *Steatomys parvus*
Total length 12 cm; tail 4 cm; mass 18 g.
Krebs's Fat Mouse *Steatomys krebsii*
Total length 13 cm; tail 5 cm; mass 24 g.
Identification pointers: Quite small size; dumpy appearance; short tail; white to off-white below; upper surface of feet white.

Description: All 3 species of fat mice show considerable size and colour variation. The Fat Mouse itself is usually rusty-brown above and white below; its tail is darker above than below. The Tiny Fat Mouse is rufous-grey above with off-white underparts and a tail which is pure white in the Botswanan part of its range but brown above and white below in the separate KwaZulu population. Krebs's Fat Mouse is ochre-yellow above and white below, with a similar colour division on its tail. The upper-surfaces of the feet in all 3 species are white, although the hindfeet of Krebs's Fat Mouse are yellowish-buff.
Distribution: The distribution ranges of all 3 species overlap in some areas. The only species occurring in the south-western and southern Cape Province is Krebs's Fat Mouse. The Fat Mouse occurs widely south of the Sahara but the other two species are more restricted in their distribution. All species have patchy distributions.
Habitat: Usually found over sandy substrates. Sometimes in cultivated lands.
Behaviour: Nocturnal, terrestrial and apparently live singly or in pairs. They live in burrows which they dig themselves. An interesting characteristic of the fat mice is their ability to lay down very thick fat deposits under the skin and around the body organs. They are also able to reduce the body temperature and decrease food intake. This has obvious advantages during drought and times of food shortage. Unlike the Pouched Mouse, the fat mice do not have cheek-pouches but they do carry food to the burrow.
Food: The fat mice are primarily seed-eaters but they have also been recorded as digging up and eating bulbs. Insects are also eaten occasionally.
Reproduction: Little known. Fat Mouse apparently gives birth during summer. Although litters of 1–9 young have been recorded, litters of 3–4 are more usual. Reproduction features are probably similar in all 3 species.

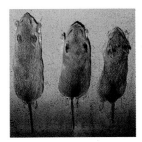

Key to fat mouse skins (l. to r.):
1. Krebs's Fat Mouse
2. Fat Mouse
3. Tiny Fat Mouse

Giant Rat: note dark ring around eye

Fat Mouse

Dendromus nyikae

Dendromus melanotis

Dendromus mesomelas

Dendromus mystacalis

Malacothrix typica

Desmodillus auricularis

CLIMBING MICE Genus *Dendromus*
Four species of climbing mice occur in the subregion. In all cases the tail is longer than the head-and-body length and a dark dorsal stripe is present.

Nyika Climbing Mouse *Dendromus nyikae*
Total length 16 cm; tail 9 cm; mass 15 g.
Grey Climbing Mouse *Dendromus melanotis*
Total length 15 cm; tail 8 cm; mass 8 g.
Brants's Climbing Mouse *Dendromus mesomelas*
Total length 17 cm; tail 10 cm; mass 14 g.
Chestnut Climbing Mouse *Dendromus mystacalis*
Total length 15 cm; tail 8 cm; mass 8 g.
Identification pointers: Small size; long, thin tails; dark diffused stripe down centre of back.

Description: All species have a dark, diffused, dorsal stripe and a long, thin tail. Grey Climbing Mouse has ash-grey fur; others are reddish-brown to chestnut-coloured. Underparts are white to off-white.
Distribution: See maps.
Habitat: Tall grass and rank vegetation.
Behaviour: Nocturnal. Good climbers with long semi-prehensile tails and toes adapted for clinging to grass-stalks. Grey and Chestnut Climbing Mice build small, ball-shaped nests of fine grass just above the ground in grass tussocks but both also use burrows dug by other species.
Food: Seeds and insects.
Reproduction: Litters of 2–8 born in summer.

Large-eared Mouse *Malacothrix typica*
Total length 11 cm; tail 3,5 cm; mass 15–20 g.
Identification pointers: Dark patterning on back and head; large ears; short tail. Should not be confused with any other species.

Description: Characterized by dark patterning on the back and head, and by large ears. Upperparts pale grey to reddish-brown; underparts grey or white.
Distribution: Drier central and western areas of subregion.
Habitat: Short grass habitats over hard soils.
Behaviour: Nocturnal. By day, shelters in deep, self-excavated burrows.
Food: Green plant material as well as seeds.
Reproduction: Summer litters of 2–8 (usually 4). Birth mass 1 g.

Gerbils Subfamily Gerbillinae

Nine species in three genera occur in southern Africa.

Short-tailed Gerbil *Desmodillus auricularis*
Total length 20 cm; tail 9 cm; mass 50 g.
Identification pointers: Tail shorter than head and body and relatively thick; diagnostic white patch at base of each ear. Soles of feet hairy.

Description: Dumpy appearance and only gerbil with tail shorter than head-and-body length. Upperparts vary from reddish-brown to grey-brown, but species is easily distinguishable by prominent white patch at base of ear; Dune and Setzer's Hairy-footed Gerbils also have small white spots behind ears, but in addition a white spot above the eye and longer tails.
Distribution: Widespread in the drier western areas.
Habitat: Hard ground with grass or karoid bush. Not sandy soils.
Behaviour: Nocturnal. It digs its own burrows and lives singly or in pairs.
Food: Seeds, mostly of grasses.
Reproduction: Year-round litters consisting of 1–7 young, but usually 4.

Climbing mouse skins (l. to r.):
1. Grey Climbing Mouse
2. Brants's Climbing Mouse
3. Chestnut Climbing Mouse

Grey Climbing Mouse

Brants's Climbing Mouse

Chestnut Climbing Mouse

Large-eared Mouse

Skin of Large-eared Mouse
showing distinctive dark
patterning on back and head

Short-tailed Gerbil

HAIRY-FOOTED GERBILS Genus *Gerbillurus*

■ *Gerbillurus paeba*
□ *Gerbillurus tytonis*

Gerbillurus vallinus

Gerbillurus setzeri

Hairy-footed Gerbil *Gerbillurus paeba*
Total length 20 cm; tail 11 cm; mass 25 g.
Brush-tailed Hairy-footed Gerbil *Gerbillurus vallinus*
Total length 20 cm; tail 12 cm; mass 35 g.
Dune Hairy-footed Gerbil *Gerbillurus tytonis*
Total length 22 cm; tail 12 cm; mass 27 g.
Setzer's Hairy-footed Gerbil *Gerbillurus setzeri*
Total length 23 cm; tail 12 cm; mass 38 g.
Identification pointers: Fairly small size; long tails—three species with tufts of longish hair at tip; large hindfeet with hairy soles; Setzer's and Dune with white patches above eyes and at ear-bases.

Description: Hairy-footed Gerbil has small tuft of long hair at tail-tip; Brush-tailed Hairy-footed Gerbil has a prominent tassel. Colour variable but Hairy-footed Gerbil commonly reddish-brown or greyish-red; Brush-tailed Hairy-footed Gerbil reddish-brown to dark grey-brown. Both have white underparts but Brush-tailed Hairy-footed Gerbil also has white forelegs. Setzer's and Dune Hairy-footed Gerbils have white spot just above eye and behind ear. Both have tufts of longish hair at tip of tail. Soles of feet hairy unlike naked soles of *Tatera* gerbils.
Distribution: See maps.
Habitat: Sandy soils in arid areas, although Hairy-footed Gerbil extends into moister environment of southern Cape coast.
Behaviour: All species are probably nocturnal and excavate their own burrows. Brush-tailed Hairy-footed Gerbil lives in colonies whereas Hairy-footed Gerbil apparently lives in smaller groups.
Food: Probably seed-eaters, but include some insects in their diet.
Reproduction: Hairy-footed Gerbil has litter of 2–5 young.

THE *TATERA* GROUP Genus *Tatera*

Tatera leucogaster

1. *Tatera afra*
2. *Tatera inclusa*

Tatera brantsii

Bushveld Gerbil *Tatera leucogaster*
Total length 28 cm; tail 15 cm; mass 70 g.
Cape Gerbil *Tatera afra*
Total length 30 cm; tail 15 cm; mass 100 g.
Highveld Gerbil *Tatera brantsii*
Total length 28 cm; tail 14 cm; mass 80 g.
Gorongoza Gerbil *Tatera inclusa*
Total length 32 cm; tail 16 cm; mass 120 g.
Identification pointers: Fairly large size; tails about same length as head and body; well-developed hindlegs and feet; ears greater length than width; eyes quite large. Soles of feet naked (see *Gerbillurus* above).

Description: All have white underparts, but eastern form of Highveld Gerbil is greyish-white underneath. Bushveld Gerbil has distinct dark line along upperside of tail and tip is never white. Its upperparts are most commonly reddish-brown, bright and silky. Many Highveld Gerbils have white-tipped tails. Cape Gerbil's long, woolly hair is usually pale fawn and mottled with brown. Its tail is uniform in colour. Gorongoza Gerbil dark brown; tail dark brown above, white underneath; some have white tip to tail.
Distribution: See maps.
Habitat: All species are found on sandy soils with the two widespread species being found in a wide variety of habitats.
Behaviour: Nocturnal; dig own burrows and live in loosely knit colonies.
Food: Grass-seed but also other plant food. Partly insectivorous.
Reproduction: Litter sizes of the Highveld Gerbil vary from 1 to 5 with a usual number of 3 and the Bushveld Gerbil has 2 to 9 with an average of 5.

Hairy-footed Gerbil

Gerbil skins (l. to r.):
1. Cape Gerbil
2. Highveld Gerbil
3. Bushveld Gerbil
4. Short-tailed Gerbil
5. Brush-tailed Hairy-footed Gerbil
6. Hairy-footed Gerbil

Brush-tailed Hairy-footed Gerbil

Setzer's Hairy-footed Gerbil

Brush-tailed Hairy-footed Gerbil (left) can be distinguished from other hairy-footed gerbils by long hair at tail-tip

Cape Gerbil

Bushveld Gerbil

SPINY MICE Genus *Acomys*

1. *Acomys spinosissimus*
2. *Acomys subspinosus*

Spiny Mouse *Acomys spinosissimus*
Total length 17 cm; tail 8 cm; mass 28 g.
Cape Spiny Mouse *Acomys subspinosus*
Total length 17 cm; tail 8 cm; mass 22 g.
Identification pointers: Spiny hairs on back; white underparts.

Description: Unmistakable with their dorsal covering of spiny hairs.
Upperparts of Spiny Mouse are reddish-grey and those of Cape Spiny Mouse
are dark grey-brown. Both species have white underparts.
Distribution: In subregion Spiny Mouse restricted to north-eastern parts.
Cape Spiny Mouse only occurs in south-western Cape.
Habitat: Rocky habitats but also woodland and other associations.
Behaviour: Nocturnal, but can be active in early morning and late afternoon in
shadows cast by rocks. Live singly or in small groups.
Food: Seeds and green plant material; also insects, millipedes and snails.
Reproduction: Spiny Mice litters of 2–5 are born during summer.

ROCK MICE Genus *Aethomys*

Five species occur in southern Africa but the Silinda Rat (*Aethomys silindensis*) and the Nyika Veld Rat (*A. nyikae*) are known from only one or two specimens from eastern Zimbabwe.

Aethomys namaquensis

Namaqua Rock Mouse *Aethomys namaquensis*
Total length 26 cm; tail 15 cm; mass 50 g.
Grant's Rock Mouse *Aethomys granti*
Total length 20 cm; tail 10 cm; mass 40 g.
Red Veld Rat *Aethomys chrysophilus*
Total length 28 cm; tail 15 cm; mass 75 g.
Identification pointers: Nondescript; typically rat-like; long, well-scaled
tail; underparts lighter than upperparts. See distribution maps.

Aethomys granti

Description: Both the Namaqua Rock Mouse and the Red Veld Rat have a tail
that is longer than the head and body; Grant's Rock Mouse has a tail equal in
length to that of the head and body. The tail of the Red Veld Rat is shorter,
thicker and more heavily scaled than that of the Namaqua Rock Mouse.
Colouration is very variable but in general Grant's Rock Mouse is dark
grey-brown above and grey below with a dark-coloured tail. The Namaqua
Rock Mouse has reddish-brown to yellowish-fawn upperparts, often pencilled
with black, and the underparts are white to greyish-white. As its name
implies the Red Veld Rat is usually reddish-brown, but is also pencilled with
black; the underparts are grey-white.
Distribution: Grant's Rock Mouse is restricted to the central Karoo of the
Cape Province and may be found together with the Namaqua Rock Mouse.
The latter is widely distributed in southern Africa. The Red Veld Rat is also
widespread, but is absent from the southern and western areas.
Habitat: Namaqua and Grant's Rock Mice largely restricted to rocky habitats.
Red Veld Rats are found in a wide range of habitats, from grassland to
savanna woodland and including rocky outcrops.
Behaviour: Nothing is known about the behaviour of Grant's Rock Mouse.
The other two species are nocturnal. The Namaqua Rock Mouse lives in
small colonies and a characteristic of its communal shelters are the large
accumulations of dry grass and other plant material dragged into the
entrances. It is also known to dig burrows at the base of bushes.
Food: All species eat grass- and other seeds.
Reproduction: The Red Veld Rat breeds throughout the year, whereas the
Namaqua Rock Mouse gives birth in the summer months. Both species
usually have 3–5 young per litter.

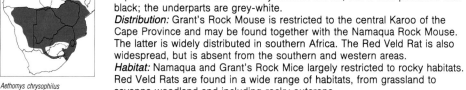

Aethomys chrysophilus

1. *Aethomys silindensis*
2. *Aethomys nyikae*

Spiny Mouse

Cape Spiny Mouse

Namaqua Rock Mouse (reddish-brown form)

Namaqua Rock Mouse (yellow-fawn form)

Red Veld Rat

Rock mouse skins (l. to r.):
1. Namaqua Rock Mouse
2. Red Veld Rat
3. Grant's Rock Mouse

Water Rat *Dasymys incomtus*
Total length 30–35 cm; tail 14–18 cm; mass 100–165 g.
Identification pointers: Similar to the vlei rats (page 118) but longer tail; dark, long, shaggy fur and white claw bases which contrast with the dark feet. Flat, disc-like face with small eyes. Incisors not grooved.

Description: Similar in appearance to vlei rats but has longer tail. Hair is relatively long and shaggy and dark grey-black in colour with brown flecks. Underparts are paler. Ears are large and rounded and the dark feet contrast with the white bases of the claws.
Distribution: The Water Rat occurs along the southern coastal belt and in the east and north-eastern areas of southern Africa.
Habitat: Well-vegetated and wet habitats, such as reed-beds, swamps, or grassy areas near streams.
Behaviour: As with the vlei rats the Water Rat uses distinct runways and in fact probably shares them with those species. It swims well and takes readily to water. Most activity takes place during the day.
Food: A variety of reeds, grasses and other plants but also insects.
Reproduction: As many as 9 young have been recorded in a litter, although the usual number is about 5. Young are born in the summer months.

Striped Mouse *Rhabdomys pumilio*
Total length 18–21 cm; tail 8–11 cm; mass 30–55 g.
Identification pointers: Four dark stripes down the back. Cannot be confused with any other species.

Description: This mouse is easily distinguished from all other species as it has four distinct longitudinal stripes running down the back. General colour is variable and ranges from dark russet-brown to almost grey-white. Similarly the underparts vary from off-white to pale grey-brown. The backs of the ears (and often the snout) are russet to yellowish-brown.
Distribution: Striped Mouse occurs widely in South Africa and South West Africa/Namibia but only patchily in Zimbabwe, Mozambique and Botswana.
Habitat: Wide-ranging, from desert fringe to high-rainfall montane areas. The only consistent requirement is the presence of grass.
Behaviour: Principally diurnal but also often active at night. Makes own burrows from which radiate numerous runways. Often around houses.
Food: Mainly seeds, but also other plant parts; insects.
Reproduction: Litters of 2–9 (usually 5–6) young are born after a gestation period of about 25 days, usually in summer.

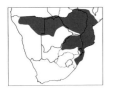

Single-striped Mouse *Lemniscomys rosalia*
Total length 27 cm; tail 15 cm; mass 60 g.
Identification pointers: Single dark stripe runs down centre of back; the climbing mice also have single dark dorsal stripes but they are much smaller than this species.

Description: The upperparts vary in colour from pale grey-brown to orange-brown and a single dark-brown or black stripe runs down the middle of the back. The underparts are white, often russet-tinged.
Distribution: Restricted to the far northern and eastern areas of southern Africa, but outside the subregion occur widely south of the Sahara Desert.
Habitat: Grass cover is essential but in associations varying from dry scrub to savanna woodland or even around agricultural land.
Behaviour: A diurnal species that excavates its own burrows. Runways lead out from the burrows to the feeding-grounds.
Food: Grass- and other seeds.
Reproduction: Litters of 2–5 young are born between September and March.

Water Rat

Striped Mouse

Striped mouse skins:
(left) Single Striped Mouse
(right) Striped Mouse

Single-striped Mouse

PYGMY MICE Genus *Mus* (part of)
Five species of pygmy mice are recorded as occurring in southern Africa.

Mus setzeri

Mus triton

> **Setzer's Pygmy Mouse** *Mus setzeri*
> Total length 9 cm; tail 4 cm; mass 7 g.
> **Grey-bellied Pygmy Mouse** *Mus triton*
> Total length 10 cm; tail 4,5 cm; mass 10 g.
> **Desert Pygmy Mouse** *Mus indutus*
> Total length 10 cm; tail 4 cm; mass 6 g.
> **Pygmy Mouse** *Mus minutoides*
> Total length 10 cm; tail 4 cm; mass 6 g.
> **Thomas's Pygmy Mouse** *Mus sorella*
> Total length 10 cm; tail 4,0 cm.
> *Identification pointers:* Very small; tail shorter than head-and-body
> length; only Grey-bellied does not have white underparts; Desert Pygmy
> Mouse has patch of white hair at base of each ear. Can be
> distinguished from the small climbing mice (*Dendromus* spp.) by their
> much shorter tails and lack of dark dorsal stripe.

Mus indutus

Description: Small, with tails shorter than length of head and body. All but
Grey-bellied Pygmy Mouse have white underparts. Upperparts range from
greyish-brown to reddish-brown. Tail of Desert Pygmy Mouse is white below
while in Pygmy Mouse it is pale brown; former also has a small patch of
white hair at base of ear.
Distribution: See maps. Desert Pygmy Mouse is found in Botswana and
north-eastern South West Africa/Namibia. Pygmy Mouse most widespread.
Habitat: Pygmy Mouse from Cape fynbos to savanna grassland and
woodland. Desert Pygmy Mouse in arid scrub savanna but also Okavango.
Behaviour: Nocturnal and terrestrial, and usually occur solitarily, in pairs or in
family parties. Although they will dig their own burrows in soft soils they
usually make use of burrows dug by other species, or shelter under dead
vegetation, rocks and the debris of human occupation.
Food: Seeds, but they also feed on green plant food and insects.
Reproduction: The Pygmy Mouse has a gestation period of 19 days and a
typical litter consists of 4 young (1–7), each weighing less than a gram at
birth. Births take place in summer. The Desert Pygmy Mouse probably has
young throughout the year with peaks in summer. Five young is the usual
litter size.

Mus minutoides

Mus sorella

> **House Mouse** *Mus musculus* (Introduced)
> Total length 16 cm; tail 9 cm; mass 18 g.
> *Identification pointers:* Nondescript; associated with human dwellings,
> store-rooms, etc. Larger than the various species of pygmy mice and
> has light-brown, not white, underparts. Could be confused with
> *Mastomys* group (page 116) but smaller and lighter.

Description: The upperparts are grey-brown with the underparts being slightly
lighter in colour. The tail is lighter brown below than above.
Distribution: This introduced species with world-wide distribution is strongly
tied to human settlement and therefore has a patchy but wide distribution. It
is widely distributed in South Africa but is also known to occur in most other
southern African countries.
Habitat: Human settlements.
Behaviour: Nocturnal and lives in pairs or family parties. Untidy nests are
constructed from a wide range of man-made and natural materials.
Food: Omnivorous. It can be extremely destructive in food stores.
Reproduction: Breeds throughout year, giving birth to 1–13 (usually 6) young
per litter; gestation about 19 days; first litters at the age of 6 weeks.

Mus musculus

Desert Pygmy Mouse

Pygmy Mouse

House Mouse

Thallomys paedulcus

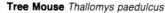

Tree Mouse Thallomys paedulcus
Total length 30 cm; tail 17 cm; mass 100 g.
Identification pointers: Arboreal habits; tail longer than head and body; dark ring around eye and extending on to muzzle; prominent ears.

Description: Characterized by having a tail longer than the head-and-body length, prominent ears and a dark ring around the eyes. Upperparts usually pale grey tinged with fawnish-yellow; underparts white; tail usually dark.
Distribution: Very widely distributed in subregion except for Lesotho and Cape south of Orange River.
Habitat: Savanna woodland – particularly areas dominated by acacias.
Behaviour: Nocturnal and arboreal. Lives in holes in trees but may also make use of large birds' nests to which it adds finer plant material. Nests may be occupied by a family group or several adults.
Food: Green leaves, fresh seeds and seed-pods but also insects.
Reproduction: Two to 5 young per litter are born during the summer.

Grammomys dolichurus

Grammomys cometes

Woodland Mouse Grammomys dolichurus
Total length 27 cm; tail 17 cm; mass 30 g.
Mozambique Woodland Mouse Grammomys cometes
Total length 30 cm; tail 18 cm.
Identification pointers: Long, thin tail; grey-brown or reddish-brown upperparts and white underparts clearly separated. Forest and woodland habitat.

Description: Both species of woodland mice have long tails well over half their total length. Colour of the upperparts may be reddish-brown with a grey tinge or much more grey-brown; underparts white. Ears are large and prominent. Mozambique Woodland Mouse sometimes has white patch at base of ear.
Distribution: Both found in woodland habitats along eastern coastal plain.
Habitat: Forest and dense woodland; Woodland Mouse sometimes in more open woodland.
Behaviour: Nocturnal and arboreal. Woodland Mouse constructs nests of grass and other fine plant material in vegetation tangles up to 2 m from the ground. It will also make use of holes in trees and even weaver-bird nests.
Food: Green plant material, wild fruits and seeds.
Reproduction: The young of the Woodland Mouse are born throughout the year, with a possible peak in summer. Litter size varies from 2 to 4.

Pelomys fallax

Uranomys ruddi
(Rudd's Mouse: no text; see plate opposite)

Grooved-toothed Rat Pelomys fallax
Total length 22–36 cm; tail 12–18 cm; mass 100–170 g.
Identification pointers: Similar in appearance to the vlei (page 118) rats but distinguished by much longer tail; tail dark above, lighter below. Face not as blunted as vlei rats. Usually indistinct dark band down back. Strong association with wet habitats.

Description: The upperparts vary from reddish-brown to yellow-brown and the rump may be more reddish than the rest of the body. An indistinct dark band is usually present down the mid-back. The tail is dark above and pale below. An interesting feature of the fur on the back is that in certain light conditions it has a distinct greenish-blue sheen.
Distribution: Restricted to eastern Zimbabwe and Mozambique but also found in well-watered parts of northern Botswana.
Habitat: The fringes of vleis, swamps, reed-beds and river-banks.
Behaviour: Mainly nocturnal and excavates its own burrows.
Food: Green plant food such as young reed shoots; seeds.
Reproduction: Litters are born in summer.

Tree Mouse

Tree Mouse

Rudd's Mouse. Only three skins of this rare species have been obtained in southern Africa. It occurs in Zimbabwe's Eastern Highlands and neighbouring Mozambique. Its total length is around 20 cm

Woodland Mouse

Grooved-toothed Rat

115

THE *MASTOMYS* GROUP Genus *Mastomys*

Four species fall within this group, two of which, the Multimammate Mouse and the Natal Multimammate Mouse, are impossible to tell apart in the field.

Natal Multimammate Mouse *Mastomys natalensis*
Total length 24 cm; tail 11 cm; mass 60 g.
Multimammate Mouse *Mastomys coucha*
Total length 24 cm; tail 11 cm; mass 60 g.
Shortridge's Mouse *Mastomys shortridgei*
Total length 22 cm; tail 10 cm; mass 45 g.
Verreaux's Mouse *Mastomys verreauxii*
Total length 25 cm; tail 14 cm; mass 40 g.
Identification pointers: Typical mouse-like appearance; underparts paler than upperparts; females of Natal Multimammate Mouse and Multimammate Mouse have up to 12 pairs of nipples; Verreaux's Mouse has darker facial markings, white upper-surfaces to feet. Shortridge's Mouse is very dark above with greyish-white underparts.

Mastomys natalensis and
Mastomys coucha

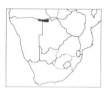

Mastomys shortridgei

Description: The various species range in colour from pale grey through grey-brown to almost black, with paler sides and grey underparts. The tail is finely scaled, with a very sparse hair covering. All species have soft, silky hair. Multimammate mice females unique with 8 to 12 pairs of nipples. Shortridge's Mouse has much darker fur and greyish-white underparts; its females have 5 pairs of nipples. Verreaux's Mouse has a dark band running between the ears and on to the muzzle, with dark hair around the eyes. The upper-surfaces of its feet are white, as is the under-surface of the tail.
Distribution: See maps; two multimammate mice liable to confusion.
Habitat: Multimammate mice have wide habitat tolerance. Other two species favour wet habitats and relatively dense vegetation.
Behaviour: Nocturnal and terrestrial. Often around houses.
Food: Seeds and fruit but also insects.
Reproduction: Multimammate Mouse most fecund of all southern African mammals, 22 foetuses having been recorded in a single female; 6–12, however, is more usual litter size. Gestation 23 days; new-born young weigh only 2 g.

Mastomys verreauxii

Rattus rattus

House Rat *Rattus rattus* (Introduced)
Total length 37 cm; tail 20 cm; mass 150 g.
Brown Rat *Rattus norvegicus* (Introduced)
Total length 40 cm; tail 19 cm; mass 300 g.
Identification pointers: Brown Rat – large size; heavy tail which is slightly shorter than head and body; restricted to coastal towns. House Rat – large size; tail slightly longer than head and body; large, naked ears; usually in association with human settlements.

Description: House Rat more slender than Brown Rat. Large feet; tail prominently scaled and is longer than head and body. Ears are large, thin and naked. Upperparts grey-brown to black; underparts white to grey. Brown Rat is bulkier, with shorter tail and smaller ears; usually greyish-brown.
Distribution: Brown Rat restricted to coastal settlements and adjacent areas; House Rat is widespread but patchy. Both occur world-wide.
Habitat: Around human settlements, but House Rat less so.
Behaviour: Nocturnal. Active diggers; swim well. House Rat more adept at climbing. Both species destructive to stored food. They build large, untidy nests from a wide range of materials and live in family groups.
Food: Both rats are omnivores, taking a wide range of foodstuffs.
Reproduction: Several litters of 5–10 per year. Gestation 3 weeks.

Rattus norvegicus

The Multimammate Mouse and the Natal Multimammate Mouse are identical in appearance

Shortridge's Mouse

Verreaux's Mouse

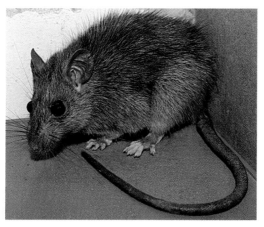

The alien House Rat

THE *PAROTOMYS* AND *OTOMYS* GROUP

These are all fairly large, short, stocky rats with blunt faces and rounded ears. The fur is quite long and shaggy and the tail length is usually less than the head-and-body measurement. With the exception of Brants's Whistling Rat all species have grooved upper incisors. The cheek-teeth are laminated.

WHISTLING RATS Genus *Parotomys*

Two species of whistling rat occur in southern Africa.

Parotomys brantsii

Parotomys littledalei

Brants's Whistling Rat *Parotomys brantsii*
Total length 25 cm; tail 10 cm; mass 120 g.
Littledale's Whistling Rat *Parotomys littledalei*
Total length 25 cm; tail 10 cm; mass 120 g.
Identification pointers: See description. Both species, as their name implies, give a sharp whistling call and this is diagnostic for *Parotomys*. Open sandy country is favoured. See 'Behaviour' below.

Description: Like other members of this group the whistling rats are stockily built, with tails shorter than the length of head and body. Body colour is very variable and ranges from pale reddish-yellow with white underparts to a brownish or greyish yellow with grey underparts. The tail may be similar in colour to the upperparts or dark above and pale below. Littledale's Whistling Rat tends to be somewhat darker on the back. The only sure way to differentiate between the two species is to examine the upper incisors. Those of Brants's Whistling Rat are not grooved, while those of Littledale's Whistling Rat are.
Distribution: The whistling rats are restricted to the arid western areas and are only found in southern Africa.
Habitat: Arid, sandy environments.
Behaviour: Largely diurnal and completely terrestrial. Brants's Whistling Rat may live solitarily in burrows but more commonly in colonies, whereas Littledale's is apparently always solitary. When alarmed they stand on their hindlegs, in close proximity to the burrow, and then give shrill whistling calls before disappearing down the burrow.
Food: They are vegetarian, eating the leaves of succulents and other green plant food, as well as seeds and flowers.
Reproduction: Nothing is known about this aspect of Littledale's Whistling Rat biology. Brants's Whistling Rat gives birth to 1–3 young during late summer. The young cling to the nipples of the female, and are dragged along when she goes out to feed.

VLEI RATS Genus *Otomys*

Six species of *Otomys* are recognized as occurring in southern Africa.

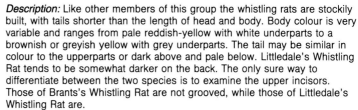

Otomys laminatus

Otomys angoniensis

Laminate Vlei Rat *Otomys laminatus*
Total length 30 cm; tail 10 cm; mass 190 g.
Angoni Vlei Rat *Otomys angoniensis*
Total length 30 cm; tail 8 cm; mass 100–250 g.
Saunders's Vlei Rat *Otomys saundersiae*
Total length 25 cm; tail 9 cm; mass 100 g.
Vlei Rat *Otomys irroratus*
Total length 24 cm; tail 9 cm; mass 120 g.
Sloggett's Rat *Otomys sloggetti*
Total length 20 cm; tail 6 cm; mass 130 g.
Bush Karoo Rat *Otomys unisulcatus*
Total length 24 cm; tail 9 cm; mass 125 g.
Identification pointers: All species have robust stocky appearance, short tails, blunt muzzles, rounded ears and grooved upper incisors. Use distribution maps and habitat preferences to assist identification.

Brants's Whistling Rat

Littledale's Whistling Rat

Angoni Vlei Rat

Vlei rat and whistling rat skins
(l. to r.):
1. Saunders's Vlei Rat
2. Littledale's Whistling Rat
3. Brants's Whistling Rat
4. Large Vlei Rat
5. Vlei Rat
6. Angonie Vlei Rat
7. Sloggett's Rat
8. Bush Karoo Rat

Otomys saundersiae

Otomys irroratus

Otomys sloggetti

Otomys unisulcatus

Petromyscus collinus

However, only examination of the teeth and skull can give positive identification. Confusion could arise with Water Rat (page 110) but it has tail more or less equal in length to that of head and body and has no grooves on upper incisors.

Description: Measurements above subject to variation. Colouration can also vary and there is a degree of colour overlap between the different species. Only certain way to distinguish between different species is to examine skull and cheek-teeth. Distribution maps can be used to eliminate species that clearly should not be present in given area. All species are densely furred and all are usually grizzled grey-brown, although Vlei Rat and Angoni Vlei Rat may be almost black. Sloggett's and the Bush Karoo rats both tend to be brown to grey-brown in colour but former has particularly short tail.

Distribution: Vlei Rat and Angoni Vlei Rat are the most widespread but only former occurs widely in the Cape Province south of the Orange River. Bush Karoo Rat only found in Cape Province. Sloggett's Rat is found in east-central parts of South Africa and in Lesotho, even on the summits of the Drakensberg Mountains. Angoni and Large Vlei Rats (the latter previously considered a full species but now accepted as a subspecies of the Angoni Vlei Rat) are shown on two separate distribution maps.

Habitat: Despite the common name 'vlei rat', only the Vlei Rat and Angoni Vlei Rat are commonly associated with moist, marshy habitats. Even these two, however, can also be found in drier habitats – grassy hillsides in the case of the former and open savanna in the case of the latter. Sloggett's Vlei Rat is the only species that is associated with rocky habitats at high altitudes, although Saunders's Vlei Rat is recorded as occurring in the mountains in close association with sedge meadows in heathland. Only the Bush Karoo Rat is found in arid areas.

Behaviour: Predominantly diurnal and live singly, in pairs or small family parties. Several species construct nests of grass and other vegetation in dense grass tussocks and vegetation tangles. Sloggett's Rat lives in rock crevices and amongst boulders. Runs are marked by small piles of discarded grass, reed and leaf segments and small cylindrical droppings.

Food: Shoots and stems of grass, sedges, reeds and other plants.

Reproduction: No information on reproduction is available for most of the species. The Angoni Vlei Rat gives birth to its 2–5 young between August and March. Only the Vlei Rat has been studied in detail; its litters of 1–4 young are born, usually in summer, after a gestation period of about 40 days. A female may have as many as 7 litters in one season.

Pygmy Rock Mouse *Petromyscus collinus*
Total length 19 cm; tail 10 cm; mass 20 g
Identification pointers: Small size; well-scaled tail; prominent ears and facial whiskers; rocky habitat.
Note: Two additional species are now recognised, namely Barbour's (*P. barbouri*) and Shortridge's (*P. shortridgei*), both falling more or less within the range of the Pygmy Rock Mouse. A related but little-known species, the Brukkaros Pygmy Rock Mouse (*P. monticularis*), is apparently restricted to the Brukkaros Mountains of southern Namibia.

Description: This small mouse is grey-yellow to brownish-yellow above; the underparts and upper surface of the feet are greyish-white. The tail is heavily scaled and sparsely haired. Prominent ears; long facial whiskers.
Distribution: Arid west of subregion.
Habitat: Dry rocky situations on mountain ranges and isolated hills.
Behaviour: Nocturnal. Although it forages alone, several may live in the same crevice. It rarely moves away from its rocky home.
Food: They feed predominantly on seeds.
Reproduction: 2–3 young per litter are born during the summer months.

Vlei Rat

Bush Karoo Rat

Bush Karoo Rats construct shelters of stick, grass and twigs

Pygmy Rock Mouse

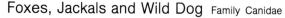

CARNIVORES <small>Order Carnivora</small>

Foxes, Jackals and Wild Dog <small>Family Canidae</small>

Cape Fox *Vulpes chama*

Total length 86–97 cm; tail 29–39 cm; shoulder height 30 cm; mass 2,5–4,0 kg.

Identification pointers: Typically fox-like appearance; long bushy tail; greyish-grizzled back and sides; light-coloured legs; muzzle generally light in colour; ears 'normal' in size. Compare with Bat-eared Fox which has black legs and muzzle and disproportionately long ears. Cape Fox normally seen singly or in pairs, whereas Bat-eared Fox usually in pairs or small groups.

Description: Only 'true' fox in subregion. Back and sides grizzled silvery-grey and neck, chest and forelegs pale tawny-brown to almost white. Throat usually white. Tail long and bushy and usually darker than rest of body. Ears long and pointed, brown at back and fringed with white hair at front.
Distribution: Restricted to subregion and south-western Angola.
Habitat: Open areas, such as grassland and arid scrub. Also wheat-lands and Cape fynbos vegetation zone in the south-west Cape.
Behaviour: Mainly nocturnal. Usually alone or in pairs. During the day it lies up in holes or dense thickets.
Food: Mainly insects, other invertebrates and rodents; also reptiles, birds, carrion and wild fruit. Rarely new-born lambs.
Reproduction: 1–4 (usually 3) pups born in spring. Gestation 50 days.

Bat-eared Fox *Otocyon megalotis*

Total length 75–90 cm; tail 23–34 cm; shoulder height 35 cm; mass 3–5 kg.

Identification pointers: Jackal-like appearance; disproportionately large ears; bushy, silvery-grey coat; black legs; bushy tail – black above and at tip; face black below eyes, paler above eyes.

Description: This small jackal-like carnivore has slender legs, a sharp-pointed, fairly long muzzle and disproportionately large ears. The ears may reach a length of 14 cm and are dark at the back, particularly at the tip; the insides of the ears are white or light in colour. The body is covered in fairly long, silvery-grey hair with a distinctly grizzled appearance and the legs are black. The tail is bushy and black above and at the tip. Although the front of the face is generally black, a light or white band runs across the forehead to the base of the ears.
Distribution: Widespread in central and western areas of subregion.
Habitat: Open country, such as short scrub and grassveld and sparsely wooded areas. Absent from mountains, dense woodland and forest.
Behaviour: Both diurnal and nocturnal activity is recorded but it lies up during the hotter hours of the day. It is an active digger but although it will excavate its own burrows, it frequently modifies those dug by other species. It is normally seen in groups numbering from 2 to 6 individuals. As pairs mate for life, the composition of groups usually consists of a pair and their offspring. Occasionally more may be seen but such groupings are temporary, perhaps associated with an abundant, localized food source. When foraging it appears to wander aimlessly, stopping periodically with ears turned to the ground; when food is located it digs shallow holes with the forepaws.
Food: Mostly insects (particularly termites) and other invertebrates; also reptiles, rodents and wild fruits.
Reproduction: Four to 6 pups born in burrow September-November; gestation 60 days. At birth pale grey and eyes closed.

Cape Fox

Bat-eared Foxes

Cape Fox

The Bat-eared Fox is both diurnal and nocturnal

Black-backed Jackal *Canis mesomelas*

Total length 96–110 cm; tail 28–37cm; shoulder height 38 cm; mass 6–10 kg.

Identification pointers: Dog-like appearance; dark, white-flecked, 'saddle' on back; black tail; fairly large, pointed, reddish-backed ears. See Side-striped Jackal where distributions overlap.

Description: Medium-sized, dog-like carnivore with characteristic black 'saddle', which is broad at neck and shoulders, narrowing to base of tail. Saddle liberally sprinkled with white hair. Face, flanks and legs reddish-brown; underparts usually paler. Lips, throat and chest are white. Fairly large pointed ears reddish on back surface and lined with white hair on inside. Black bushy tail.

Distribution: Very widely distributed in subregion but absent from parts of north-east and eradicated by farmers in other areas.

Habitat: Wide habitat tolerance, from coastal Namib Desert to moist Drakensberg. Unlike Side-striped Jackal, however, it prefers drier areas.

Behaviour: Mainly nocturnal when in conflict with man, but in protected reserves is frequently seen during day. Normally solitary or in pairs but also occurs in family parties. Pairs form long-term pair-bond, with both the male and the female marking and defending a territory which varies considerably in size, depending on the availability of food and competition with other jackals. It is well known for its wariness and cunning and is generally able to avoid all but the most sophisticated of traps. When resting, it may lie up in a burrow dug by other species, or under a bush or other vegetation. Its call is characteristic and has been described as a screaming yell, finished off with 3 or 4 short yaps. Calling is more frequent during the winter months when mating takes place.

Food: It takes an extremely wide range of food items, from young antelope, rodents, hares, birds, reptiles and insects to wild fruits and berries. It also feeds on carrion and in fact there is little that it has not been recorded eating. Unfortunately, it has proved to be a problem in sheep- and goat-farming areas, but only certain individuals take to stock-killing – not all.

Reproduction: Seasonal breeder with the 1–6 (usually 3) pups being born between July and October. Gestation approximately 60 days. New-born dark-brown pups are helpless and are born in burrows dug by other species. Both male and female bring food to young, as will 'helpers' – subadults from the previous breeding season. They start to forage with the parents when they are about 14 weeks old.

Side-striped Jackal *Canis adustus*

Total length 96–120 cm; tail 30–40 cm; shoulder height 40 cm; mass 7,5–12 kg.

Identification pointers: Overall grey appearance with a light-and-dark stripe along each side; lacks dark, silver-mottled saddle typical of the Black-backed Jackal; tail usually with white tip; ears fairly large but smaller and less pointed than those of Black-backed Jackal. Habitat can be useful aid to identification. Also see distribution maps of the two jackals.

Description: From a distance this jackal has a uniform grey appearance but at close quarters a light-coloured band, liberally fringed with black, can be seen along each flank. These side-stripes give the jackal its name. The underparts and throat are paler than the upperparts. The tail is quite bushy, mostly black and usually has a white tip.

Distribution: Only found in the far northern and eastern areas of Southern African Subregion, but has a wide distribution elsewhere in sub-Saharan Africa, excluding the equatorial forest zone.

Habitat: It shows a preference for well-watered wooded areas, but not forest.

Black-backed Jackal

Side-striped Jackal

Black-backed Jackal

Behaviour: Although it is mainly nocturnal it may be seen in the early morning and late afternoon. Most sightings are of single animals, although pairs and family parties are often encountered. Call has been likened to owl-like hoot, quite unlike long-drawn-out howl of the Black-backed Jackal.
Food: It is an omnivorous species taking a wide variety of food items from small mammals, birds, reptiles, insects and carrion to wild fruits.
Reproduction: Between 4 and 6 pups are born between August and January, in the abandoned burrows of other species.

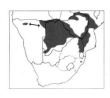

Wild Dog *Lycaon pictus*
Total length 105–150 cm; tail 30–40 cm; shoulder height 65–80 cm; mass 20–30 kg.
Identification pointers: Heavily blotched black, white and yellow-brown; slender body, long legs; white-tipped tail; large, dark, rounded ears; black muzzle and stripe from between eyes over top of head.

Description: Unmistakable; similar in size to domestic Alsatian dog. It has large, rounded ears, long legs and a bushy, white-tipped tail. Body irregularly blotched with black, white, brown and yellowish-brown. Muzzle is black, with black continuing as line from muzzle to between ears. Forehead on either side of black line is pale fawn to white.
Distribution: In South Africa the Wild Dog only occurs permanently in the Kruger National Park but a number have been introduced to the Hluhluwe and Umfolozi game reserves in Natal. In the other southern African countries it only survives in the larger reserves and uninhabited areas. It previously occurred widely in Africa, outside the equatorial forests, but has been greatly reduced in numbers by man. Probably rarest large carnivore in subregion.
Habitat: As it hunts by sight it is usually associated with open country. It avoids dense woodland, forest and extensive areas of tall grass.
Behaviour: It is a highly specialized hunter, living in packs usually numbering from 10 to 15 animals although smaller and larger groups have been observed. It is predominantly diurnal, undertaking most of its hunting in the cooler morning and late afternoon hours. Hunting is undertaken by the pack, which moves slowly towards its intended prey at first, increasing the pace as the quarry starts to move away. Once an individual has been singled out the pack rarely deviates from its goal and a chase may continue for several kilometres. Smaller prey may be pulled down immediately but larger prey is bitten and torn whilst on the move until it weakens from shock or loss of blood and can be overpowered. Despite its reputation as a wanton killer, the Wild Dog kills only for its immediate needs. During hunts it is able to reach speeds of over 50 km/h. When pups begin to eat solids, the adults regurgitate meat at the den for the pups, as well as for the adults that remained to guard the young and any sick animals unable to take part in the hunts. Wild Dogs do not establish territories but have very large home ranges. The average home range size in Kruger National Park has been estimated to be 450 km^2, but in arid areas home ranges are considerably larger. It is a very vocal species with a wide range of calls. Normally, only a single female comes into breeding condition (oestrus) at any one time and she is mated by the dominant male.
Food: Wild Dogs hunt a wide range of mammals, ranging in size from Steenbok to Buffalo. They also take rodents, hares and birds. Impala is the most important prey species in the Kruger National Park, with Springbok being very important throughout much of the Wild Dog's Botswanan range.
Reproduction: Young are born during the dry, winter months (March to July) when grass is short and hunting conditions at their best. Between 2 and 10 pups are born after a gestation period of 69 to 73 days. The young are born in the abandoned burrows of other species and for the first 3 months of their life remain in close proximity to the den.

Wild Dog

Wild Dog: note rounded ears

Unlike the jackals, the Wild Dog hunts in organized packs

Otters, Badger, Weasel and Polecat Family Mustelidae

Cape Clawless Otter *Aonyx capensis*
Total length 110–160 cm; tail 50 cm; mass 10–18 kg.
Identification pointers: Quite large size; dark-brown coat (appears black when wet) with white lips, chin, throat and upper chest. On land ambles along with back arched. Finger-like digits. Larger than Spotted-necked Otter, and lacks neck spots. Unlike Spotted-necked Otter, the Cape Clawless Otter may be found away from permanent water. Occasionally confused with the Water Mongoose (page 138).

Description: Larger of two otter species occurring in subregion. Soft dark-brown coat, with lips, chin and throat being silvery-white; white colouration sometimes extends to upper part of chest. Legs short and stout and tail long, heavy at base and tapering towards tip. On land it walks with back arched. Toes distinctively finger-like, and lack claws although there are small, flat, rudimentary nails on some digits of hindfeet.
Distribution: Absent from most of the dry interior of subregion.
Habitat: Rivers, marshes, dams and lakes; also dry stream-beds in most terrain if pools of water exist. May wander several kilometres from water. Utilizes intertidal zone of Cape Province, Transkei and Natal.
Behaviour: Active during early morning and late afternoon but may hunt at any time of day or night. Lies up in cover or shade during hotter hours. Occurs singly, in pairs, or small family parties. 'Latrine' areas with numerous droppings made up largely of crushed crab-shell are useful indication of its presence. Otters crush and eat entire crab; Water Mongoose usually leaves carapace, pincers and legs of larger crabs. Cape Clawless Otter will hunt by sight but much of prey is found by feeling with fingers. It therefore thrives in dirty water with poor visibility. (Compare with Spotted-necked Otter).
Food: Freshwater crabs but also fish and frogs. Takes molluscs, small mammals, birds and insects. Freshwater mussels are smashed on rocks.
Reproduction: Usually 2–3 cubs per litter; gestation 60–65 days.

Spotted-necked Otter *Lutra maculicollis*
Total length 100 cm; tail 30–50 cm; mass 3–5 kg.
Identification pointers: Upperparts uniform brown to dark brown; underparts lighter with pale blotching on throat and upper chest and occasionally between hindlegs. Considerably smaller than Cape Clawless Otter; closer in size to Water Mongoose but lacks long hair of latter. Closely associated with water and rarely seen far from it.

Description: Smaller of two otter species occurring in subregion. Body slender and long, with somewhat flattened tail. Feet fully webbed and toes clawed. Uniform dark brown to reddish-brown, with throat and upper chest mottled or blotched with creamy-white. Appear black when wet.
Distribution: Patchy distribution in subregion. Declining in numbers perhaps because of soil erosion, consequent muddy rivers and poor visibility for otter.
Habitat: Larger rivers, or those with large permanent pools, as well as lakes, dams and well-watered swamps. More closely tied to water than Cape Clawless Otter; not associated with estuaries or coastal environment.
Behaviour: Diurnal. Normally in groups of 2–6, but sometimes larger groups or single. Prey usually taken to bank to eat but also eaten in water. It is quite vocal, with whistles being most frequently heard, probably as a means of maintaining group contact. Uses 'latrine' sites close to water's edge. Droppings are smaller than those of Cape Clawless and similar in size to those of Water Mongoose. Those of latter species, however, usually contain greater quantity of mammal hair and are rarely so white.
Food: Mostly fish but also crabs, frogs, birds and insects.
Reproduction: 2–3 cubs probably born in summer. Gestation 60 days.

Cape Clawless Otter

Cape Clawless Otter

'Latrine' site of Cape Clawless Otter

Spotted-necked Otter

Honey Badger *Mellivora capensis*
Total length 90–100 cm; tail 18–25 cm; shoulder height 30 cm; mass 8–14 kg.
Identification pointers: Stocky build and short legs; silver-grey upperparts including top of head; black underparts and legs; short, bushy black tail — often held erect when walking. Cannot be confused with any other species.

Description: Unmistakable animal, with its thickset form, silver-grey upperparts and black underparts and legs. Top of head and upper neck usually paler than rest of upperparts. Tail short, bushy and black and often held erect when walking. Ears are small and barely noticeable. Spoor distinctive with clear impressions in prints left by long, heavy claws of forefeet (page 256).
Distribution: Widespread in subregion, but apparently absent from Orange Free State, parts of Cape Province and central Botswana.
Habitat: Found in most major habitats, but absent from coastal Namib Desert.
Behaviour: Tough and aggressive; records of attacks on elephant and buffalo and also humans when threatened. Usually seen singly, but pairs and family groups may also be observed. Mainly nocturnal, but where not disturbed is active in early morning and late afternoon.
Food: Wide range of food items but insects, other invertebrates and rodents are the most important. Reptiles, birds, other small mammals, wild fruit and carrion are also eaten. Common name is derived from their tendency to break into beehives (both natural and man-made) to eat honey and larvae. 'Rogue' individuals may take to killing poultry, sheep and goats.
Reproduction: It appears that young may be born at any time of the year. One to 4 young are born after a gestation period of about 180 days, in a grass- and leaf-lined burrow.

Striped Weasel *Poecilogale albinucha*
Total length 40–50 cm; tail 12–16 cm; shoulder height 5 cm; mass 220–350 g.
Identification pointers: Long thin body; fairly long, bushy white tail and very short legs; overall colour black with white cap on head and 4 white to yellowish stripes running from neck to base of the tail. Often confused with the Striped Polecat, but latter has much longer hair and white patches on face.

Description: This is a long, slender carnivore, with short legs. The overall colour is black with 4 off-white to yellowish stripes running from the neck to the base of the tail, combining into a white cap on the top of the head. The tail is quite bushy and white but the body hair is coarse and short.
Distribution: The Striped Weasel has a wide distribution in the eastern areas of southern Africa, with single records from South West Africa/Namibia, Botswana and Mozambique.
Habitat: It has a wide habitat tolerance but most of the records are from grassland areas.
Behaviour: Occasionally sighted during the day but predominantly nocturnal. Although usually solitary, pairs and family parties may be observed. When it walks or runs, the back has an arched appearance. It is an efficient digger in soft soil but probably uses rodent-burrows as well as its own for shelter.
Food: It hunts small, warm-blooded prey, particularly rodents. Food may be hoarded or carried to the shelter to be eaten. Its build is well adapted for the pursuit of rodents in their burrows.
Reproduction: Most records of births are in the summer months, from November to March. Litters consist of 1 to 3 young, each with a mass of about 4 g; the gestation period is about 32 days. At birth the young are almost hairless and their eyes are closed. They open after about 2 weeks.

The ears of the Honey Badger are barely noticeable

Honey Badger

Striped Weasel (see also skin photograph on page 133)

Striped Polecat *Ictonyx striatus*
Total length 57–67 cm; tail 26 cm; shoulder height 10–15 cm; mass 0,6–1,4 kg.
Identification pointers: Small size and long white and black hair; white hair in 4 stripes down back; white patch between eyes and one at base of each ear. (See Striped Weasel page 130.)

Description: Conspicuous black-and-white markings warn would-be predators that they can expect a squirt of foul-smelling liquid from its anal glands. Long body hair is shiny black with 4 distinct white stripes extending from top of head to base of tail along back and flanks. White patch on forehead between eyes and larger white patch at base of ear. The tail is predominantly white but black shows through.
Distribution: Throughout subregion except for Namib Desert coast.
Habitat: Found in all the major habitat types.
Behaviour: Strictly nocturnal; usually solitary, but also in pairs and family parties. Shelter is sought in other species' burrows, on rocky outcrops, amongst matted vegetation and even under the floors of buildings; can dig own burrow. If threatened it adopts threat posture, with rump towards aggressor, back arched and tail held erect. If threat persists, it squirts foul-smelling fluid at aggressor.
Food: Mostly insects, rodents and other small animals.
Reproduction: After gestation of 36 days, litter of 1–3 young (up to 5) born in summer.

Mongooses, Genets and Civets Family Viverridae

Banded Mongoose *Mungos mungo*
Total length 50–65 cm; tail 18–25 cm; mass 1,0–1,6 kg.
Identification pointers: Small size; usually 10–12 dark-brown to black transverse stripes on grey to grey-brown back. Superficially similar to the Suricate but the banding is much more distinct and tail bushier. Also occurs in groups. Compare the distribution maps and habitat preferences.

Description: This small, very distinctive mongoose has 10–12 dark-brown to black transverse bands on back, from behind shoulders to base of tail. Colour varies from grizzled grey to grey-brown. Tail bushy and usually darker in colour towards tip. Head relatively long and pointed.
Distribution: It is restricted to the eastern and northern areas of southern Africa and is absent from the drier central and western regions.
Habitat: Wide habitat tolerance but absent from desert, semi-desert and rain-forest. Preference for woodland with adequate ground cover.
Behaviour: Highly gregarious and social species; troops number 5–30 or more. When foraging maintain contact with constant soft calls. Troop's home range will include several shelters, usually in termitaria. Size of home range depends on number of pack members and availability of food, from 80 ha to over 4 km². Frequent marking with anal gland secretions is performed on rocks and logs. Encounters between different troops may result in conflict but apparently they do not defend territories.
Food: Insects and other invertebrates are the most important food items but they also take reptiles, amphibians, birds, carrion and probably small rodents. When feeding on birds' eggs they use the front feet to throw the eggs between the hindlegs against a rock or other hard object.
Reproduction: Usually 2 to 6 (up to 8) young, each weighing about 20 g, are born after a gestation period of approximately 60 days. The young suckle from any lactating female, not just the mother, and all the adults perform guard duties over the young animals. Juveniles begin following the troop about 5 weeks after birth.

Striped Polecat

Banded Mongoose

Skin of Striped Polecat (left) and
Striped Weasel (right)

Banded Mongoose

Meller's Mongoose *Rhynchogale melleri*
Total length 60–90 cm; tail 30–38 cm; mass 1,7–3 kg.
Identification pointers: May have black, brown or white tail; individuals with white tails may be confused with the White-tailed Mongoose but are smaller and have blacker overall appearance than latter. Check also with Selous's Mongoose with which it may also be confused. The crest-like parting on the neck is a useful character if a good view can be obtained of the animal. The distribution ranges of White-tailed, Meller's and Selous's Mongooses overlap in north-eastern areas of subregion.

Description: Hair shaggy. Colour above varies from light to dark brown; underparts lighter. Mongoose tail colour often aids identification but in this species is variable. Although near base it is usually brown, towards the tip it may be black, brown or white; dark brown to black, however, is the most usual. At close quarters upperparts have grizzled appearance. Legs are black. Useful distinguishing characteristic is a distinct crest-like parting in the hair on either side of the neck. Head quite short; muzzle swollen.
Distribution: Patchy distribution in north-eastern parts of southern Africa.
Habitat: Open woodlands but extends marginally into grassland savanna, nearly always in the vicinity of dense ground-cover and water.
Behaviour: Nocturnal and usually solitary.
Food: Mainly termites. Also other invertebrates, reptiles, amphibians and wild fruit.
Reproduction: 2–3 young born in summer in burrows or rock crevices.

Bushy-tailed Mongoose *Bdeogale crassicauda*
Total length 65–72 cm; tail 23–30 cm; mass 1,5–2,1 kg.
Identification pointers: Overall black appearance; should not be confused with any other mongoose species occurring in southern Africa.

Description: Overall body and tail colour appears black, but at close quarters appears grizzled. Legs and long-haired bushy tail are jet-black.
Distribution: Apparently very rare in subregion and seldom seen. Restricted to extreme northern and eastern Zimbabwe and central Mozambique.
Habitat: Open woodland with grass, often in rocky outcrops.
Behaviour: Apparently solitary and nocturnal, although day-time sightings have been made. Little is known of the way of life of this mongoose.
Food: Insects, other invertebrates, but also rodents, reptiles and amphibians.
Reproduction: Nothing known.

Selous's Mongoose *Paracynictis selousi*
Total length 63–90 cm; tail 28–43 cm; mass 1,4–2,0 kg.
Identification pointers: Smaller and more slender than the White-tailed Mongoose. Tail only white towards the tip, whereas in White-tailed Mongoose it is white for three-quarters of its length.

Description: The overall body colour of this mongoose is pale speckled grey to tawny-grey; the legs are brown to black. The fairly long-haired tail is usually light-coloured but only white towards the tip.
Distribution: Restricted to north-east and far north of subregion.
Habitat: Savanna grass- and woodland.
Behaviour: Nocturnal and usually solitary, but pairs and females with young are not uncommonly seen. It digs its own burrows. This mongoose is probably overlooked because of its relatively small size and its nocturnal habits.
Food: It feeds mainly on invertebrates but also takes a wide range of small rodents, amphibians, reptiles and birds.
Reproduction: Litters of 2–4 born August to March.

Meller's Mongoose

Selous's Mongoose

Small Grey Mongoose *Galerella pulverulenta*
Total length 55–69 cm; tail 20–34 cm; mass 0,5–1,0 kg.
Identification pointers: Small size; uniform grey colouring; only marginally overlaps distribution range of the Slender Mongoose. Lacks the latter's black tail-tip and holds tail horizontally when running, whereas Slender Mongoose holds tail vertically or curved slightly over the body. See distribution maps. Much smaller than the Large Grey Mongoose which in any case has black tail-tip.

Description: Uniform light to dark grey above, appearing grizzled at close quarters. In north-west some animals may appear more brown. Legs darker than rest of body. Head quite long and muzzle pointed. Tail long, bushy and uniform grizzled grey.
Distribution: It occurs widely in the Cape Province south of the Orange River and extends through the southern Orange Free State, Lesotho and marginally into Natal.
Habitat: It has a very wide habitat tolerance, from forest to open scrub. Particularly common in the southern coastal areas and adjacent interior.
Behaviour: Active by day, although tends to lie up during the hottest part of the day in summer. Usually solitary but pairs and family parties are occasionally seen. It makes use of regular pathways within home range. Home ranges overlap considerably and although this species marks with glandular secretions it is not known whether it is territorial.
Food: Invertebrates (mainly insects) and small rodents; also carrion, birds, reptiles, amphibians and wild fruits.
Reproduction: From 1–3 young are born in holes, amongst rocks or in dense vegetation, from about August to December.

Large Grey Mongoose *Herpestes ichneumon*
Total length 100–110 cm; tail 45–58 cm; mass 2,5–4,0 kg.
Identification pointers: Large size; long grey-grizzled body hair; black tail-tip and black lower legs. Much larger than Small Grey Mongoose which has a completely grey tail and no black at tip.

Description: This, as its name indicates, is a large, grey mongoose. The tail is prominently black-tipped and the lower parts of the legs are black. The hair on the sides and hindquarters is almost long enough to hide the hindlegs from view. Tail hair is long but becomes shorter towards the black tip.
Distribution: It occurs in a narrow belt along the southern coast from close to Cape Town in the west and then northwards into Natal. It is fairly widely distributed in the eastern areas of southern Africa and marginally in the far north. It is widespread elsewhere in Africa, although absent from much of the equatorial forest zone and desert. It extends to the Mediterranean along the broad Nile River valley and then along the coast of North Africa to Spain and Portugal. It also occurs in parts of the Middle East.
Habitat: Riverine vegetation and around lakes, dams and marshes. When foraging , however, it may wander several kilometres from its usual habitat.
Behaviour: Although nocturnal activity has been recorded it is mainly diurnal. It is usually seen solitarily or in pairs, but family parties are not an uncommon sight. Such parties may walk along in line, nose to anus, giving the group a snake-like appearance. It will frequently stand on its hindlegs to view the surrounding area. Droppings are deposited at regular latrine sites and it also marks objects within its home range with anal gland secretion.
Food: Small rodents are very important in its diet but it also eats other small mammals, reptiles, birds, amphibians and a wide range of invertebrates, as well as wild fruits. It is known to eat snakes, including fairly large puff-adders.
Reproduction: Young are probably born in the summer months but there is no information available for southern Africa. Litter size has been recorded as 2 to 4, born after a gestation period of about 75 days.

Small Grey Mongoose

Large Grey Mongoose

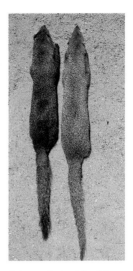

Colour variants of Small Grey Mongoose: (left) dark form from north-west of range; (right) more typical grey form

Slender Mongoose *Galerella sanguinea*
Total length 50–65 cm; tail 23–30 cm; mass (male) 500–800 g, (female) 370–560 g.

Identification pointers: Small size and slender body; colour grey, brown or chestnut-orange; short legs and fairly bushy tail with black tip – raised or vertical but with forward curve when running; compare with Small Grey Mongoose where range overlaps, but latter lacks black-tipped tail. See maps.

Description: Body colour of this slender species varies from grizzled yellow-brown to rich red-brown; latter colour most frequently encountered in the north-western areas of subregion. In central and northern South West Africa/Namibia are usually dark brown but reddish-brown specimens also occur. Tail bushy and black-tipped. When the animal runs, tail typically held well clear of ground and often vertical, but curving forward over back and not rigidly upright as is the case with the Suricate.
Distribution: Widespread in subregion north of Orange River.
Habitat: It is found in areas of high and low rainfall, and from forest to open savanna, as long as there is adequate cover.
Behaviour: Terrestrial but climbs well. Usually solitary. One of most commonly seen small carnivores within its range, particularly along roads.
Food: Insects and other invertebrates; also takes reptiles, small rodents, birds and amphibians as well as wild fruits.
Reproduction: Litter size 1–2, sometimes 3, born in summer. Gestation period approximately 45 days.

Water Mongoose *Atilax paludinosus*
Total length 80–100 cm; tail 30–40 cm; shoulder height 22 cm; mass 2,5–5,5 kg.

Identification pointers: Large; generally uniform dark-brown in colour; associated with water. Sometimes confused with the two otter species, but much smaller than the Cape Clawless Otter, and lacks the pale markings on throat and neck of the Spotted-necked Otter. The head is long and pointed and typically mongoose-like.

Description: Large, usually uniformly dark-brown, shaggy-haired animal. Short hair on feet and face. Some are reddish-brown or almost black.
Distribution: Widespread in subregion but absent from arid interior. It penetrates the Karoo along length of Orange River to the west coast.
Habitat: The Water Mongoose is usually associated with well-watered areas, along rivers and streams, and around dams, lakes, estuaries and swamps wherever there is cover. It utilizes temporary stream-beds where there are pools and may wander some distance from water.
Behaviour: This mongoose is active mainly by night but is also crepuscular (active at dusk and dawn). It is probably territorial and sightings are mostly of single animals, although pairs and females with young are occasionally seen. The home ranges tend to be linear, in that they follow rivers and streams or the perimeters of other waterbodies. Droppings accumulate at latrine sites which are usually situated near the water's edge; these latrines are not, however, as dispersed as those of otters and the droppings are usually darker in colour. When foraging it follows regular pathways. It swims readily.
Food: Mainly crabs and amphibians but also small rodents, birds, fish, insects, reptiles and occasionally wild fruits. Aquatic food hunted in shallows where feet are used to dig in the mud and explore under rocks. It smashes freshwater mussels by throwing them with front feet between hindlegs against rocks. It forages along beaches and in rock-pools in coastal areas.
Reproduction: Most of the young probably born August to December. There are usually 1 to 3 young, each weighing about 120 g at birth, and they are born in burrows, rock crevices or amongst dense vegetation.

Slender Mongoose

Water Mongoose

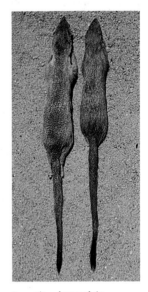

Two colour forms of the
Slender Mongoose; the
chestnut-red form is found
in the Kalahari thornveld of
the northern Cape and
southern Botswana

Dwarf Mongoose *Helogale parvula*
Total length 35–40 cm; tail 14–20 cm; shoulder height 7 cm; mass 220–350 g.
Identification pointers: Very small size; uniform dark brown, glossy coat; always in troops.

Description: The Dwarf Mongoose is the smallest carnivore occurring in southern Africa. Its body is a uniform dark brown and from a distance appears to be almost black. The fur is glossy and has a slightly grizzled appearance at close quarters.
Distribution: The Dwarf Mongoose is restricted to the northern and eastern regions of the Southern African Subregion. Elsewhere in Africa it extends through central and East Africa to as far north as Somalia.
Habitat: Open woodland and grassland savanna. It is absent from very dry areas and forest but is often associated with rocky areas.
Behaviour: A strictly diurnal mongoose usually living in troops of up to 10 individuals, although as many as 30 have been recorded. They have a fixed home, frequently in termitaria but will use burrows dug by other species or excavated by themselves. Dwarf Mongoose troops have a rigid social system with a dominant male and female, the rest of the members falling into a 'pecking order'. Usually only the dominant female breeds, and apart from suckling the young she leaves their care to the other troop members. When disturbed, Dwarf Mongooses will dive for cover but they are inquisitive and will soon re-emerge, standing on their hindlegs to look around.
Food: Insects and other invertebrates are by far the most important prey items but they will also eat reptiles, birds and birds' eggs. Several troop members may co-operate to overpower larger prey.
Reproduction: Two to 4 young are born in the summer months after a gestation period of some 50–54 days. The young are covered with hair at birth but the eyes are closed.

White-tailed Mongoose *Ichneumia albicauda*
Total length 90–150 cm; tail 35–48 cm; mass 3,5–5,2 kg.
Identification pointers: Large size; white tail, dark body and legs. The superficially similar Selous's Mongoose is smaller and the tail is only white towards the tip. When walking the head is held lower than the rest of the body.

Description: This very large mongoose has a coarse shaggy coat and a distinctively long, white tail. The body and the long legs are brown-grey to almost black but the head is usually somewhat lighter in colour. When it walks, its hindquarters appear to be higher than the shoulder region.
Distribution: This large mongoose is only found in the eastern parts of the Southern African Subregion. Further north it occurs widely in central and East Africa, extending as far north as Egypt, and also through the savannas of West Africa to Senegal.
Habitat: Woodland savanna but marginally in forest. Largely absent from equatorial forest and desert.
Behaviour: Nocturnal and usually solitary but occasionally pairs or family parties may be seen. It lies up in burrows dug by other species, or in rock crevices and amongst dense vegetation. Little is known about the biology of this mongoose however.
Food: Insects and other invertebrates are by far the most important food but it also takes rodents, amphibians, reptiles, birds and wild fruits. It is recorded as catching mammals up to the size of hares and cane-rats.
Reproduction: The young are probably born in spring and early summer. There are between 1 and 4 young per litter.

Dwarf Mongooses

Dwarf Mongoose

White-tailed Mongoose

Yellow Mongoose *Cynictis penicillata*
Total length 40–60 cm; tail 18–25 cm; mass 450–900 g.
Identification pointers: Small size; yellowish body and tail but white tail-tip; in parts of northern range, however, specimens are more grey and lack white tail tip; pointed face.

Description: Usually reddish-yellow to tawny-yellow with prominent white tip to tail. However, in northern parts of range, particularly Botswana, it is more grey and usually lacks white tip to tail. Tail quite bushy. Chin, throat and upper chest paler than rest of body and eyes are orange-brown.
Distribution: Western and central areas of subregion, extending as far east as north-western Natal and the Transvaal.
Habitat: This is a mongoose of open habitats, short grassland, and semi-desert scrub, but it also occurs in the more open areas along the coast of the western and eastern Cape. It is absent from forest, dense vegetation and the coastal Namib Desert.
Behaviour: A diurnal species but although usually seen alone it lives communally in warrens of 5 to 10 (sometimes as many as 20) individuals. It may dig its own burrows but will readily occupy those dug by the Suricate and Ground Squirrels, sometimes with all three species living in the same burrow systems. Each morning the Yellow Mongoose colony disperses along regularly used pathways to forage. The droppings are deposited in latrines in close proximity to the entrances to the burrows.
Food: Mostly insects and invertebrates, but also takes small rodents, amphibians and reptiles and occasionally carrion.
Reproduction: In the southern parts of its distribution range the litters of 2–5 young are born between October and January but in the north this extends through to March. It is possible that births also occur at other times of the year as well.

Suricate *Suricata suricatta*
Total length 45–55 cm; tail 20–24 cm; mass 620–960 g.
Identification pointers: Small size; pale body colour with several irregular transverse bands on the back; thinly haired tail, usually with darker tip, and often used as a fifth 'leg' when standing on hindlegs and held rigidly vertical when running. Occurs in groups. Could only be confused with the Banded Mongoose but ranges only overlap marginally (see maps) and banding much more distinct in that species. Habitat preferences also differ.

Description: The body is fawn to silvery-grey with a number of darker, irregular transverse bars running from behind the shoulders to the base of the tail. The tail is thin, tapering and short-haired. The head is broad at the back and the muzzle is pointed. Frequently stands on hindlegs and the tail is used for support. When running, tail held vertically (but see Slender Mongoose). The front claws are very long and are used for digging for prey.
Distribution: The Suricate is widely distributed in the central and western parts of the subregion, extending eastwards into the southern Transvaal.
Habitat: Open, arid, lightly vegetated country.
Behaviour: It is completely diurnal in habit and lives in groups numbering from 5 to 40 individuals. It will dig its own burrow complexes ('warrens') but will also make use of those dug by Ground Squirrels and Yellow Mongooses, often living in harmony with both of these species. When foraging or on the move it maintains communication with a constant soft grunting.
Food: Predominantly insects and other invertebrates, but it will also eat reptiles and birds. Much of the food is obtained by digging with the long claws of the forefeet.
Reproduction: 2–5 young born in summer; gestation period 73 days.

Yellow Mongoose (reddish-yellow phase)

Yellow Mongoose (grey phase)

Suricates

The Suricate can stand upright on its hindlegs using its tail for support to survey its surroundings

Genetta genetta

Genetta tigrina

Small-spotted Genet *Genetta genetta*
Total length 86–100 cm; tail 40–50 cm; mass 1,5–2,6 kg.
Large-spotted Genet *Genetta tigrina*
Total length 85–110 cm; tail 40–50 cm; mass 1,5–3,2 kg.
Identification pointers: Genets have long, slender bodies and tails;
Small-spotted Genet – *white tail-tip*; smaller dark to black spots; crest of
longish hair only raised when alarmed. Large-spotted Genet – *usually
black tail-tip*; larger, rusty-brown spots; no crest along back. Compare
distribution maps and habitat requirements. Sometimes confused with
Civet but very much smaller.

Description: Both genet species have long, slender bodies and tails and
short legs. The ears are long, rounded and thin. The Small-spotted Genet is
usually off-white to greyish-white, spotted with dark-brown to almost black
spots and bars. The tail is black-ringed and usually has a white tip. A crest of
fairly long, black-tipped hair runs along the back and is raised when the
animal is frightened or angry.
In the Large-spotted Genet the spots are generally larger and rusty-brown in
colour and the legs are usually paler. There is no prominent crest down the
back and the hair is generally shorter and softer. The tail-tip is usually dark
brown to black. The black-and-white facial markings are usually more
prominent in the Small-spotted Genet than in the Large-spotted Genet; the
chin of the former is dark and in the latter usually white.
It should be noted that the systematics of the various species of African
genet – including the two southern African species – have not yet been fully
clarified. There is enormous variation in colour and patterning and all grades
of intermediate between the two may be encountered.
Distribution: Small-spotted Genet – this genet is widespread in southern
Africa but is absent from much of Mozambique and northern and eastern
Zimbabwe; it only occurs marginally in Natal. Elsewhere it occurs widely in
southern Angola and the extreme west of Zambia; it is absent from central
Africa but a separate population extends from Tanzania northwards to Sudan
and through the Sahel to West Africa, North Africa, the Middle East and parts
of Europe. Large-spotted Genet – largely restricted to the eastern areas of
southern Africa but extends in a narrow belt along the south coast west to
Cape Town. It occurs widely in the rest of Africa.
Habitat: The Small-spotted Genet has a very wide habitat tolerance, ranging
from desert margins to areas with high rainfall. This includes woodland,
riverine margins and even isolated rocky outcrops on open plains. The
Large-spotted Genet is more associated with well-watered areas and fairly
dense vegetation. Both species occur together in some areas of southern
Africa.
Behaviour: Both species of genet are mainly nocturnal, lying up under cover
during the day. They are excellent climbers although much of their foraging is
done on the ground. Normally solitary, pairs are occasionally seen.
Droppings are deposited at latrine sites and these are usually in open or
conspicuous places.
Food: Both genet species have a similar diet. Invertebrates, particularly
insects, are very important sources of food, as are small rodents. Reptiles,
amphibians, birds and other small mammals are taken, as well as wild fruits.
They can be a problem to poultry-owners and if they gain access to a
poultry-run or hen-house often kill far more than they require.
Reproduction: Young of both species are born in the summer months in
holes, rock crevices or amongst dense vegetation. Between 2 and 4 young
(up to 5 have been recorded for the Large-spotted Genet) are born after a
gestation period of about 70 days. The eyes are closed at birth.

Small-spotted Genet; black and white facial markings more prominent than those of Large-spotted Genet (below)

Large-spotted Genet

Facial markings of Large-spotted Genet are less bold than those of Small-spotted Genet

Large-spotted Genet

Civet *Civettictis civetta*
Total length 120–140 cm; tail 40–50 cm; shoulder height 40 cm; mass
9–15 kg.
Identification pointers: Large size; white, black and grey facial markings;
grey body heavily marked with black spots, blotches and irregular
stripes; black legs; white and black neck bands; bushy tail with white
bands below and black tip; walks with back arched and head held low.
Sometimes confused with genets but is much larger, with shorter tail.
See the genets (page 144).

Description: Long-bodied, heavily built and long-legged – about the size of a
medium-sized dog. When moving, it holds its back in an arched position and
its head low. Hair long and coarse. Forehead light grey, muzzle white, and
broad black band runs horizontally between forehead and muzzle and
extends round head on to throat. Distinct light band extends from ear base
towards chest. Greyish to grey-brown overall with many black spots, blotches
and bands covering the body. Spotting is less distinct on, or may be absent
from the shoulder and neck. Legs black. Ridge of dark hair along spine to
tail, erected when Civet is threatened or under stress. Ears small with black
tip. Bushy tail banded white and black below; upperside and tip black.
Distribution: Restricted to the northern and eastern parts of subregion.
Habitat: Fairly wide habitat tolerance but preference for more densely
vegetated areas, for example open woodland; near permanent water.
Behaviour: Mainly nocturnal but often active in early morning and late
afternoon. Solitary or in pairs. Regular 'latrine' sites known as 'civetries'.
Marks points within its range with secretions from anal glands.
Food: Insects, other invertebrates, wild fruits, small rodents, reptiles, birds
and carrion. Largest prey recorded are hares and guinea-fowl.
Reproduction: Litter 2–4 usually born in summer, in burrows excavated by
other species, in rock crevices, or in dense vegetation. Gestation period
60–65 days.

Tree Civet *Nandinia binotata*
Total length 87–97 cm; tail 45–50 cm; mass 1,5–3,0 kg.
Identification pointers: Long, fairly slender body and tail; generally dark
appearance in the field, but at close quarters seen to be lighter brown
with numerous darker, irregular spots. Forest habitat. Compare with the
two genet species. Tree Civets have a very limited distribution in
southern Africa. See distribution map.

Description: Similar to but stouter than genets. Head rounder with short ears.
At a distance appear uniformly dark brown but at close quarters, upperparts
noticeably spotted with small, irregularly shaped, dark-brown, almost black
spots, on a lighter-brown background. More or less visible white or yellowish
spot above shoulder-blade. Sides and lower parts of limbs not spotted. Hair
soft and woolly on body and quite long on the long tail.
Distribution: In subregion only in eastern Zimbabwe and adjacent areas of
Mozambique. Widespread in the equatorial forest zone.
Habitat: High forest or montane rain-forest receiving an annual rainfall of
1 000 mm or more.
Behaviour: It is nocturnal, solitary and largely arboreal. Usually moves in the
taller trees but does descend to the ground.
Food: Its principal food is wild fruit, although it also feeds on birds, rodents
and insects. It has also been recorded as catching and eating fruit-bats.
Carrion is eaten and they may take to raiding poultry-runs.
Reproduction: Virtually nothing is known about the Tree Civet's biology in
southern Africa but it seems likely that it may breed at any time of the year.
Usually 2 young, but up to 4, are born in holes in trees after a gestation
period of about 64 days.

Civet

Civet

Civet: coarse hair and spots in close-up

Captive Tree Civet showing two white shoulder spots and banding on tail

Captive Tree Civet showing detail of body colour

Hyaenas Family Hyaenidae

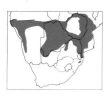

Spotted Hyaena *Crocuta crocuta*

Total length 120–180 cm; tail 25 cm; shoulder height 85 cm; mass 60–80 kg.

Identification pointers: Large size; shoulders higher than rump; short-haired fawn-yellow coat with numerous dark-brown spots or blotches; lacks the long hair and pointed ears of the Brown Hyaena. See Brown Hyaena. Characteristic repertoire of whooping, giggling and cackling calls.

Description: Unmistakable. Heavily built forequarters stand higher than rump. Large head with prominent rounded ears; black muzzle. Body usually fawn-yellow to grey-fawn with scattering of dark-brown spots and blotches, less distinct in old animals. Head, throat and chest not spotted. Short tail has coarse hair covering. Short erect mane along neck and shoulders.

Distribution: Formerly occurred as far south as Cape Town. Now only in northern and eastern parts of subregion.

Habitat: Open country but also rocky areas and in open woodland. Absent from forest and the Namib coastal belt. Requires access to drinking water.

Behaviour: Usually live in family groups or 'clans' led by a female. Clan members share the same range and dens and may number from 3 or 4, to 15 or more individuals. Territories are defended against other clans and are marked with anal gland secretions, urine and the distinctive bright white droppings – usually deposited in 'latrine' sites. Mainly nocturnal but frequently seen during day. Very vocal with whoops, groans, grunts, whines, yells and giggles.

Food: In the past regarded as a cowardly scavenger, now known to be an efficient and regular hunter. Hunts singly, in small groups or in packs, depending on type of food taken. Diet ranges from insects to large game such as zebra, wildebeest and giraffe. Scavenges and will chase other predators from their kills. Raids dustbins and rubbish-heaps at camps.

Reproduction: One or two cubs is usual, very rarely more; largely a non-seasonal breeder although seasonal peaks can be discerned in some regions. Two or more females may keep young in same burrow for several months. Uniform dark brown at birth with lighter heads.

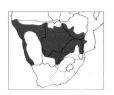

Brown Hyaena *Hyaena brunnea*

Total length 130–160 cm; tail 17–30 cm; shoulder height 80 cm; mass (male) 47 kg, (female) 42 kg.

Identification pointers: Large size with shoulders higher than the rump; long dark-brown hair, lighter in colour on neck and shoulders; large head with long pointed ears; long-haired tail. Spotted Hyaena has shorter hair, a spotted coat to lesser or greater extent and has shorter, more rounded ears.

Description: The Brown Hyaena is higher at the shoulder than at the hindquarters; the shoulders and chest are heavily built. The body is covered in a long, shaggy coat, with a dense mantle of hair on the back and shoulders. The mantle is lighter in colour than the rest of the body. The body colour varies from light to dark brown and the legs are striped black and light brown. The tail is short, bushy and dark. Ears are long, erect and pointed.

Distribution: The Brown Hyaena used to occur widely in southern Africa but is only occasionally seen south of the Orange River today. It is most frequently encountered in the Kalahari. Wanderers may, however, be expected to turn up far outside their main range.

Habitat: Although today it is found mainly in drier parts of southern Africa, even occurring along the arid Namib Desert coastal belt, its past distribution range shows that it has a potentially wide habitat tolerance.

Spotted Hyaena group

The Brown Hyaena has longer, pointed ears

The Spotted Hyaena has shorter, rounded ears

Hyaena droppings are characteristically white

Behaviour: Brown Hyaenas are mainly nocturnal and are usually seen singly. Several animals may share a territory, altough foraging is usually an individual activity. Territory size varies considerably, from about 19 km² in a Transvaal study to between 235 km² and 481 km² in the southern Kalahari. The animals sharing a territory are apparently an extended family unit consisting of 4 to 6 individuals and all will assist in raising cubs. Territories are marked with droppings and secretions of anal glands. Unlike the Spotted Hyaena, the Brown Hyaena is not particularly vocal.

Food: Brown Hyaenas are mainly scavengers but it also eats a wide range of small vertebrates, insects and fruits. Hunting and killing of large prey is rare, although on occasion it has been recorded as killing sheep and goats in farming areas. Surplus food may be hidden in holes or under vegetation.

Reproduction: Nomadic males, overlapping the territories of several groups, mate with receptive females, while the males resident with groups do not. Two to 3 cubs are born after a gestation of 90 days. The eyes are closed at birth and open after 2 weeks. Young are born from August to January.

Aardwolf Family Protelidae

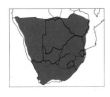

Aardwolf *Proteles cristatus*
Total length 84–100 cm; tail 20–28 cm; shoulder height 50 cm; mass 6–11 kg.
Identification pointers: Hyaena-like appearance; prominent mane of long hair down neck and back; pale-buff background colour with dark vertical body stripes, with black bands on upper part of legs; feet, muzzle and much of distal part of tail black; long, pointed ears. Much smaller than the two hyaena species.

Description: The Aardwolf is a medium-sized carnivore which is higher at the shoulders than at the rump. The hair is quite long and coarse, with a long mane of erectile hair down the neck and back, raised only when the animal is frightened or threatened. The general background colour varies from pale tawny to yellow-white and there are several vertical black stripes on the body and black bands on the upper parts of the legs. The muzzle and feet are black. At its base the bushy tail is yellow-fawn but the remainder is black. The ears are large and pointed.

Distribution: The Aardwolf is very widely distributed in the subregion and extends into southern Angola and marginally into Zambia. It is absent from central Africa but there is another population in East Africa and north along the Red Sea to Egypt.

Habitat: This carnivore has a very wide habitat tolerance, occurring in both low- and high-rainfall regions. It shows a marked preference for open habitats and avoids forest. Its distribution is dictated by the availability of termites, its principal food.

Behaviour: Although mainly active at night it may be seen during the early morning and late afternoon, as well as on overcast days. It occurs singly, in pairs, or in family parties. A home range may be occupied by two or more animals and several females may drop their pups in the same den. Although it often digs its own burrows it will also use those dug by other species. Droppings are usually deposited at a number of latrine sites within the home range and grass-stalks are marked with a secretion from the anal glands.

Food: Mostly termites but it will occasionally take other insects. Despite the frequent claim that it kills and eats sheep there is no evidence of this. Although the canine teeth are well developed, the cheek-teeth are greatly reduced in size and are not capable of dealing with flesh.

Reproduction: One to 4 young are born in a burrow, after a gestation period of about 60 days. Although most young are dropped between October and February, they have also been recorded at other times of the year.

Aardwolf

Aardwolf head showing all-black muzzle

Cats Family Felidae

African Wild Cat *Felis lybica*
Total length 85–100 cm; tail 25–37 cm; shoulder height 35 cm; mass 2,5–6,0 kg.
Identification pointers: Very similar in appearance to domestic cat but distinguishable from it by the rich reddish-brown colour of back of ears, over belly and on back of hindlegs. Vertical body stripes are present but range from very distinct to very faint.

Description: Similar in appearance to domestic cat but larger with proportionately longer legs. Colour ranges from pale sandy brown in drier areas to light or dark grey in wetter parts of subregion. Body marked with more or less distinct dark vertical stripes. Relatively long tail dark-ringed with black tip. Chin and throat white and chest usually paler than rest of body. Belly usually reddish. Back of each ear coloured rich reddish-brown. Interbreeds readily with domestic cats and hybrids can cause confusion.
Distribution: Throughout subregion but absent from Namib Desert coastal belt.
Habitat: Wide habitat tolerance but requires cover.
Behaviour: Solitary except when mating or when female is tending kittens. Droppings usually buried in the same way as domestic cat but they also establish small 'latrines' where droppings accumulate.
Food: Mainly small rodents but they also eat other small mammals, birds, reptiles, amphibians, insects and other invertebrates. The largest recorded prey items are hares, springhares and birds up to the size of guinea-fowl.
Reproduction: 2–5 kittens are born in summer amongst dense vegetation cover, rocks or in burrows dug by other species; gestation period 65 days.

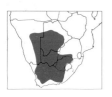

Small Spotted Cat *Felis nigripes*
Total length 50–63 cm; tail 16 cm; shoulder height 25 cm; mass 1,0–2,0 kg.
Identification pointers: Small size; pale body colour well covered with smallish dark-brown to black spots; white chin and throat; back of ears same colour as body. Smaller and more distinctly marked than African Wild Cat, also lacks reddish-ginger colour at back of ears; can be distinguished from genets by short tail and typical short cat-like face.

Description: Also called Black-footed Cat, this is the smallest cat species occurring in subregion. Colour ranges from reddish-fawn in southern parts of range to much paler in north. Numerous black (or red-brown in north) spots and bars on body, legs, head and tail. Tail is short, black-ringed and -tipped. Chin and throat are white but there are two or three distinct dark bands on the throat. Back of ear is usually same colour as rest of body but lacks markings.
Distribution: The Small Spotted Cat is restricted to the more arid southern and central parts of southern Africa. Only recently found to occur on the west coast and south-western interior of the Cape Province.
Habitat: Open, dry habitats with some vegetation cover.
Behaviour: The Small Spotted Cat is nocturnal and rarely seen. It is nowhere common and little is known about its behaviour. Most sightings are of solitary animals and it lies up in burrows dug by other species and in hollow termite-mounds. For this reason it is sometimes called the 'Anthill Tiger'.
Food: It feeds mostly on small rodents but also takes reptiles, birds and insects. The largest recorded prey item is a Ground Squirrel.
Reproduction: The litter of 1–3 kittens is born in the summer months after a gestation period of about 68 days.

African Wild Cat:
note pale-reddish belly

Domestic Cats, significant predators
on small vertebrates

The African Wild Cat may be distinguished from the Domestic Cat
by the rich red-brown colour of the ears

Small Spotted Cat

Serval *Felis serval*
Total length 96–120 cm; tail 25–38 cm; shoulder height 60 cm; mass 8,0–13,0 kg.
Identification pointers: Pale, usually yellowish-fawn coat, black-spotted and black-barred; large, rounded ears each with two black bands separated by white patch at back; short, black-banded and-tipped tail. Much smaller then either Leopard and Cheetah—proportionately shorter tail, large ears.

Description: Slender, long-legged, spotted cat with short tail and large, rounded ears. Body colour very variable but usually yellowish-fawn with scattered black spots and bars. Black bars and spots on neck; black bands extend down legs. Underparts paler but usually also spotted. Back surface of ear has black band, separated from black tip by white patch. Tail banded with black and has black tip.
Distribution: North and east of subregion; formerly to southern Cape. Widespread elsewhere in Africa.
Habitat: Usually environments with water, adjacent tall grassland, reed-beds or rank vegetation fringing forest.
Behaviour: Usually nocturnal but sometimes active in early morning and late afternoon. Usually solitary but also in pairs and family groups. Mainly terrestrial but a good climber.
Food: Small mammals (particularly vlei rats, but up to hares and cane-rats), birds, reptiles and insects. Perhaps young of smaller antelope species.
Reproduction: Most young are born in summer after a gestation of 68–72 days. Usually 1–3 (up to 5) kittens each weighing about 200 g are born in burrows dug by other species or in dense vegetation.

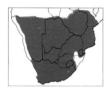

Caracal *Felis caracal*
Total length 70–110 cm; tail 18–34 cm; shoulder height 40–45 cm; mass 7–19 kg.
Identification pointers: Hindquarters slightly higher than shoulders; general reddish-fawn colouration; short tail; pointed ears with tuft of black hair at tip and black at back sprinkled with white hairs.

Description: A robustly built cat, its hindquarters slightly higher than its shoulders. Coat thick but short and soft; colour varies from pale reddish-fawn to a rich brick-red. Underparts off-white with faint spotting or blotching. Long, pointed ears with tuft of longish black hair at the tip are characteristic. Backs of ears are black, liberally sprinkled with white hairs. Face prominently marked with black and white patches, notably around eyes and mouth. Short reddish tail.
Distribution: Widespread in subregion but absent from much of Natal and Namib coastal strip. Occurs widely in the rest of Africa, but absent from equatorial forest, and extends into Middle East and as far east as India.
Habitat: Semi-desert to savanna woodland; hilly country to coastal forests.
Behaviour: Mainly nocturnal, but partly diurnal if undisturbed. Solitary, except when mating or females accompanied by kittens. Stalks its prey as close as possible and then relies on a direct pounce or short, fast run.
Food: The Caracal hunts mainly small- to medium-sized mammals, ranging from mice to antelope (up to the size of Bushbuck ewes). It also catches birds and reptiles. In some small-stock farming areas it is considered to be a major problem because of its depredations on sheep and goats.
Reproduction: Litters of 1–3 kittens may be born at any time of the year, although there is a summer peak. The gestation period is about 79 days and the birth mass is around 250 g. Kittens may be born in burrows excavated by other species, in rock crevices or amongst dense vegetation.

Serval: note characteristic colouration of back of ear

The Serval's tail is proportionately shorter than that of the cheetah (p. 157)

Caracal: black and white markings on face

The black tuft of hair at the top of the Caracal's ear is characteristic

Cheetah *Acinonyx jubatus*
Total length 180–220 cm; tail 60–80 cm; shoulder height 80 cm; mass 40–60 kg.
Identification pointers: Large size; slender, greyhound-like build; long, spotted white-tipped tail, black-ringed towards tip; spotted coat – single, rounded, black spots; rounded face with a black line from inner corner of eye to corner of mouth ('tear-mark'). Leopard has heavier build, its spots form rosettes, it has no black lines on face and it usually frequents different habitats. Serval much smaller and has disproportionately short tail.

Description: The Cheetah, sometimes referred to as the 'greyhound of cats', is probably the most elegant member of the cat family. It is tall and slender, with long legs and a short muzzle with a rounded head. The body colour is off-white to pale fawn and is liberally dotted with black, rounded, spots more or less uniform in size. A clear black line (the 'tear-mark') runs from the inner corner of each eye to the corner of the mouth. Numerous small black spots are present on the forehead and top of the head. The tips of the ears are white. The long tail is black-ringed with a white tip. A short erectile crest is situated on the back and sides. The Cheetah is the only cat that does not have fully retractile claws and the impressions of the claws can be seen in their tracks. The well-publicized 'King Cheetah' is merely an aberrant colour form, albeit an attractive one.
Distribution: Formerly widespread in southern Africa, the Cheetah has disappeared from the Cape Province (except for the Kalahari Gemsbok National Park), Orange Free State and much of the Transvaal. It has been reintroduced to Natal. It is still widespread in Botswana and South West Africa/Namibia but nowhere common. It is estimated that between 4 000 and 6 000 survive in southern Africa. It occurs widely but patchily throughout much of Africa, except in the equatorial forest regions, although in greatly reduced numbers. Previously it occurred as far east as India, where it is now extinct, but small numbers apparently survive in parts of the Middle East, Iran and Pakistan.
Habitat: Open savanna and light woodland, but also hilly country on occasion. The availability of drinking water is not essential.
Behaviour: The Cheetah is normally seen singly, in pairs or small family parties consisting of female and cubs. It is principally diurnal, but tends to hunt in the cooler hours. Adult males move singly or in bachelor groups and females establish territories from which they will drive other females. Males are apparently not territorial and may move over areas held by several females. Favoured lying-up spots are usually raised above the surrounding area and are urine-marked by both males and females. When hunting, Cheetah stalk to within a short distance of their intended prey and then sprint in for the kill. Although they may top speeds of more than 70 km per hour this can only be sustained for a few hundred metres.
Food: Normally Cheetah hunt medium-sized mammals up to a mass of about 60 kg, although if two or more cheetah hunt together larger prey may be overpowered. Antelope are the principal prey items. In the Kruger National Park the Impala is the most important prey. It also catches birds up to the size of Ostrich.
Reproduction: Cheetah have a long-drawn-out courtship. The litters of 1–5 (usually 3) young may be born at any time of the year. The cubs are blind and helpless and weigh between 250 g and 300 g at birth. For the first 6 weeks they are usually hidden in dense plant cover, thereafter following the mother.
General: Cheetah used to be tamed and used for hunting, particularly in Asia. Akbar the Great was said to have kept a 'stable' of 1 000 Cheetah.

Cheetah

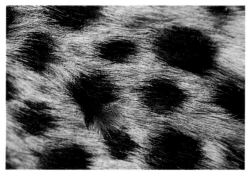

Cheetah spots are 'solid'; compare with Leopard spots (p. 161)

Cheetah: note black 'tear-mark' from eye to mouth

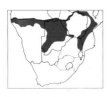

Lion *Panthera leo*
Male: total length 2,5–3,3 m; tail 1,0 m; shoulder height 1,2 m; mass 150–225 kg.
Female: total length 2,3–2,7 m; tail 1,0 m; shoulder height 1,0 m; mass 110–152 kg.
Identification pointers: Large size; usually uniform tawny colour; males with long mane; dark-tipped tail. Cannot be confused with any other species.

Description: Largest of the African cats and adult males and females are easy to tell apart. Body colour ranges from reddish-grey to pale tawny with lighter underparts. Although faint spots are present on the sides of cubs these are usually lost by adulthood. Tail is short-haired and same colour as rest of body but has a dark tip. Only the adult male carries a mane of long hair, extending from the sides of the face on to the neck, shoulders and chest. Mane colour ranges from pale tawny to black. 'White' lions from the Transvaal Lowveld are not true albinos but are genetic variants with strongly reduced pigmentation.
Distribution: In the recent past occurred throughout subregion but now only in northern and eastern areas. It is largely restricted to the major conservation areas. Reintroduced to Hluhluwe and Umfolozi game reserves in Natal. Lions once occurred widely in parts of Europe, Asia, the Middle East and throughout most of Africa. They now have a patchy distribution in Africa and are only found south of the Sahara, excluding the equatorial forest regions.
Habitat: The Lion has a very wide habitat tolerance, from desert fringe to woodland or open savanna, but is absent from equatorial forest.
Behaviour: It is the most sociable member of the cat family, living in prides of 3–30 individuals. Pride size varies according to the area and prey availability. In Botswana prides usually 6 or fewer individuals, whereas average pride size in Kruger National Park is about 12. Prides normally consist of from 1 to 4 adult males, several adult females (one of which is dominant) and a number of subadults and cubs. A pride area or territory is defended against strange Lions by both the males and females but some prides and solitary males are nomadic. Territories are marked by urine, droppings and by earth-scratching. The mighty roars of the Lion – audible over several kilometres – also serve to indicate that an area is occupied. Most of their activity takes place at night and during the cooler daylight hours. The females undertake most of the hunting, and despite the fact that the males play little part in most kills they feed before the females. Cubs compete for what remains once the adults have finished their meal.
Food: Although the Lion is mainly a hunter of medium to large-sized mammals, particularly ungulates, it will take anything from mice to young elephant as well as a wide range of non-mammalian prey. It also scavenges and often chases other predators from their kills.
Reproduction: No fixed breeding season; 1–4, (occasionally 6) cubs each weighing about 1,5 kg are born after gestation of 110 days. Lioness gives birth under cover, soon returning to the pride. Any lactating lioness allows any pride cub to suckle. Pride females often conceive at approximately the same time, this having the advantage that maximum food and maternal care are available to cubs. Cubs may remain with mother for two years or longer.
General: Unless provoked, Lions will rarely attack humans, but it is useful to know the warning signs: an angy Lion will drop into a coruch, flatten its ears and give vent to growls and grunts, meanwhile flicking its tail-tip rapidly from side to side. Just prior to a charge the tail is usually jerked up and down.

Male Lion

Female Lion

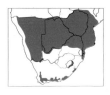

Leopard *Panthera pardus*
Total length 160–210 cm; tail 68–110 cm; shoulder height 70–80 cm; mass (male) 20–90 kg, (female) 17–60 kg.
Note: Leopards from the mountain ranges of the Cape Province are generally much smaller than those from further north; males are considerably larger than females.
Identification pointers: Large size; rosette spots on body, solid black spots on legs, head, sides and hindquarters; lacks the black face-lines of Cheetah and is more heavily spotted. See Cheetah. Size, long tail and different form of spots make easy differentiation from Serval.

Description: An elegant, powerfully built cat, with a beautifully spotted coat. The basic body colour varies from almost white to orange-russet, with black spots on the legs, flanks, hindquarters and head. The spots on the rest of the body consist of rosettes or broken circles of irregular black spots. The tail is about half of the total length, with rosette spots above and a white tip. The ears are rounded and white-tipped. The underparts are usually white to off-white. Cubs have dark, woolly hair and less-distinct spots.
Distribution: Extremely widely distributed in southern Africa, but now absent from the sheep-farming areas of central South Africa. Widely distributed in the rest of sub-Saharan Africa, the Middle East and through Asia into China. By far the most successful of the large cats.
Habitat: It has an extremely wide habitat tolerance, from high mountains to coastal plain, from low- to high-rainfall areas. In the Cape Province south of the Orange River it has been eradicated from all but the more mountainous and rugged areas. Although drinking water is not essential, cover is an essential requirement.
Behaviour: Normally solitary except when a pair come together to mate or when a female is accompanied by cubs. Although it is mainly active at night, in areas where it is not disturbed it can be seen moving during the cooler daylight hours. Although it is mainly terrestrial it is a good climber and swimmer. Males mark and defend a territory against other males, and a male's territory may overlap that of several females. Territories are marked with urine, droppings and tree-scratching points. Home ranges may be as small as 10 km^2 or cover areas of several hundred square kilometres. The size is largely dependent on the availability of food. Although normally silent the Leopard does have a characteristic call that has been likened to the sound of a coarse saw cutting wood. Leopard stalk and then pounce on their prey and do not rely on running at high speed like the Cheetah.
Food: A broad diet, ranging from insects, rodents and birds to medium-sized and occasionally large antelope. In some rocky and mountainous areas dassies make up an important part of the diet. It will on occasion kill more than its immediate needs, the surplus being stored for later use. Kills may be dragged under dense bush, amongst rocks, or in some areas into trees out of reach of other predators. Leopard readily feed from rotten carcasses.
Reproduction: Litters of 2–3 cubs, each weighing around 500 g, are born in dense cover, rock crevices or caves after a gestation of about 100 days. There is no fixed breeding season.
General: Although Leopards may take to man-eating, this has not apparently been recorded for southern Africa. Trapped, wounded or threatened, the Leopard can be extremely dangerous, but under normal circumstances it is shy and withdraws from disturbance.

Leopard

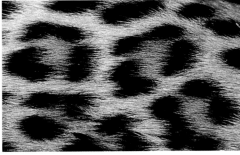

Leopard spots are mostly in the form of 'rosettes'

The Leopard has no facial 'tear-mark' (see Cheetah, p. 157)

AARDVARK Order Tubulidentata Family Orycteropodidae

Aardvark *Orycteropus afer*
Total length 140–180 cm; tail 45–60 cm; mass 40–70 kg.
Identification pointers: Unmistakable; large size; elongated pig-like snout; tubular ears; generally heavy build; walks with back arched.

Description: The Aardvark resembles no other mammal occurring in southern Africa, with its long pig-like snout, elongated tubular ears, heavily muscled kangaroo-like tail and very powerful, stout legs which terminate in spade-like nails. It has only a sparse covering of hair and the skin is grey-yellow to fawn-grey. The hair at the base of the tail and on the legs tends to be quite dark. Normally, however, an Aardvark will be of a colour similar to the soil in the area in which it lives. The back is distinctly arched.

Distribution: This strange mammal is found throughout southern Africa with the exception of the coastal Namib Desert. It is widespread in Africa south of the Sahara but is absent from the equatorial forest region.

Habitat: The Aardvark is found in a wide range of habitats and the limiting factor is probably the availability of suitable food. It shows a preference for open woodland, sparse scrub and grassland. This is one of the few species that has benefited from man's overstocking of areas with domestic stock. By trampling the grass, stock make it more accessible to the termites on which the Aardvark feeds.

Behaviour: It is rarely seen during the day, most of its activity taking place at night. Although normally solitary, females may be accompanied by a single young; they excavate extensive burrow-systems. Males usually dig quite shallow burrows to lie up in during the day and are greater wanderers than the females. Occupied burrows are often characterized by numerous small flies in the entrance-way. Aardvarks may walk several kilometres to feeding grounds each night, where they appear to wander aimlessly, nose close to the ground. When they locate an ant or termite colony they rip into it with the massive claws on the front feet. In areas where the Aardvark is present, numerous termite-mounds have holes excavated at their bases. It is generally unpopular with farmers because it excavates holes in roads and dam-walls.

Food: Mainly ants and termites. Termites predominate in the diet in the rainy season and ants during the dry season. Once a colony has been opened the long, sticky tongue probes for the small insects, their larvae and eggs. It occasionally eats other insects and the fruit of the wild cucumber.

Reproduction: There are very few records of births but it is probable that its single young is born during the rainy season; it has a mass of almost 2 kg and the gestation period is about 7 months. A baby Aardvark will start following its mother in its third week.

Aardvark

Aardvark

ELEPHANTS Order Proboscidea Family Elephantidae

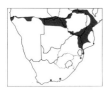

Elephant *Loxodonta africana*
Male: tail 1,5 m; shoulder height 3,2–4,0 m; mass 5 000–6 300 kg.
Female: tail 1,5 m; shoulder height 2,5–3,4 m; mass 2 800–3 500 kg.
Identification pointers: Massive size; long trunk; usually carries tusks; large ears. Cannot be mistaken for any other species.

Description: Apart from its vast size – it is the largest land mammal in the world – it is characterized by the long trunk, large ears and the (normal) presence of tusks. The trunk is extremely mobile and is almost as efficient as the human hand. The large ears serve a display function but also assist in cooling the body. The backs of the ears are well supplied with blood vessels, and as the ears are flapped the blood is cooled. Elephants may also squirt water behind the ears to cool the blood. Tusks are characteristic of most elephants, although some individuals and even populations may be tuskless. The heaviest pair of tusks on record came from an Elephant from Kenya – respectively 102,3 kg and 97 kg. Elephant tusks continue to grow throughout life but because of continuous wear and breakages they never reach their full potential length.
Distribution: The Elephant once occurred virtually throughout southern Africa but it is now restricted to the extreme northern and eastern areas. An isolated, natural population is present in the Addo Elephant National Park and 2 or 3 individuals survive in the forests near Knysna, Cape Province. It still occurs widely in Africa south of the Sahara but the populations are becoming increasingly isolated and numbers are being reduced by poaching.
Habitat: Elephant have an extremely wide habitat tolerance as long as sufficient food, water and shade are available.
Behaviour: Live in small family groups, each led by an older cow, the matriarch. Each group consists of the matriarch and her offspring and may include other related cows with their young. A number of family groups may come together to form larger herds, not infrequently numbering several hundreds. The family group retains its identity during these gatherings and normally the smaller groups move off on their own. These large congregations gather when food is abundant or at water, but there are no reproductive or social benefits. If left uncontrolled herds may destroy their habitat, not only for themselves but for other species as well, and culling becomes essential. Adult bulls usually only join the family herds when cows are in breeding condition and leave to join bachelor groups afterwards. A cow may mate with several bulls during oestrus. Although the Elephant is active both by night and by day, it usually rests in shade during the heat of the day. It is normally a peaceful animal but when wounded, sick, or in defence of a small calf it can be dangerous.
Food: A very wide variety of plants. Although not specialized feeders they do show a marked preference for certain species, for which they will travel long distances. During the rains green grass forms a large percentage of their diet. An adult Elephant may eat as much as 300 kg per day.
Reproduction: A single calf, weighing approximately 120 kg, is dropped after a 22-month gestation period. Calves may be born at any time of the year but in some areas there is a peak in births that coincides with the rainy season. The calf is pinkish-grey and hairier than the adults. Cows are very protective of calves and should anything happen to a nursing mother another lactating female will usually take over the nursing of the orphan.
General: Elephant face a number of threats including poaching for the ivory market and encroachment by humans on their traditional areas. When confined to limited areas by outside pressures they can inflict considerable damage on vegetation and it is for this reason that control programmes are often essential.

Elephant mother and calf   An Elephant requires an average of 160 litres of water daily

Feeding Elephants will pull down branches and even trees

DASSIES (HYRAX) Order Hyracoidea Family Procaviidae

Although dassies may appear rodent-like at first sight, their evolutionary relationships in fact lie with the elephant and the dugong. Four species occur in southern Africa. Three of these species are associated predominantly with rock habitat while the fourth, the Tree Dassie, lives in forested areas.

Procavia capensis

Procavia welwitschii

Heterohyrax brucei

Rock Dassie *Procavia capensis*
Total length 45–60 cm; mass 2,5–4,6 kg.
Kaokoveld Rock Dassie *Procavia welwitschii*
Total length 36–50 cm.
Yellow-spotted Rock Dassie *Heterohyrax brucei*
Total length 45–55 cm; mass 2,5–3,5 kg.
Identification pointers: Small but stocky build; no tail; small rounded ears; rocky habitat; where Rock Dassie overlaps with either of the other two species the colour of the erectile hair in the middle of the back is the most certain character – black for Rock Dassie and white to off-white or yellowish in the other two species.

Description: The three species of rock dassie or hyrax are small, stoutly built, tail-less animals with short legs. Their ears are small and rounded. Hair colour varies considerably in all three species. All species have a patch of erectile hair overlying a glandular area in the centre of the back. The colour of this hair around the gland is a very important character for distinguishing the different dassie species.

	Rock Dassie	Kaokoveld Rock Dassie	Yellow-spotted Rock Dassie
General colour	Yellow-fawn to dark-brown	Yellow-fawn to dark-brown	Grey to dark-brown
Dorsal gland	Black	White or yellowish	White or yellowish
Underparts	Slightly paler; never white	White to off-white	White to off-white
Other	(Inconspicuous) Fawn-buff patch above eye and at ear-base	Off-white patch at ear-base	Conspicuous white patch above eye

Distribution: The Rock Dassie is the most widespread of the three rock-dwelling dassies occurring in southern Africa. However, it is absent from the north-central areas, the Namib Desert coastal belt and most of Mozambique. The Kaokoveld Rock Dassie is restricted to north-western South West Africa/Namibia but extends into south-western Angola. Yellow-spotted Rock Dassies only occur in the north-eastern parts of southern Africa but thence as far north as northern Egypt.

Habitat: Rocky areas, from mountain ranges to isolated rock outcrops. Rock Dassie and Yellow-spotted Rock Dassie frequently occur together where ranges overlap. Rock dassies as a group generally favour drier areas but with the exception of the Kaokoveld Rock Dassie are also found in higher rainfall areas. Rock Dassie may sometimes be found living in holes in erosion gulleys (dongas) and amongst the roots and leaves of sisal, prickly pear and spekboom.

Behaviour: The behaviour of all three rock-dwelling dassie species is similar. They are predominantly diurnal but on warm, moonlit nights they may emerge to feed. Normally they only become active after sunrise when they lie for some time on the rocks in the sun to warm up before moving off to feed. Whilst the group basks in the sun an adult animal (either a male or a

Rock Dassies

Dassie urine leaves characteristic white and brown streaks on rocks

Yellow-spotted Rock Dassie

Rock Dassies (left) and a single Yellow-spotted Rock Dassie (right)

female) keeps watch for predators. If disturbed, the 'guard' gives a sharp cry and the dassies scuttle for cover amongst the rocks. Groups usually number from 4 to 8 but much larger numbers may live together depending on the available habitat. Each group or colony has a dominant male and female and the other animals fit into a hierarchy or pecking order. During the mating period males may fight fiercely. Most feeding is done in the morning and late afternoon and they retreat to the shelter of the rocks during the hotter hours. Although they will move several hundred metres to feeding areas they usually feed closer to shelter. Rock dassies will readily climb into trees and bushes to feed and because of this they are often thought to be Tree Dassies (see page 168). If a food shortage develops, a dassie colony will move to a more favourable area. Dassies deposit their droppings at fixed latrine sites and accumulations of their pellets may become very large. Dassie urine leaves white and brown streaks on rocks and often serves as an indication of their presence.

Food: Grazers and browsers, with quantities of each varying according to the season. Feeding usually takes place on ground but they will climb trees to feed on leaves, bark and fruits. They eat a very wide range of plants.

Reproduction: All three species give birth to precocious young: fully haired, with eyes open and able to move about soon after birth. They are perfectly proportioned miniatures of the adults. There is a distinct birth season in the Rock Dassie but the timing varies considerably in different regions. For example, in the south-western Cape births normally occur in September and October and in Zimbabwe in March and April. In the lower Orange River area of the north-western Cape, with its extremely hot summer temperatures, the young are dropped in the cooler months of June and July. One to 4 young may be born but 2–3 is usual. Birth weight varies according to the size of the litter and may range between 150 and 300 g.

The Kaokoveld Rock Dassie gives birth during February and March to 2 or 3 young, rarely 4.

Yellow-spotted Rock Dassies apparently give birth at any time of the year to litters with an average of 2 offspring, each weighing approximately 200 g.

Tree Dassie *Dendrohyrax arboreus*
Total length 42–52 cm; mass 2,0–3,5 kg.
Identification pointers: Similar in size to rock dassie species; hair quite long and woolly in appearance; upperparts grey, flecked with white or brown; white to creamy underparts and dorsal gland; forest or dense bush habitat; distinctive, nocturnal screaming call.

Description: Similar in size to the rock dassies but body hair is much longer and has a woolly appearance. Upperparts vary from grey flecked with white to grey-brown. Underparts are white to creamy white, as is the long hair around the dorsal gland in the centre of the back. No external tail.

Distribution: Their distribution is limited to suitable habitat. They occur along the coastal plain in the eastern Cape and extend into Natal. Another isolated population occurs in south-central Mozambique. Elsewhere, they are found in Zambia, eastern Zaïre and throughout the western parts of East Africa.

Habitat: Tree Dassies inhabit suitable forest and bush areas, including coastal dune forest. Fairly dense cover is an essential habitat requirement.

Behaviour: Solitary, arboreal and nocturnal, but may bask in the sun, particularly in the early morning. They are rarely seen but their hair-raising screaming call at night is characteristic. For those unfamiliar with this bloodcurdling shriek it can be a disturbing experience. Droppings accumulate on lower branch forks and particularly at base of trees.

Food: Probably a browser but it may feed on grasses and herbs.

Reproduction: It probably breeds throughout the year, with 1 to 3 young being born after a gestation period of 7–8 months.

Tree Dassie

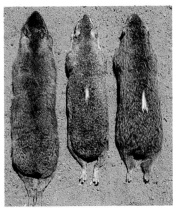

Dassie skins (l. to r.):
1. Rock Dassie
2. Kaokoveld Rock Dassie
3. Tree Dassie

Tree Dassie: note white underparts

ODD-TOED UNGULATES Order Perissodactyla

Zebras Family Equidae

Equus zebra zebra
(Cape Province only)
Equus zebra hartmannae
(S.W.A./Namibia only)

Cape Mountain Zebra *Equus zebra zebra*
Hartmann's Mountain Zebra *Equus zebra hartmannae*
Cape subsp.: shoulder height 1,3 m; tail 40 cm; mass 250–260 kg.
Hartmann's subsp.: shoulder height 1,5 m; tail 40 cm; mass 250–350 kg.
Identification pointers: Black and white stripes without shadow stripes; legs striped to the hoofs; grid-iron pattern on rump; throat with dewlap. Range of Hartmann's overlaps marginally with that of Burchell's Zebra in north-western South West Africa/Namibia. Hartmann's introduced to farms and reserves outside normal range.

Description: Both subspecies of the Mountain Zebra are similar in appearance but with Hartmann's being slightly larger and with some variations in striping on the hindquarters. Both, however, are white with black stripes, the legs being striped to the hoofs; underparts are white. No 'shadow' stripes (see opposite page) and over top of rump above tail there is a series of transverse black stripes forming a 'grid-iron' pattern characteristic of the species. Tip of muzzle is black with orange-brown hair extending a short way towards eyes. An erect mane runs from the top of the head to the shoulders. A dewlap is present on the throat; this feature is also diagnostic of the species and does not occur in other zebras.
Distribution: Formerly Cape Mountain Zebra widespread in Cape mountains south of Orange River; now restricted to a small group of nature reserves. Hartmann's restricted to the montane escarpment of South West Africa/ Namibia but occurs marginally in south-western Angola.
Habitat: Mountainous areas and adjacent flats.
Behaviour: Breeding herds consist of an adult stallion with mares and their foals and usually number 4 or 5 but occasionally more. In the dry season, however, Hartmann's may congregate in loose associations of up to 40.
Food: Predominantly grazers but also browse occasionally.
Reproduction: A single foal is born after gestation of about 360 days.

Equus burchellii

Burchell's Zebra *Equus burchellii*
Shoulder height 1,3 m; tail 45 cm; mass 290–340 kg.
Identification pointers: Stocky and horse-like; black and white stripes with shadow stripes superimposed on white stripes; stripes extend on to underparts; lacks dewlap on throat.

Description: Burchell's Zebra shows considerable variation in colouration and patterning but is normally striped in black and white with a fainter 'shadow' stripe superimposed on the white stripe, particularly on the hindquarters. No 'grid-iron' pattern on rump and striping extends on to underparts. Long, erect mane extends from top of head to shoulders. Striping may or may not extend to the hoofs.
Distribution: North and east of subregion but widely reintroduced.
Behaviour: Burchell's Zebra associate in family herds consisting of an adult stallion, mares and their foals; other stallions form bachelor herds or run alone. Family units normally number 4 to 6. Much larger herds usually consist of numerous smaller herds coming together temporarily. They have a characteristic call that has been likened to a bark – '*kwa-ha-ha*' – which was also the call of the extinct Quagga, hence the name.
Food: Grazers but they do occasionally browse.
Reproduction: Single foal with mass of 30–35 kg born usually in summer; gestation period 375 days.

Cape Mountain Zebra stallion: note dewlap and 'grid-iron' pattern on rump

Burchell's Zebra lacking 'shadow' stripes
(see photograph below)

Hartmann's Mountain Zebra

Burchell's Zebra normally possess 'shadow' stripes (see photograph above left)

Rhinoceroses Family Rhinocerotidae

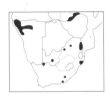

Hook-lipped Rhinoceros *Diceros bicornis*
Shoulder height 1,6 m; tail 70 cm; mass 800–1 100 kg.
Record front horn length 1,2 m (East Africa), 1,05 m (Natal).
Identification pointers: Large size but much smaller than Square-lipped Rhinoceros; lacks neck hump present in Square-lipped; characteristic pointed upper lip; shorter head than Square-lipped; two horns on face.

Description: Although frequently called the Black Rhinoceros this species is also more appropriately known as the Hook-lipped Rhinoceros. Dark grey with slightly lighter underparts. Body colour influenced by its habit of wallowing in dust and mud. Sparse scattering of body hair. No raised hump on neck, unlike the Square-lipped Rhinoceros. Two horns on face, one behind other, the front horn usually being the longer. Rhino horn is composed of numerous, matted, hair-like filaments which are attached to the skin, not to the bone; it is not a sheath-like covering to a bony core as is the case with antelope horns. The triangular-shaped prehensile upper lip is characteristic. The spoor or footprint is rounded at the back, whereas that of the Square-lipped Rhinoceros is sharply indented (see page 258).

Distribution: Once widely distrubuted throughout subregion, but now occurs naturally only in some Zululand reserves, north-western Namibia, the Zambezi Valley of Zimbabwe, and possibly in parts of southern Mozambique. Reintroduced to Addo Elephant National Park, Vaalbos National Park and to the Double Drift Nature Reserve in the Eastern Cape. There are approximately 1 600 Hook-lipped Rhinoceros in southern Africa, and these now make up 62 per cent of the world total of the species. Previously common throughout central and East Africa, extending into West Africa, but has been brought to the verge of extinction over much of its former range through the relentless predations of poachers.

Habitat: The Hook-lipped Rhinoceros requires areas with shrubs and trees reaching to a height of about 4 m, with dense thickets for resting. Although it requires water for drinking and wallowing it may go several days between visits to water in arid areas. It occupies a wide range of habitats where these basic requirements are met, from the arid plains of Kaokoveld to the rich savanna woodland of the Natal game reserves.

Behaviour: Hook-lipped Rhinoceros are solitary animals although groups may come together temporarily at water. Bulls and cows only come together for mating and cows are often accompanied by calves. Serious fighting may take place when bulls compete for a receptive cow. During the heat of the day they usually lie up in dense thickets, feeding in the early morning and late afternoon but also after dark. The dung may be dropped in latrine or midden areas or at random through the home range. Bulls kick the dung vigorously with the hindfeet at the latrine sites leaving distinct grooves in the ground. The dung balls, apart from being smaller, can be distinguished from those of the Square-lipped Rhinoceros by their content of light-coloured, coarse woody material. The Square-lipped Rhinoceros, being a grazer, has much finer, darker material in the dung. Hook-lipped Rhinoceros are notoriously bad-tempered, this being particularly true of bulls associating with receptive cows, and of cows with calves. Despite their cumbersome appearance they are surprisingly fast and agile; they rely on their hearing and sense of smell to locate a threat as their eyesight is poor.

Food: The Hook-lipped Rhinoceros uses its pointed mobile upper lip to grasp twigs and shoots which are either snapped off or cut through by the cheek-teeth. It is a selective feeder and tends to reject dry plant material. During the rains it will on occasion take grass.

Reproduction: There is no fixed breeding season and a single calf, weighing about 40 kg, is born after a gestation period of about 450 days. It is able to walk and suckle within 3 hours of birth. The calf either walks alongside or

Hook-lipped (or Black) Rhinoceros

Hook-lipped (or Black) Rhinoceros

The triangular prehensile upper lip of the Hook-lipped Rhinoceros is ideally suited for browsing selected shoots

behind the mother, the reverse of the situation with the Square-lipped Rhinoceros.

General: The rapid decline in numbers of both African rhinoceros species is a result of the demand for their horns. Most of the horns find their way to Yemen, where they are carved into dagger handles for tribesmen, and to the Far East where they are used in the production of traditional medicines. The best chance for the survival of both species at present appears to lie in southern Africa, and particularly in South Africa.

Square-lipped Rhinoceros *Ceratotherium simum*
Shoulder height 1,8 m; tail 1,0 m;
mass (bull) 2 000–2 300 kg, (cow) 1 400–1 600 kg.
Record front horn length (southern Africa) 1,58 m.
Identification pointers: Large size; broad, square muzzle; hump on neck; large, pointed ears; two horns on face. See Hook-lipped Rhinoceros.

Description: The Square-lipped Rhinoceros, also known as the White Rhinoceros, is much larger than the Hook-lipped Rhinoceros. The skin colour is grey but this is often influenced by the colour of the mud and dust in which it rolls. A large, distinctive hump is present on the neck. The head is long and carried low, frequently only a few centimetres above the ground, and terminates in a broad square muzzle – hence the common name. There are two horns on the face, the front one usually being the longer. The ears are large and pointed.

Distribution: Restricted by the beginning of the 20th Century to the Umfolozi Game Reserve in Natal, the southern subspecies of the Square-lipped Rhinoceros was strictly protected and spread naturally into the Hluhluwe Game Reserve; it has since been widely reintroduced and introduced to other reserves and game-farms throughout the subregion. Square-lipped Rhinoceros previously had a very wide distribution, with the northern subspecies occurring in Sudan, Chad, Uganda and Zaïre, and the separate southern subspecies in South Africa, Mozambique, Zimbabwe, Botswana, South West Africa/Namibia and Angola. Tiny population pockets of the endangered northern subspecies may still survive in southern Sudan and definitely in Zaïre but it is possible that they may still be exterminated as has happened with the animals that were present in Uganda into the 1970s.

Habitat: This species shows a preference for short-grassed areas, with thick bush cover and water. Where adequate food and water is available it will occupy a wide range of open woodland associations.

Behaviour: The Square-lipped Rhinoceros is much more sociable than the Hook-lipped Rhinoceros. Territorial bulls occupy clearly defined territories which they will defend against neighbouring bulls; subordinate bulls may be allowed to remain within a territory if they remain submissive. The home range of cows may overlap with the territories of several territorial bulls but when a cow is receptive for mating the bull will attempt to keep her within his area. Family groups usually number between 2 and 5 individuals, although larger numbers may come together for short periods. The home ranges and territories are only left when water is not readily available. When they move to watering points they follow the same paths each time. Feeding takes place during the cooler morning and afternoon hours but they are also active at night. Bulls have a number of fixed latrine sites within their territories.

Food: Square-lipped Rhinoceros are grazers, with a preference for short grass. A reliable source of drinking water is an essential requirement.

Reproduction: Calves, weighing about 40 kg, are dropped at any time of the year after a gestation period of approximately 480 days. The cow moves away from the rhinoceros group to give birth and remains separated with her new-born calf for several days. In contrast to the Hook-lipped Rhinoceros, the calf of the Square-lipped Rhinoceros walks in front of the mother.

The mouth of the Square-lipped (or White) Rhinoceros is adapted for grazing

The hump on the neck of the Square-lipped Rhinoceros is diagnostic

Square-lipped Rhinoceros

EVEN-TOED UNGULATES Order Artiodactyla

Pigs and Hogs Family Suidae

Warthog *Phacochoerus aethiopicus*
Male: shoulder height 70 cm; tail 45 cm; mass 60–105 kg.
Female: shoulder height 60 cm; tail 45 cm; mass 45–70 kg.
Identification pointers: Pig-like appearance; grey, sparsely haired body; wart-like lumps on face; thin tail with dark tufted tip, held erect when running; curved, upward-pointing tusks in adults.

Description: Often described as ugly and grotesque but not without appeal. Grey with sparse, dark, bristle-like hairs scattered over body, and mane of long erectile hair along back which lies flat except when Warthog is under stress; mane may be yellowish-brown to black in colour. Tufts of pale-coloured whiskers lie along side of face. Snout is typically pig-like and prominent wart-like protuberances are present on face – two pairs in male, one less-conspicuous pair in female. Canine teeth of adults develop into long curved tusks; those of the boar may reach considerable lengths and make effective defensive weapons. Thin tail with its tuft of black hair is held erect when Warthog runs, unlike that of Bushpig.
Distribution: Northern and eastern areas of subregion.
Habitat: Open country but also lightly wooded areas; savanna.
Behaviour: Predominantly diurnal but sometimes nocturnal. Groups or 'sounders' of Warthog usually consist of sows and their young, or bachelor groups. Sexually active boars usually move freely and alone except when with a sow. Can dig own burrows but usually take over Aardvark holes.
Food: Mostly short grasses and grass roots. When grazing they usually kneel. Browse occasionally and rarely feed on animal matter.
Reproduction: Sow separates from sounder to give birth to litter of 2–3 (up to 8) piglets in burrow; gestation period 170 days. New-born piglets weigh 480–850 g. Emerge from burrow about 2 weeks after birth. Seasonal breeders with most births taking place early summer.

Bushpig *Potamochoerus porcus*
Shoulder height 55–88 cm; tail 38 cm; mass 60 (up to 115) kg.
Identification pointers: Pig-like appearance; well-haired body; tufts of hair on ear tips; long head; tail held down when running – unlike the Warthog whose tail is held vertically upwards; facial hair much lighter in colour than rest of body.

Description: More typically pig-like than Warthog. Boar slightly larger than sow. Body is well covered with long bristle-like hair and although variable usually reddish-brown to grey-brown. Mane of longer and paler hair extends from the back of neck to shoulders and facial hair is usually grey-white. Head is long and ears are pointed with tuft of longish hair at tip. Older boars may develop a pair of warts on muzzle, but not as large as those of Warthog. Thin tail has tassel of black hair at tip. Piglets dark brown with several longitudinal pale stripes along body.
Distribution: Northern and eastern areas of subregion south to Mossel Bay.
Habitat: Forest, dense bush and riverine woodland, reed-beds and stands of long grass where there is water. Can be a problem in farming areas.
Behaviour: Mainly nocturnal but in areas where they are not disturbed they may be seen during the day. Live in 'sounders' of 4–10 individuals but larger groups have been recorded. Sounder consists of dominant boar, a dominant sow, other sows and young. Solitary animals also occur, as well as bachelor groups. If wounded or cornered, Bushpigs can be dangerous.
Food: Bushpigs use their hard snouts to root for rhizomes, bulbs and tubers;

Female Warthog (centre) has one pair of warts just below eyes; young male (left) has a second pair lower down on the cheeks

Warthog wallow regularly

Male Warthog with two pairs of warts

Bushpig: note no facial warts

Bushpig: note mane of pale hair

Some Bushpigs develop extremely hairy coats

areas where they have been active look like small ploughed plots. In some areas they do considerable damage to crops. They also browse. Animal matter may feature quite prominently in their diet and may include insects, other invertebrates, frogs and carrion; rarely sheep and goats.

Reproduction: Most births in summer. Sow constructs 'haystack' of grass, in bush cover, up to 3 m in diameter and 1 m in height. 2–4 piglets but up to 8, each weighing approximately 750 grams are born in centre of stack.

Hippopotamuses Family Hippopotamidae

Hippopotamus *Hippopotamus amphibius*
Shoulder height 1,5 m; tail 40 cm; mass 1 000–2 000 kg (bull), 1 000–1 700 kg (cow).
Identification pointers: Large size; barrel-shaped body and short legs; massive head with broad muzzle; in water by day.

Description: Large rotund animal with smooth naked skin, short, stocky legs and a massive, broad-muzzled head. Mouth equipped with an impressive set of tusk-like canines and incisors. Short, flattened tail is tipped with a tuft of black hair. Body colour greyish-black with pink tinge at the skin folds, around eyes and ears, while underparts are pinkish-grey. Four-toed feet leave a characteristic track.

Distribution: The Hippopotamus is restricted to the extreme northern and the eastern parts of southern Africa. At the present time the most southerly natural population is in northern Natal, but until hunted out by European settlers was found in the vicinity of Cape Town, along the southern coastal belt and along the entire length of the Orange River. It has a patchy distribution over the rest of sub-Saharan Africa but is widespread.

Habitat: The Hippopotamus requires sufficient water to allow submergence and a preference is shown for permanent waters with a sandy substrate. This includes rivers, dams and lakes.

Behaviour: This semi-aquatic mammal spends much of the day lying in water; it emerges at night to move to feeding-grounds. It also lies up on sand- or mud-banks in the sun, particularly during the winter months. Although it normally occurs in herds or schools of 10 to 15 animals, larger groups and solitary bulls are not uncommon. Schools are usually composed of cows and young of various ages with a dominant bull in overall control. The territories are narrow in the water but broaden out towards the feeding-grounds. Dominant bulls mark their territories by scattering dung with a vigorous sideways flicking of the tail on to rocks, bushes and other objects. Territoriality is apparently strongest closer to the water but virtually absent in the feeding-grounds. Fixed pathways are used and these are characterized by a 'double' trail – each one made by the feet of one side. Exceptionally, up to 30 km may be travelled to feeding areas, depending on the availability of food. An adult hippopotamus can remain under water for up to six minutes. Skin glands secrete a reddish fluid which is frequently mistaken for blood but probably acts as a skin lubricant and moisturizer. The hippopotamus is extremely vocal and its deep roaring grunts and snorts constitute one of the typical sounds of Africa. Provoked, it can be extremely dangerous, particularly solitary bulls and cows with calves.

Food: The Hippopotamus is a selective grazer. In areas with high populations considerable damage can be done to grazing areas near water.

Reproduction: Mating takes place in the water, and after a gestation period of between 225 and 257 days a single calf is born weighing between 25 and 55 kg (usually about 30 kg). The cow gives birth on land in dense cover and she and the calf remain separated from the school for several months. The calves may be produced at any time of the year but there is some evidence of seasonal peaks.

Hippopotamus often lie on sand- and mud-banks

Hippopotamus sunbathing

The Hippopotamus can open and close its nostrils at will

Hippopotamus showing tusk-like canines and incisors

Giraffe Family Giraffidae

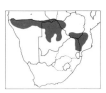

Giraffe *Giraffa camelopardalis*
Male: height to top of head 3,9–5,2 m; height to shoulder 2,6–3,5 m; tail 96–150 cm; mass 970–1 400 kg.
Female: height to top of head 3,7–4,7 m; height to shoulder 2,0–3,0 m; tail 75–90 cm; mass 700–950 kg.
Identification pointers: Large size; long legs and neck; patchwork patterning. Cannot be mistaken for any other species.

Description: The Giraffe apparently gets its name from the Arabic '*xirapha*', which means 'one who walks swiftly', and anyone who has observed Giraffe on the move would agree that this is entirely appropriate. The Giraffe is the tallest animal in the world and with its long neck and legs is unmistakable. A beautiful lattice pattern consisting of large, irregularly shaded patches separated by networks of light-coloured bands covers the body. The colouring of the patches is very variable, ranging from light fawn to almost black. Old bulls are often very dark. Knob-like horns are present on the top of the head and these are well developed in adult bulls.
Distribution: In southern Africa the population occurring in the eastern Transvaal and adjacent areas of Mozambique and Zimbabwe is isolated. They also occur in western Zimbabwe, northern South West Africa/Namibia and from there extending into Angola and Zambia. Once occurring widely and continuously in savanna country south of the Sahara, they are now broken up into numerous isolated populations scattered throughout West and East Africa. They are absent from equatorial forest areas.
Habitat: Dry savanna woodland.
Behaviour: Giraffe are active during the day and at night but usually rest during the hot midday hours. Although they occupy large home ranges that are usually between 20 km² and 85 km², they do not establish defended territories. They are usually seen in herds of from 4 to 30 individuals, but these groups are unstable and much wandering takes place. Bulls only associate with cows temporarily. Although Giraffe are generally believed to be silent they do have a range of grunting and snorting calls.
Food: Giraffe are browsers, only rarely eating grass. Their long neck and legs give them access to a food supply beyond the reach of all other browsers. Although they feed from a fairly wide range of trees and bushes they are selective in what they eat. Twigs are pulled into the mouth by the lips and the long prehensile tongue, which may reach 45 cm in length, and the leaves are shredded off into the mouth. Between 15 and 20 hours of each day may be spent feeding.
Reproduction: Calves weighing about 100 kg may be born at any time of the year after a gestation period of about 450 days. The newly born calf can stand and walk within an hour of birth but remains isolated from the herd for up to 3 weeks. There is a very high mortality of calves in their first year.

Giraffe drinking; dark bull in foreground, lighter coloured cow in background

The tops of the 'horns' are ringed with black hair

Older giraffe bulls are usually darker in colour

Buffalo and antelopes Family Bovidae

Buffalo *Syncerus caffer*
Shoulder height 1,4 m; tail 70 cm; mass 550 kg (cow), 700 kg (bull).
Average horn length 100 cm along curve from centre of boss to tip.
Record horn length for southern Africa (Zimbabwe) 124,8 cm.
Identification pointers: Cattle-like appearance: large size; uniform dark-brown or black colouring; heavily built; characteristically massive horns.

Description: Buffalo are massive, heavily built, cattle-like animals. Adult bulls are dark brown to black in colour but the cows are usually not so dark and calves are reddish-brown. They have stocky, relatively short legs, with large hoofs, those on the forefoot being larger than those on the hindfoot. The horns are heavy and massive, and the central horn base or 'boss' is particularly well developed in the bulls. The horns first curve down and outwards and then upwards and inwards, narrowing towards the tips. When viewed from the front the horns form a shallow 'W'. The horn boss of the cow is much less pronounced and is absent in younger animals. Ears are large and hang below the horns. The tail is cow-like with a tip of long brown or black hair.
Distribution: Once widely distributed in southern Africa, the Buffalo is now restricted to the northern and eastern parts of the region with an isolated natural population occurring in the Addo Elephant National Park in the south-east Cape Province. An isolated population is also found in the Hluhluwe/Umfolozi area of Natal/KwaZulu. Despite its wide distribution south of the Sahara, many Buffalo populations have been fragmented by human expansion and the species now has a markedly discontinuous distribution. It has, however, been reintroduced to several nature reserves and game-farms, for example the Andries Vosloo Kudu Reserve in the Eastern Cape.
Habitat: The Buffalo has a fairly wide habitat tolerance but requires areas with abundant grass, water and cover. It shows a preference for open woodland savanna and will utilize open grassland as long as it has access to cover.
Behaviour: The Buffalo is a gregarious animal occurring in herds that may number several thousands. Smaller groups may break away from the main concentration only to rejoin it later. Bachelor groups may form away from the main herd and solitary bulls are quite commonly encountered. Adult bulls within the mixed herd maintain a dominance hierarchy, the complexity of which is influenced by the size of the herd. The cows also establish a 'pecking order' amongst themselves. The dominant bull or bulls will mate with the cows that are receptive or in breeding condition. Buffalo herds have clearly defined home ranges and herd areas rarely overlap. They come to water in the early morning and late afternoon and seek out shade during the heat of the day. Most feeding takes place at night.
Food: Predominantly grazers but Buffalo also occasionally browse.
Reproduction: Buffalo are seasonal breeders with the majority of calves being dropped in the wet and warm summer months. A single calf, weighing about 40 kg is born after a gestation period of about 340 days. Calves are born within the herd and are able to keep up within a few hours of birth.

Buffalo bull with heavy 'boss' to horns

Buffalo cow with lightly developed 'boss'

Buffalo bull

Eland *Taurotragus oryx*
Male: shoulder height 1,7 m; tail 60 cm; mass 700 kg (but up to 900 kg).
Female: shoulder height 1,5 m; tail 60 cm; mass 450 kg.
Average horn length (both sexes) 60 cm.
Record horn length (Botswana) 102,3 cm.
Identification pointers: Massive size; fawn/tawny with some grey on forequarters; both sexes with straight horns, each with a slight twist or spiral.

Description: The largest living antelope, the Eland has a cow-like appearance. Its general colour is usually fawn or tawny, turning blue-grey with age, particularly on the neck and shoulders. Adult bulls develop a patch of fairly long, dark, coarse hair on the forehead. A short, dark mane runs down the back of the neck. The tail is fairly long with a tuft of black hair at the tip. Older bulls typically develop a large dewlap on the throat. Both sexes have horns but those of the bull are thicker and the shallow spiral is marked by a prominent ridge.

Distribution: Once occurred widely in southern Africa but now restricted to the northern parts except for a natural population in the Drakensberg and numerous localities where it has been reintroduced to farms and reserves. Occurs widely in central and East Africa but is absent from the forested areas of equatorial Africa.

Habitat: The Eland occupies a wide range of habitats from desert scrub to montane areas but shows a preference for open scrub-covered plains and woodland savanna.

Behaviour: Normally occurs in herds of 25 to 60 individuals but temporary associations numbering more than 1 000 are occasionally seen. The larger gatherings usually occur during the rainy season. In some areas Eland tend to be more or less sedentary, whereas in others, such as the Kalahari, they may move considerable distances in search of suitable sources of food. Although a hierarchy exists within Eland herds, there appears to be no defence of territories. Eland are predominantly diurnal but also feed at night, particularly during the summer months.

Food: Predominantly browsers, Eland do occasionally eat grass. They dig for roots and bulbs with their front hoofs and also use their horns to knock down foliage. They are independent of water but will drink when it is available.

Reproduction: The dominant bulls mate with the receptive cows and a single calf weighing 22–36 kilograms is born after a gestation period of approximately 270 days. The calf remains hidden for the first two weeks after birth. Calves may be dropped in any month of the year but there is a peak in summer. They grow rapidly and can achieve a mass of 450 kg by the end of their first year.

General: The Eland features frequently in Bushman paintings. Despite its massive size it is an excellent jumper and can easily clear a two-metre fence. Captive herds of Eland have been domesticated in Zimbabwe and the U.S.S.R. Moving Eland make a distinct clicking noise which is believed to be caused by the two halves of each hoof striking together. This sound carries quite well and is sometimes the first indication of the species' presence.

Eland bull

Eland bull has tuft of hair on forehead

The Eland cow has no forehead tuft

Kudu *Tragelaphus strepsiceros*
Shoulder height 140–155 cm; tail 43 cm; mass 250 kg (bull), 180 kg (cow).
Average horn length 120 cm.
Record horn length (along the curve) 181,6 cm.
Identification pointers: Large size; long legs; 6 to 10 vertical white stripes on grey-brown sides; large rounded ears; bushy tail, blackish or brownish above, white underneath; characteristic long, spiral horns of bull.

Description: This large and handsome antelope is grey-brown to rufous in colour, with the bulls being more grey than the cows and calves. The sides are clearly marked with six to ten vertical white stripes. There is a distinct white band across the face, with white spots on the cheeks. The bull has a prominent mane from the neck to beyond the shoulders and a fringe of longer hair on the throat and lower neck. The blackish or brown bushy tail is white underneath with a black tip. The ears are very large, showing pink on the inside. Only the male has the long, spiral horns.

Distribution: Kudu occur principally in the northern and eastern parts of southern Africa with apparently isolated populations in the Cape Province. Elsewhere they occur widely in central Africa south of the equatorial forests, through East Africa to Ethiopia, Sudan and Chad.

Habitat: The Kudu is an antelope of wooded savanna. It may occur in arid areas but only where there are stands of bush that provide cover and food. It does not occur in open grassland or forest. It has, however, been able to penetrate the Karoo and Namib Desert along wooded watercourses. In many areas it shows a preference for acacia woodland and rocky hill country.

Behaviour: Although it normally occurs in small herds of from 3 to 10 animals, larger groups are occasionally seen. Outside the midwinter rutting period the adult bulls are either solitary or join small bachelor herds. At the time of the rut an adult bull will run with a group of cows and their young. Although usually active in early mornings and late afternoons, in areas where they are disturbed or hunted they have taken to nocturnal activity. They are well known for their jumping ability, having no difficulty in clearing 2-metre-high fences.

Food: Although predominantly a browser, it does occasionally graze. It eats a wider variety of browse species than any other of our local antelopes. It is considered a pest in some areas because it feeds on crops such as lucerne, mealies (maize) and vegetables.

Reproduction: Calves are born throughout the year but most births take place in the summer months, the main rutting period being in midwinter. As in the case of the Sable Antelope and Roan Antelope, the Kudu cow moves away from the herd to drop its single calf which weighs about 16 kg. The gestation period is around 210 days. The calves hide for a few days, until they are strong enough to keep up with the herd.

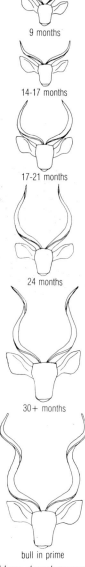

9 months

14-17 months

17-21 months

24 months

30+ months

bull in prime

Horn development
(after C.D. Simpson, 1966)

186

Kudu cow and calf

Kudu cow

2-year-old Kudu bull

Adult Kudu bull

Nyala *Tragelaphus angasii*
Male: shoulder height 115 cm; tail 43 cm; mass 108 kg.
Female: shoulder height 97 cm; tail 36 cm; mass 62 kg.
Average horn length 60 cm.
Record horn length 83,5 cm.
Identification pointers: Ram slate-grey overall with long mane along entire length of back and long fringe hanging below underbelly from throat to between hindlegs; lower part of legs rufous or yellow-brown; 3–14 vertical white stripes on sides; tail quite bushy and white below; horns spiralled but much shorter, lighter and less spiralled than those of Kudu. Ewe is smaller, has no horns, and is yellow-brown to chestnut in colour with up to 18 vertical white stripes on sides.

Description: Between Kudu and Bushbuck in size. Like other members of genus *Tragelaphus* only male has horns, but sexes are markedly different in other respects. Ram has fringe of long hair hanging from underparts from just behind chin to between hindlegs, and a mane of hair from back of head to rump. Mane normally lies flat but is raised during certain behavioural interactions such as on encountering another ram. Buttocks and upperparts of hindlegs are also lined with long hair. From 8 to 14 vertical white stripes are present on the sides but these disappear or become less distinct in older rams. Ground colour is slate-grey to dark brown. Lower parts of legs are rufous to yellow-brown. There are 2–3 white cheek spots and chin and upper lip are also white. Shallow V-shaped white line runs between eyes. Ewe is very different from ram being much smaller and lacking long shaggy hair. In addition ewes and lambs have yellow-brown to chestnut ground colour and up to 18 vertical white lines on sides of body. Ram's slightly spiralled horns curve outward after the first turn. Horn tips are whitish-yellow.
Distribution: Occurs patchily in the north-eastern parts of southern Africa, with a marginal occurrence north of the Zambezi in Mozambique and southern Malaŵi.
Habitat: Restricted to dry savanna woodland and along watercourses. It may be seen grazing in open areas adjacent to bush or tree cover.
Behaviour: Nyala rams are not territorial. Commonly seen in small groups, either ewes and lambs, or rams together. Solitary rams are commonly seen. Group composition is constantly changing although ewe-and-lamb groups are the most stable.
Food: Principally a browser, eating from wide variety of plants. Fresh grass taken during rains.
Reproduction: Single calf weighing 4,2–5,5 kg born at any time of year. Gestation period 220 days. Remains hidden for first 2 weeks.

Nyala ram (right) and ewe (left)

The slightly spiralled horns of the Nyala ram are white at the tips

Sitatunga *Tragelaphus spekei*
Shoulder height 90 cm; tail 22 cm; mass 115 kg (ram).
Average horn length 60 cm; record horn length 92,4 cm.
Identification pointers: Semi-aquatic habitat requirements totally different from those of Nyala; considerably larger than Bushbuck. Hindquarters higher than front; fairly long, shaggy hair. Spoor unmistakable (page 259).

Description: Adult rams larger than ewes; shaggy-haired drab dark brown with no body stripes – sometimes lighter marks on back. Ewes also dark brown or reddish-brown but have black band down centre of back, four vertical stripes on side, white lateral band and white spots on haunches. Both sexes have an incomplete white band between eyes and white spots on cheeks. White patch above chest and another below chin. Dark-brown tail is white below; not very bushy. Hoofs are extremely widely splayed and up to 18 cm long – an adaptation to marshy habitat. Only rams have horns; quite long and similar in form to Nyala.
Distribution: In subregion occurs only in Botswana's Okavango Delta and adjacent areas in Caprivi Strip. Patchy distribution northwards to Lake Chad.
Habitat: Semi-aquatic and spends most of its time in dense reed-beds, with water to a depth of a metre. Swims in deeper water to escape danger.
Behaviour: Common grouping is adult ram with ewes and juveniles, but solitary animals and groups of subadults are also seen. Active throughout day, but lies up during hottest hours on trampled mats of reeds or other vegetation. Will also feed at night. If alarmed will swim to safety.
Food: Papyrus and other reeds; also grass and occasional browse.
Reproduction: Single calf born after 220-day gestation, usually in midwinter.

Bushbuck *Tragelaphus scriptus*
Male: shoulder height 80 cm; tail 20 cm; mass 45 kg.
Female: shoulder height 70 cm; tail 20 cm; mass 30 kg.
Average horn length 26 cm; record horn length 52,07 cm.
Identification pointers: Presence of vertical white stripes and spots on sides of the body to a greater or lesser extent, more so in north; broad ears; short bushy tail, dark above and white below; ram has short, almost straight horns with slight spiral and ridge. Much smaller than Nyala.

Description: Small bright-chestnut to dark-brown antelope; those in north of subregion more brightly coloured and clearly marked than those from south. Nevertheless, considerable variation in colour and markings even within one population. Patterns of white lines and spots are present on the flanks to a greater or lesser extent, more so in the north. No white band or chevron between eyes as in Sitatunga, Nyala and Kudu, but there are two white patches on throat. Crest of longish hair down back of ram but only raised when it displays or threatens. Bushy tail white below and dark brown above. Only ram has horns; they project backwards with a single spiral and have a prominent ridge along edge. Can be extremely sharp-pointed in young rams.
Distribution: Southern coastal belt and east and north parts of subregion.
Habitat: Riverine woodland and bush associated with water, from coastal dune bush to montane forest.
Behaviour: Usually single but occasionally in pairs or small groups of ewes and lambs. Mainly nocturnal but also active during day in cooler or overcast weather.
Food: Predominantly browsers but will take grass. May damage young trees in forestry plantations or agricultural crops.
Reproduction: Single young weighing 3,5–4,5 kg born after gestation period of 180 days. Follows mother regularly after 4 months of remaining hidden.

Sitatunga ram

Young Sitatunga ram swimming

Bushbuck ewe typical of those from south-east of subregion

Bushbuck ewe from Chobe, Botswana, showing brighter colouring and clearer markings of the northern populations

The Bushbuck ram has short, slightly spiralled horns

Roan Antelope *Hippotragus equinus*
Shoulder height 110–150 (average 140) cm; tail 54 cm; mass 220–300 (average 270) kg.
Average horn length (bull) 75 cm; record horn length (Zimbabwe) 99,06 cm.
Identification pointers: Large size; greyish-brown colour with lighter underparts; black and white facial pattern; heavily ridged, swept-back, curving horns; long, narrow, tufted ears. See Sable Antelope.

Description: After the Eland, the Roan Antelope is the second-largest antelope species occurring in Africa. It has a somewhat horse-like appearance with a general colouring of greyish-brown, often with a reddish tinge ('roan' colouration). The underparts are lighter. The face is distinctly marked with black and white, giving it a slightly clown-like appearance and the long, narrow ears have prominent tassels of hair at the tip. The tail is long and tufted. A distinct, light-coloured but darker-tipped mane, runs from between the ears to just beyond the shoulders. Both sexes carry the back-curved horns but those of the cow are lighter and shorter than the bull's.

Distribution: Restricted to the northern and north-eastern areas of southern Africa where it is considered to be rare. Beyond the Southern African Subregion it occurs widely in central Africa, western East Africa and through the savanna zone to West Africa. However, despite this wide distribution, it is considered to be rare and endangered throughout much of its range.

Habitat: Roan Antelope require open or lightly wooded grassland with medium to tall grass and access to water. They avoid areas with short grass.

Behaviour: They live in small herds (5 to 12) usually led by an adult bull. Larger herds (30–80) have been recorded. Nursery herds, consisting of cows and young animals, occupy fixed areas which are defended by dominant bulls from approaches by other bulls. The herd itself is usually led by a cow which becomes dominant over the other cows and juveniles. The bull is responsible for breeding and keeping competitors away and the lead cow selects feeding and resting areas. Two-year-old bulls are driven away from the herd by the herd bull and these join together to form small bachelor herds. Adult bulls (5–6 years old) move off to live alone or to take over nursery herds. Most activity takes place during the day.

Food: Roan Antelope are principally grazers, selecting for medium or long grasses. They rarely browse.

Reproduction: Calves may be dropped at any time of the year after a gestation period of about 280 days. Shortly before the birth the cow moves away from the herd and remains in bush cover until the calf is born. For the first few days the cow remains close to the calf, but then rejoins the herd, only visiting her calf in the early morning and late afternoon. When it is about two weeks old the calf joins the herd. Although its facial markings are similar to those of the adults, its body colour is light to rich rufous brown.

Roan Antelope

Sable Antelope *Hippotragus niger*
Shoulder height 135 cm; tail 50 cm; mass 180–270 (average 230) kg. Average horn length (bull) 102 cm; record horn length (southern Africa) 127,6 cm.

Identification pointers: Large size; contrasting black or dark-brown upperparts with pure white underparts; long, transversely ridged, back-curved horns in both sexes. Different body colour from the Roan Antelope, with a somewhat lighter build, longer horns and no tuft of hair at the tip of the ear.

Description: The adult bull Sable Antelope is shiny black with sharply contrasting white underparts and inner thighs. Cows and younger bulls are usually reddish brown above. The black-and-white facial markings are conspicuous. The face is mainly white, with a broad black blaze from the forehead to the nose and a black stripe from below the eye almost to the muzzle. There is an erect, fairly long mane running from the top of the neck to just beyond the shoulders. The ears are long and narrow but lack the tufted tips found in Roan. Both sexes carry horns but those of the bull are longer and more robust. The transversely ridged horns rise up from the skull and then sweep backwards in a pronounced curve.

Distribution: Restricted to the north-eastern parts of southern Africa but even here distribution is patchy and not continuous. It occurs as far north as southern Kenya and marginally in south-western Angola. An isolated population occurs in northern Angola and is considered to be a separate subspecies – the so-called Giant Sable.

Habitat: Sable are usually associated with dry, open woodland with medium to tall grass. They avoid dense woodland and short grassveld. Water is essential.

Behaviour: The Sable Antelope lives in herds usually numbering from 10 to 30 individuals but occasionally larger groups come together. Territorial bulls establish themselves in territories overlapping those of nursery herds (cows and young animals). The nursery herds move within a fixed home range. During the rut the bull tries to keep the cows within his territory. As with Roan Antelope, a cow takes over leadership of a nursery herd. The young bulls grow up within bachelor herds, only seeking out their own territories in their fifth or sixth year. Most Sable activity takes place in the early morning and late afternoon.

Food: Sable are principally grazers but will take browse, particularly in the dry season.

Reproduction: The Sable is a seasonal breeder, dropping its calves between January and March; this varies according to area. A single reddish-brown calf, weighing 13 to 18 kg, is born after a gestation period of about 270 days. The cow leaves the herd to give birth and the calf remains hidden for some time before joining the other animals. After each suckling, only once or twice each day, the calf moves to a new hiding-place and in this way reduces the chances of being found by a predator.

Sable Antelope cow

Sable Antelope bull

Sable Antelope calves are red-brown

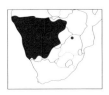

Gemsbok *Oryx gazella*
Shoulder height 1, 2 m; mass 240 kg (bull), 210 kg (cow).
Average horn length 85 cm; record horn length (Botswana) 121,9 cm.
Identification pointers: Heavily built with thick neck; distinct black facial and body markings; long horse-like tail and long straight horns. Should not be confused with any other species.

Description: Heavily built with a short, thick neck and distinct black-and-white markings on the head, body and legs; has long, black, horse-like tail. Body colour greyish-fawn, separated from white underparts by black streak along flanks. Black patches on upper part of legs and along top of rump. Black stripe runs down front of neck. Calves fawn and lack black body markings. Both sexes carry the long, almost straight, transversely ridged, rapier-like horns; those of bull are shorter and more robust.
Distribution: Arid north-west of subregion, extending north into Angola. Another separate population in East Africa.
Habitat: Open, dry country but also open woodland, grassveld and dune country. Availability of water is not an essential habitat requirement.
Behaviour: Gregarious, occurring in herds of about 15. Sometimes in larger numbers, particularly during rains. They may occur in mixed herds (consisting of bulls, cows and young of different ages) or nursery herds (cows and young); solitary bulls are often seen. A territorial bull will herd a mixed or nursery herd into his territory and only he will mate with receptive cows. Gemsbok are usually forced by the nature of their hostile environment to be nomadic, moving to fresh vegetation growth following rain.
Food: Although mainly grazers they also include browse, seed-pods and fruits such as tsama melons in their diet.
Reproduction: Single calf after a gestation period of about 264 days, usually in summer. The calf hides and will move with the mother at night to a new resting-place. Calves usually 3–6 weeks old before joining the herd.

Waterbuck *Kobus ellipsiprymnus*
Shoulder height 1,3 m; tail 35 cm; mass 250–270 kg (bulls).
Average horn length 75 cm; record horn length (Transvaal) 99,7 cm.
Identification pointers: Large size; broad white ring around rump; coarse, shaggy grey-brown coat; long, ringed, forward-swept horns of the bull.

Description: Waterbuck are large, robust antelope with coarse and long coats. The body colour is grey-brown with either grey or brown being dominant, scattered through with grey or white hairs. A broad white ring encircles the rump and a white band is present from throat to the base of the ears. The flanks are lighter in colour than the back and the hair around the mouth, nose and above the eyes is white. The ears are short, rounded, white on the inside with a black tip. The tail is quite long with a black tuft of hair at the tip. Only the bull has the long, heavily ringed horns which curve backwards and then forwards towards the tips.
Distribution: Waterbuck occur patchily in eastern southern Africa and then northwards through East Africa to southern Somalia.
Habitat: Always associated with water, preferring areas with reed-beds or tall grass as well as woodland. They will utilize open grassland adjacent to cover.
Behaviour: Waterbuck are gregarious, occurring in small herds of 5–10 but sometimes as many as 30. Nursery herds may move through territories of several bulls. Younger bulls form bachelor herds. Waterbuck can often be detected by the strong musky scent given off by their oily hair.
Food: Principally grass but also take browse.
Reproduction: A single calf may be dropped at any time of the year but mostly in summer; the gestation period is about 280 days. After 3 or 4 weeks in hiding the calf begins to follow the mother and joins the herd.

Gemsbok bull

Gemsbok cow (foreground)

Herd of Gemsbok

Waterbuck

Waterbuck cow with calves

Only the Waterbuck bull has horns

Lechwe *Kobus leche*

Male: shoulder height 100 cm; tail 34 cm; mass 100 kg.
Female: shoulder height 96 cm; tail 34 cm; mass 80 kg.
Average horn length 70 cm; record horn length 93,98 cm.
Identification pointers: Chestnut upperparts and white underparts; black lines on front of forelegs (absent in Puku); long, ridged, forward-pointing horns of the ram much longer than those of Puku. Semi-aquatic nature of habitat sets Lechwe aside from most other species. Very different in appearance from Sitatunga.

Description: The hindquarters of the Lechwe are noticeably higher than the shoulders and its muzzle is quite short. Upperparts are bright chestnut and the underparts from chin to belly are white. There are conspicuous black lines down the front of the forelegs. Only the ram has the long, strongly ridged, lyre-shaped horns. The tail has a tip of black hair.
Distribution: In subregion Lechwe restricted to Okavango and Chobe areas of northern Botswana and Caprivi Strip.
Habitat: Floodplains and seasonal swamps; rarely ventures more than 2 or 3 km from permanent water.
Behaviour: Next to Sitatunga the Lechwe is the most water-loving antelope. It takes readily to water to feed and when threatened. It usually occurs in herds of up to 30 individuals, but occasionally many thousands may be seen together. Rams form small territories within which they keep small groups of ewes for mating. On edges of mating grounds small groups of non-territorial rams congregate. Ewe herds with their young move freely between ram territories. Lechwe are active during the early morning and late afternoon, lying up during the heat of the day and at night. Although quite slow on land they can move rapidly in shallow water and swim readily.
Food: Almost entirely semi-aquatic grasses.
Reproduction: Most calves in the Okavango Swamps are born during the period from October to December, but they may be dropped at any time of the year. A single calf weighing approximately 5 kg is born after a gestation period of about 225 days. Calves remain hidden for the first 2–3 weeks.

Puku *Kobus vardonii*

Shoulder height 80 cm; tail 28 cm; mass 74 kg (ram), 62 kg (ewe).
Average horn length 45 cm; record horn length 53,98 cm.
Identification pointers: Can be distinguished from Lechwe by the absence of black markings on the front of the forelegs and by the shorter horns of rams. Very restricted southern African distribution.

Description: The upperparts of this medium-sized antelope are golden-yellow with slightly paler sides. The underparts are off-white, as are the throat, the sides of the muzzle and around the eyes. The legs are uniform brown in colour. The tail is golden-yellow. Only the ram has the relatively short, stout, lyre-shaped, well-ringed horns.
Distribution: In subregion only on Pookoo Flats and vicinity on Chobe River, Botswana but widely scattered through central and East Africa.
Habitat: Open flatland adjacent to rivers and marshes but usually not on open floodplains favoured by Lechwe.
Behaviour: Herds of Puku usually number from 5 to 30. Adult rams defend small territories for short periods, during which time they attempt to herd the ewes, which will however move across the territories of several rams.
Food: Predominantly grasses.
Reproduction: Young may be dropped at any time of the year but there is a peak in births during the dry winter months. The gestation period is approximately 240 days. The lamb hides for the early part of its life and on joining the herd usually moves with the other lambs as the mother/lamb bond is weak in comparison with other antelope species.

Lechwe ram

Lechwe ram and ewes

Small herd of Puku ewes

Puku ram

Mountain Reedbuck *Redunca fulvorufula*
Shoulder height 72 cm; tail 20 cm; mass 30 kg.
Average horn length 14 cm; record horn length 25,4 cm.
Identification pointers: Grey-fawn upperparts; white underparts; bushy tail, grey above and white below; short, forward-curved horns of male. May be confused with Grey Rhebok where they occur together, but the horns of the latter are straight and vertically set, and not forward-curved. Similar to Reedbuck but smaller, and has no dark-brown line on front of the forelegs; different habitat.

Description: Upperparts grey-fawn and underparts white. Hair of the head and neck is usually more yellow-fawn. Bushy tail, grey-fawn above and white below, is held vertically when animal flees, prominently displaying white under-surface. Ears are long and narrow. Only male has horns; they are short, stout and forward-curved.
Distribution: Patchy distribution in eastern parts of subregion.
Habitat: The Mountain Reedbuck is restricted to mountainous and rocky areas. Preference for broken hill country with scattered bush, trees or grassy slopes but avoids steep rock-faces. Water is essential.
Behaviour: Territorial rams occupy their areas throughout the year but small groups of 2 to 6 ewes and young are unstable and move from herd to herd and over several ram territories. Bachelor groups may also be observed. This species is active both at night and during the day but lies up during the hottest hours.
Food: Grasses.
Reproduction: Breeding takes place throughout the year with a birth-peak in the summer months. A single lamb with a mass of 3 kg is born after a gestation period of approximately 242 days. The ewe gives birth to the lamb under cover and away from the group. The lamb remains hidden for 2 to 3 months before joining with the other group members.

Reedbuck *Redunca arundinum*
Shoulder height 80–95 cm; tail 25 cm; mass 50–70 kg.
Average horn length 30 cm; record horn length 45 cm.
Identification pointers: Forward-curved horns of the ram; white, bushy underside of tail is prominent when the animal is running away. Differs from Mountain Reedbuck in being larger, having black lines on front surface of forelegs, and by ram having considerably longer horns. Habitat requirements of the two species are different and they are rarely found together.

Description: Medium-sized antelope with brown or greyish-fawn upperparts, although head and neck are slightly lighter. Underparts are white. Short, bushy tail is grey-fawn above and white below. There is a vertical black stripe on the forward-facing surface of forelegs. Ears are broad and rounded and white on the inside. Only the ram has horns and they are curved forward and transversely ridged from the base for two-thirds of their length.
Distribution: Reedbuck has patchy distribution dictated by availability of suitable habitat. Restricted to east and north of subregion.
Habitat: Reedbuck requires tall-grass areas and reed-beds as well as permanent water. It avoids bush areas.
Behaviour: Usually in pairs or family groups but up to 20 on occasion. A pair occupies a territory which is defended by the ram. Both nocturnal and diurnal. Loud alarm whistle emitted through the nostrils when the animal is disturbed, or by rams advertising their territories.
Food: Reedbuck are predominantly grazers but do take browse on occasion.
Reproduction: Birth peak in summer. Gestation 220 days. Single lamb weighs 4,5 kg; hidden for 2 months, then accompanies ewe; both join ram at 3 to 4 months.

Mountain Reedbuck ram

Mountain Reedbuck ewe

Reedbuck ram

Reedbuck ewe

Grey Rhebok *Pelea capreolus*
Shoulder height 75 cm; tail 10 cm; mass 20 kg.
Average horn length 20 cm; record horn length 29,21 cm.
Identification pointers: Woolly grey coat; long, narrow ears; large black nose; straight, upright horns of ram. May be confused with Mountain Reedbuck where the two species occur together, but the latter's horns curve forwards at the tip.

Description: A gracefully built antelope with a grey, thick woolly coat. The underparts are pure white. The short, bushy tail is grey above and white underneath and at the tip. Ears are long and narrow. Only the male has the vertical, almost straight horns. The large black nose has a somewhat swollen appearance.
Distribution: Restricted to South Africa, Lesotho and Swaziland.
Habitat: Usually hill or mountain country but also in the wheat-lands of the south-western Cape, particularly in the Bredasdorp and Swellendam districts.
Behaviour: Normally in small family parties consisting of a territorial adult ram, several ewes and their young. Active by day. Gives vent to a sharp snort at regular intervals when disturbed or alarmed. Runs with 'rocking-horse' motion displaying white underside of tail as warning signal.
Food: Grasses.
Reproduction: Single lambs born in November-December; gestation period 260 days.

Black Wildebeest *Connochaetes gnou*
Shoulder height 1,2 m; mass 100–180 kg. Average horn length 52 cm; record double horn length (tip to tip) 69,9 cm.
Identification pointers: Overall black appearance; long, white, horse-like tail; characteristic horn shape; extensive facial 'hair-brush'. Could be confused with Blue Wildebeest but range does not overlap except where introduced; the white tail is, however, characteristic (Blue Wildebeest has black tail).

6 months

12 months

24 months

36 months

48 months

Horn development
(after W. von Richter, 1971)

Description: More dark brown than black, but from a distance the Black Wildebeest does look black. Long, white, horse-like tail contrasts with body colour. Somewhat grotesque in appearance: shoulders are higher than rump and it has a large, broad-snouted head. Face covered in brush-like tuft of hairs which points outwards and there is long hair on throat and on chest between forelegs. Erect mane runs from top of neck to shoulders. Horns of cow are thinner and less robust than those of bull. They bend steeply downward, forward and upward; in mature bulls horn base forms a 'boss' over top of head.
Distribution: Formerly distributed over a wide area of Cape Province, Orange Free State, southern Transvaal and Natal but brought to brink of extinction last century. Numbers are now over 3 000 in total. Widely reintroduced even beyond former range.
Habitat: Low karoid scrub and open grassland.
Behaviour: Bulls set up territories and during rut will attempt to 'herd' cows within their areas. The herds, consisting of cows and their young, normally wander freely over bull territories. Bulls mark their territories with urine, droppings and scent secretions and reinforce the effect by performing elaborate displays. Bachelor herds consist of bulls of all ages.
Food: Principally grasses but browse on occasion. Drinking water essential.
Reproduction: The majority of calves are dropped during the midsummer months but the peak period varies in different areas. A single calf is dropped after a gestation period of about 250 days and can move with the herd shortly after birth.
General: Also known as the White-tailed Gnu, the latter part of the name coming from the characteristic nasal call 'ge-nu'.

Grey Rhebok with long, straight horns; the ewe lacks horns

Black Wildebeest

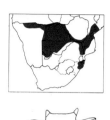

Blue Wildebeest *Connochaetes taurinus*

Male: shoulder height 1,5 m; tail 60 cm; mass 250 kg.
Female: shoulder height 1,3 m; tail 60 cm; mass 180 kg.
Average horn length 60 cm; record horn length (measured like black wildebeest from tip to tip along both horns) 83,8 cm.

Identification pointers: Forequarters higher and much heavier than hindquarters; dark grey with some brown in younger animals and cows and with darker, vertical stripes on neck and chest; broad snout; superficially buffalo-like horns but much lighter than Buffalo's. Distinguished easily from Black Wildebeest by black tail (as opposed to white tail of the latter).

Description: The Blue Wildebeest has lightly built hindquarters and is more robust at the shoulders. The head is large with a broad snout. Adult animals are dark grey tinged with brown, and in certain light conditions a silvery sheen is discernible. A number of vertical, darker stripes are present from the neck to just behind the rib-cage. It is frequently referred to as the Brindled (= brown-streaked) Gnu for this reason. There is a mane of long black hair down the back of the neck and a beard of black hair on the throat. The front of the face is almost black, although an area of brown hair may be present at the horn base, particularly in younger animals. The calf is rufous fawn with a darker face and has a dark vertebral stripe. Both sexes have horns, although those of the cow are less robust. The horn bases form a boss over the top of the head and the horns themselves grow outwards, turn sharply up and then inwards. The tail is black and horse-like.

Distribution: Largely restricted to the northern areas of southern Africa but it has been introduced widely to reserves and farms further south. It extends from northern South West Africa/Namibia into southern Angola and western Zambia, with an isolated population in the Luangwa Valley. There is then a break in distribution with a separate population occurring in Tanzania and Kenya.

Habitat: It shows a preference for open savanna woodland and open grassland. Access to drinking water is essential.

Behaviour: Although Blue Wildebeest occur in herds of usually up to 30 individuals, much larger concentrations may be observed, numbering many thousands. These large concentrations are formed during migrations to new feeding-grounds but the smaller herd units maintain their identity. Such mass movements still take place in Botswana but the erection of veterinary cordon fences in that country have disturbed a number of the traditional routes. Territorial bulls defend a zone around their cows, even when on the move. A bull may have between 2 and 150 cows with their young within his territorial control. However, cows may move through the territories of a number of bulls and mate with more than one. Outside the mating season the cow herds move freely and are not herded by the territorial bulls. Bachelor herds are usually found around the edge of the main concentration. Blue Wildebeest are active by day but they seek out shade during the hottest hours.

Food: Blue Wildebeest are essentially grazers, showing a preference for short green grass.

Reproduction: The mating season is usually from March to June, with most of the calves being dropped from mid-November to the end of December. However, this varies in different areas and may be influenced by such factors as drought or early rains. A single calf weighing about 22 kg is born after a gestation period of approximately 250 days. The calf is able to run with the mother a few minutes after birth.

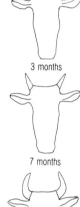

3 months

7 months

10 months

16 months

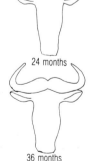

24 months

36 months

Horn development
(after J. Kingdon, 1982)

204

Blue Wildebeest cow with calf

Blue Wildebeest

Blue Wildebeest bull

Alcelaphus buselaphus

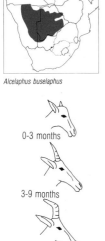

0-3 months

3-9 months

9-18 months

18-30 months

30-36 months

36+ months

Horn development
(after O.B. Kok, 1975)

Sigmoceros lichtensteinii

Red Hartebeest *Alcelaphus buselaphus*
Shoulder height 1,25 m; tail 47 cm; mass 150 kg (bull), 120 kg (cow).
Average horn length 52 cm; record horn length 70,5 cm.
Identification pointers: Much higher at shoulder than at rump;
golden-brown colour with black leg markings; long face with black blaze;
unusual horn shape. Lichtenstein's Hartebeest similar but distributions
do not overlap (see maps). Also similar to Tsessebe, but their horns
have a completely different shape.

Description: High-shouldered, rather awkward-looking antelope with long
pointed head. Body colour fawn to golden-brown, but darker from shoulders
down centre of back to rump, particularly in bulls. Rump and upper thighs are
paler than rest of body. Black blaze down front of face and black markings on
all four legs. Tail is pale at base, with black hair over remainder. Horns in
both sexes; those of bull are heavier but both are set close together at the
base, curving forwards and out and then twisting in and back.
Distribution: Now restricted to arid western parts of subregion but formerly as
far south as Cape Town. Reintroduced widely within former range.
Habitat: Open savanna country, but also open woodland. Drinking water not
essential.
Behaviour: Normally in herds numbering from about 20 to several hundred,
but occasionally in thousands. Larger groups usually formed at onset of
summer rains. In arid areas it will travel great distances in search of fresh
grass. Adult bulls are territorial. Harem herds consisting of cows, young
animals and a territorial bull occupy the best grazing, with bachelor herds
having to make do with what is left. Mostly active by day.
Food: Mainly grasses but also browse.
Reproduction: Single calf born away from herd, after gestation period of 240
days, usually in early summer. It remains hidden until it is strong enough to
keep up with the other animals.

Lichtenstein's Hartebeest *Sigmoceros lichtensteinii*
Shoulder height 1,25 m; tail 48 cm; mass 170 kg (bull).
Average horn length 52 cm; record horn length 60,33 cm.
Identification pointers: Higher at shoulders than rump; yellow-tawny
body colouring; characteristic horn shape. Compare with Tsessebe
where range overlaps.

Description: Like the Red Hartebeest, Lichtenstein's Hartebeest is a
clumsy-looking antelope with its shoulders higher than its hindquarters.
Yellow-fawn body with slightly darker 'saddle' from shoulders to rump. Flanks
and underparts are lighter with an off-white area on rump. Dark stripe runs
down front of forelegs. Tail base is white but remainder of tail has a covering
of longish black hair. Both sexes have horns flattened at base, strongly
ringed, except at the tips, and have a 'Z'-shaped curvature similar to those of
Red Hartebeest.
Distribution: Lichtenstein's occurs in Mozambique and south-eastern
Zimbabwe. Recently introduced to Kruger National Park from Malawi.
Habitat: Savanna woodland where it abuts on vleis or floodplain. Surface
water essential.
Behaviour: Small herds of up to 10 individuals but occasionally larger groups.
A territorial bull stays with a number of cows and calves within a fixed area.
Bachelor herds subsist in less favourable habitat. Mainly active by day but
partly nocturnal.
Food: Grasses but occasionally browse.
Reproduction: Single calf weighing about 15 kg is born after a gestation
period of 240 days, usually in September. Can follow mother soon after birth
but usually lies up between feeds; makes no attempt to hide.

Red Hartebeest

Lichtenstein's Hartebeest

Damaliscus dorcas dorcas
(S.W. Cape)
Damaliscus dorcas phillipsi
(E. Cape to Transvaal)

Bontebok

Blesbok

Facial blaze

Bontebok *Damaliscus dorcas dorcas*
Shoulder height 90 cm; mass 62 kg (ram).
Blesbok *Damaliscus dorcas phillipsi*
Shoulder height 95 cm; mass 70 kg (ram).
Average horn length (both subspecies) 38 cm.
Record horn length 50,8 cm (Blesbok), 43 cm (Bontebok).
Identification pointers: Bontebok rich dark-brown body colour with pure white buttocks and open white blaze from muzzle to between horns; Blesbok reddish-brown colour with pale brown buttock patch and white blaze on muzzle broken by brown between the eyes. No other hartebeest-like antelope has white on face.

Description: The Bontebok and Blesbok are separate and distinct subspecies of *Damaliscus dorcas*. The differences between the two are outlined below. Both subspecies are higher at the shoulder than at the rump and have long, pointed heads with both sexes carrying simple lyre-shaped horns. They are thus similar in general appearance to the other hartebeests and the Tsessebe. The ewe's horns are more slender than those of the ram.

	Bontebok	Blesbok
Body colour	Rich, dark brown with purple gloss, particularly rams; darker on sides and upper limbs.	Reddish-brown; no gloss.
Face	White blaze usually unbroken but narrows between eyes. (This character not 100%).	White blaze usually broken by brown band between eyes. (This character not 100%).
Buttocks	Always white.	Usually pale but rarely white.
Limbs	Lower part usually white.	Rarely as white as in Bontebok.
Horns	Usually black on upper ringed surface.	Usually straw-coloured on upper ringed surface.

Distribution: Bontebok historically restricted to Bredasdorp and Mossel Bay areas of Cape. After near-extinction, now safe on several reserves and private farms. Largest single population in the De Hoop Nature Reserve near Bredasdorp. Blesbok occur throughout the Orange Free State, southern Transvaal and in eastern Cape, as well as marginally in Natal.
Habitat: Bontebok: coastal plain within Cape fynbos vegetation zone; require short grass, water and some cover. Blesbok: open grassland with water.
Behaviour: Bontebok and Blesbok are diurnal, but are less active during hotter midday hours. Both characteristically stand head down in groups facing the sun. Territorial Bontebok rams hold their areas throughout the year and ewe/lamb groups numbering some 6 to 10 wander at will through adjoining territories. Ewe groups are herded during January-March rut. Bachelor herds usually establish home ranges away from those held by territorial rams. Blesbok ewes move in harem herds numbering from 2 to 25, each herd attended by a territorial ram. Unlike Bontebok, where herd structure remains largely unchanged throughout the year, Blesbok do not occupy the same home range throughout the year and during the dry winter months come together in large mixed herds.
Food: Grasses but will browse occasionally.
Reproduction: Most Bontebok lambs born September–October with a few being dropped as late as February. Most Blesbok lambs born November–January with a peak in December. Gestation period is approximately 240 days and the lamb has a mass of 6 or 7 kg at birth. It is pale fawn to creamy in colour and can run with the mother within 20–30 minutes of birth.

On hot days Bontebok herds characteristically orientate towards the sun with head bowed, a habit they share with Blesbok

Bontebok ram (right) 'testing' ewe (left)

Young Bontebok

Bontebok (left) showing continuous facial blaze and white rump, and Blesbok (right) showing broken blaze and pale rump

Tsessebe *Damaliscus lunatus*
Shoulder height 1,2 m; tail 45 cm; mass 140 kg (bull), 126 kg (cow).
Average horn length 34 cm; record horn length 46,99 cm.
Identification pointers: Higher at shoulder than rump; characteristic horn
shape; head dark in contrast to reddish-brown body. See Red
Hartebeest and Lichtenstein's Hartebeest where distributions overlap.

Description: Rather hartebeest-like in general appearance, with long face and
sloping back. Upperparts dark reddish-brown with distinct purplish sheen.
Bulls darker than cows. Head, lower shoulder and upper parts of legs darker
in colour than rest of body. Lower parts of legs are brownish-yellow, with
pale-fawn tail base and inner thighs. Black tassel on end half of tail. Both
sexes have horns; lyrate and ringed except at the tip.
Distribution: Occurs patchily in north and north-eastern areas of subregion.
Habitat: Open savanna woodland with adjacent grassland and surface water.
Behaviour: Small herds of 5 or 6 individuals but sometimes number up to 30
or more, especially near water or favourable grazing. A territorial bull
maintains a defended area, within which the cows and young animals live
permanently.
Food: Grasses.
Reproduction: Single young, with a mass of 10–12 kg, born after gestation of
240 days, usually October-December. Calves can run with the herd shortly
after birth.

Aepyceros melampus melampus
(from Caprivi eastwards)
Aepyceros melampus petersi
(north-west S.W.A./Namibia only)

Impala *Aepyceros melampus*
Shoulder height 90 cm; tail 28 cm; mass 50 kg (ram), 40 kg (ewe).
Average horn length 50 cm; record horn length 80,97 cm.
Identification pointers: Long, graceful, lyrate horns of the ram; black tuft
of hair above the hoof on the rear surface of hindleg; thin black line
down centre of white tail and vertical black line on each buttock.

Description: Medium-sized, lightly built antelope. Upperparts reddish-fawn
becoming paler on sides; chest, belly, throat and chin are white. Tail is white
with central black line on upper surface, and each buttock has vertical black
blaze. Tuft of black hair on lower rear edge of hindleg, a characteristic unique
to the Impala. Ears are black-tipped. Only rams carry the long graceful lyrate
horns. The Black-faced Impala (*Aepyceros melampus petersi*) of northern
South West Africa/Namibia differs at subspecies level from the eastern
populations of Impala (*A. melampus melampus*); black blaze down front of
face of *petersi* is distinctive.
Distribution: Widespread in north-eastern areas of subregion and then
northwards to Kenya. An isolated subspecies, the Black-faced Impala, occurs
in north-western South West Africa/Namibia and extends into Angola.
Habitat: Open or light savanna woodland; avoids open grassland unless there
is scattered bush cover. Absent from mountains. Surface water must be
available.
Behaviour: Rams are extremely vocal during the mating season and give
vent to growls, roars and snorts. They are only territorial during the rut, from
January to May, spending the rest of the time in bachelor herds. The home
range of a breeding herd, consisting of ewes and young animals, may
overlap with the territories of several territorial rams. The rams separate out
harem herds of 15–20 ewes (with their young) for mating. This disrupts the
composition of the herds but they reunite at the conclusion of the rut.
Bachelor herds tend to occupy areas away from the breeding herds. Impala
are active mainly during the cooler daylight hours but there is some nocturnal
activity.
Food: Short grasses and browse; proportions vary with area and season.
Reproduction: Single lamb, weighing approximately 5 kg, is born in early
summer after gestation of 196 days.

Tsessebe

Impala ram

Black-faced Impala ewe

Black-faced Impala ram

Impala ewe

Impala is only antelope with tuft of black hair above hoof

Springbok *Antidorcas marsupialis*
Shoulder height 75 cm; tail 25 cm; mass 41 kg (ram), 37 kg (ewe).
Average horn length (ram) 35 cm; record horn length (ram) 49,22 cm.
Identification pointers: Dark-brown band separating upper- from underparts; white head with brown stripe through eye to corner of mouth; short lyrate horns in both sexes; broad white crest on back visible when pronking.

Description: Hindquarters of this distinctive antelope appear to be slightly higher than shoulders. Dark red-brown band along flanks separates fawn-brown upperparts from white underparts. Head is white with a brown stripe running through eye to corner of upper lip. A large white patch on rump is bordered by brown stripe. There is a long-haired, white dorsal crest extending from the midpoint of the back to the rump; this is normally seen only when the crest is erected, for example during 'pronking'. The pronk is a jump performed with stiff legs accompanied by arching of the back. Tail is white with tuft of black hairs at tip. Both sexes have heavily ridged, lyre-shaped horns but ram's are thicker and longer.
Distribution: More arid western areas of subregion and into Angola. Now one of South Africa's most important game-farming animals.
Habitat: Open, arid plains. Surface water not essential.
Behaviour: Normally in small herds but when moving to new feeding-grounds may congregate in herds of many thousands. Small herds may be mixed or consist of rams only; solitary rams are frequently encountered. Springbok rams are territorial and in rut herd ewe groups; they do not, however, remain on their territories throughout the year. Springbok are active during the cooler daylight hours but also partly at night.
Food: Grass and browse; will dig for roots and bulbs.
Reproduction: A single lamb weighing about 3,8 kg is born after a gestation period of about 168 days, usually during rains. Joins herd after 2 days.
General: Springbok are farmed in parts of the Cape Province and Orange Free State for their venison and skins. Aberrant Springbok with white or black coats appear from time to time; these are often selectively bred by farmers as they fetch high prices at sales of game animals.

Damara Dik-dik *Madoqua kirkii*
Shoulder height 38 cm; tail 5 cm; mass 5 kg.
Average horn length 8 cm; record horn length 10,2 cm.
Identification pointers: Small size; elongated nose; crest of long hair on the forehead. No similar species occur within its southern African distribution range.

Description: Very small; characterized by having elongated, very mobile nose. Upperparts yellowish-grey with grizzled appearance; neck paler than shoulders and flanks. Underparts white to off-white. Tuft of long hair on forehead is erected when the Dik-dik is alarmed or displaying. Rams have short, spike-like horns that slope back at angle of facial profile.
Distribution: Central and north-western South West Africa/Namibia and north into south-western Angola. A separate population occurs in East Africa.
Habitat: Damara Dik-dik show a strong preference for fairly dense, dry woodland. They penetrate deep into the Namib Desert along riverine woodland. Bush-covered hillsides and adjacent scrub are also occupied.
Behaviour: Usually single, in pairs or in small family parties. Pairs establish communal dung middens within home range. Both nocturnal and diurnal.
Food: Although they are chiefly browsers they do take some grass during the rainy season. They will utilize leaves, pods and flowers knocked down by larger species such as elephant and kudu.
Reproduction: After a gestation period of approximately 170 days a single fawn with a mass of 620–760 g is dropped during the summer months.

Springbok ram showing dorsal gland fold   Springbok ram

'Black' Springbok

Springbok ewe

Damara Dik-dik ram

Damara Dik-dik ewe: note elongated, mobile nose

213

Suni *Neotragus moschatus*
Shoulder height 35 cm; tail 12 cm; mass 5 kg.
Average horn length 8 cm; record horn length 13,34 cm.
Identification pointers: Very small size; constantly flicking white-tipped tail; pink-lined and translucent appearance of ears. Much smaller than Sharpe's Grysbok; white flecks on upperparts distinguish it from similar-sized Blue Duiker.

Description: Tiny, elegant antelope with rich rufous-brown upperparts flecked with white hairs, and white underparts. Two slightly curved white bars on throat. Above each hoof is narrow dark band. Tail fairly long and is dark brown above with a white tip and is regularly flicked from side to side. Pink-lined ears give the appearance of being almost transparent. Only ram has horns and these are quite thick, prominently transversely ridged and slope backwards in line with facial profile. Prominent gland in front of each eye of ram.
Distribution: Widespread in Mozambique but only occurs marginally in northern Natal/Zululand and in south-east and north-east Zimbabwe.
Habitat: Dry thickets and riverine woodland with dense underbrush.
Behaviour: Suni usually occur in pairs or small groups consisting of 1 adult ram and up to 4 ewes. Chiefly nocturnal but they are probably also active during early mornings and late afternoons. When disturbed they take off in a rapid zigzag resembling that of a startled hare. They follow regular pathways and use communal dung-heaps.
Food: Principally browse, but take a wide range of plant food.
Reproduction: Single fawn is born during summer; gestation 180 days. Remains hidden for several weeks, only emerging to suckle.

Klipspringer *Oreotragus oreotragus*
Shoulder height 60 cm; tail 8 cm; mass 10 kg (ram), 13 kg (ewe).
Average horn length 8 cm; record horn length (eastern Transvaal) 15,9 cm.
Identification pointers: Stocky appearance; short muzzle; only antelope walking on hoof-tips; always associated with rocky areas where it displays great agility.

Description: A small, stocky antelope with coarse, spiny hair. General colour yellow-brown to grey-yellow, with an overall grizzled appearance. Underparts, chin and lips are white. Ears are rounded, broad and bordered with black. Heavily built appearance caused by hair standing on end instead of lying flat as with other antelope. Characteristically walks on tips of hoofs. Only ram has horns; these are short, widely separated at the base, vertically placed and ringed only near base.
Distribution: Wide but patchy distribution in rocky habitats.
Habitat: Rocky habitat only.
Behaviour: Occur in pairs or small family groups. Adult ram is territorial. Extremely agile in moving across rocky terrain and up steep rock-covered slopes. Frequently stop to look back when running from a disturbance and both sexes give loud nasal alarm whistles. Use communal dung-heaps which are usually situated on flat areas. Active in morning and in later afternoon but throughout day when cool.
Food: Predominantly browse but grass taken occasionally.
Reproduction: Klipspringer probably give birth at any time of the year. A single lamb weighing about 1 kg is born after a gestation period of 210 days. The lamb remains hidden for the first 2 to 3 months after birth.
General: Popular opinion has it that the coarse, bristly, hollow hair of the Klipspringer has a cushioning function when the animal falls. It is, however, more likely that it serves as a heat regulator. Klipspringer hair was formerly prized for stuffing saddles.

Suni ram

Suni ram

Klipspringer ram

Klipspringer ewe marking twig with facial gland

Steenbok *Raphicerus campestris*
Shoulder height 50 cm; tail 5 cm; mass 11 kg; average horn length 9 cm; record horn length 19,05 cm.
Identification pointers: Small size; large ears; clearly demarcated reddish-fawn upperparts and white underparts; very short tail; only ram has short, vertical horns. Could be confused with Oribi, but the latter is larger, has smaller ears, a longer neck and has black tail tuft. The Oribi ram's horns are ridged for part of their length. Also see Cape and Sharpe's Grysbok.

Description: Small, elegant, large-eyed antelope normally rufous-fawn above but can vary from pale fawn to reddish-brown. Underparts including insides of legs are pure white, and there is a white patch on throat and above eyes. Rufous-fawn tail is very short. Only ram carries the short, sharp-pointed, smooth-surfaced, vertical horns.
Distribution: Widespread in subregion; separate population in East Africa.
Habitat: Open country but some cover required. In arid areas inhabit dry river-bed associations.
Behaviour: Occur singly or in pairs. Territorial. Unlike other small antelope Steenbok defaecate and urinate in shallow scrapes dug by front hoofs; these are then covered. Lie up in cover during heat of day, feeding in early morning and late afternoon. Also active at night, particularly in areas where they suffer disturbance.
Food: Mixed feeders taking grasses, browse, seed-pods and fruit. Dig for roots and bulbs with the front hoofs.
Reproduction: A single lamb weighing approximately 900 g is born after gestation of 170 days, usually in summer. Hidden for first few weeks.

Oribi *Ourebia ourebi*
Shoulder height 60 cm; tail 6–15 cm; mass 14 kg.
Average horn length 10 cm; record horn length 19,05 cm.
Identification pointers: Steenbok-like but larger; yellow-orange rufous above, white below; short, black-tipped tail (not black-tipped in Steenbok); long neck. The ram has erect, partly ridged horns, unlike the smooth horns of the Steenbok ram.

Description: Largest of the 'small' antelope. Upperparts rufous yellow-orange and underparts white. White hair extends on to front of chest. Relatively long neck, medium-sized ears and short tail with distinguishing black tip. Has pale throat patch and off-white areas on either side of nostrils and above eyes. Hair on back and underparts may have a curly appearance, particularly during winter. Only ram has horns and these are stout, erect and partly ridged.
Distribution: Widely separated areas in eastern and northern parts of subregion. Rare but widespread in sub-Saharan Africa.
Habitat: Open short grassland with taller grass patches for cover.
Behaviour: Occur in pairs or small parties consisting of 1 ram and up to 4 ewes. The ram is vigorously territorial. Communal dung-heaps serve a territorial marking function. When disturbed Oribi give a sharp whistle or sneeze and run off rapidly with occasional stiff-legged jumps displaying black-tipped tail. Inquisitive, however, and will turn to look back at source of disturbance after running a short distance. Also lie down in taller grass if disturbed, with head erect; in this position they are difficult to detect.
Food: Oribi are principally grazers but occasionally browse. They show a marked preference for short grass and will move if grass becomes too long. They are independent of drinking water.
Reproduction: Births have been recorded throughout the year but the majority of lambs are dropped during the wet summer months. A single lamb is born after a gestation period of about 210 days. The lamb remains hidden for as long as 3 to 4 months before joining the group.

Steenbok ram

Steenbok ewe

Oribi ram

Oribi ram (left) and ewe (right) resting in long grass

Cape Grysbok *Raphicerus melanotis*
Shoulder height 54 cm; tail 5,5 cm; mass 10 kg.
Average horn length 8 cm; record horn length 12,38 cm.
Identification pointers: Similar to Sharpe's Grysbok but their distribution ranges do not overlap (see map). The rufous-brown upperparts flecked with white distinguish it from the Steenbok, as do the brown underparts.

Description: A small, squat antelope characterized by rufous-brown upperparts abundantly flecked with white hairs. Flanks and neck have fewer white hairs and underparts are lighter brown than upperparts. Tail very short and grey-brown ears are proportionately large with white hairs on inside. Only ram has short, smooth, slightly back-angled horns. Pair of 'false hoofs' above the fetlock.
Distribution: Restricted to a narrow belt along south-western and southern Cape coastal belt and the adjacent interior.
Habitat: An inhabitant of relatively thick scrub-bush, it is almost entirely restricted to the 'fynbos' vegetation of the Cape. It is found in a variety of situations, from scrub-covered sand-dunes to wooded gorges on mountain slopes. In the areas where it enters the extreme southern Karoo it is found along rivers and on scrub-covered hillsides. It is frequently found along the fringes of agricultural land where belts of natural vegetation remain.
Behaviour: Mainly nocturnal but active in early morning and late afternoon if not disturbed, or on overcast and cool days. Usually single except when mating or when ewes are tending lambs. Males probably territorial.
Food: It is said to be mainly a grazer but it does take browse. In south-western Cape vineyards it is considered to be a nuisance as it eats the young grapes and terminal buds.
Reproduction: Although lambs may be dropped at any time of the year most are born from September to December. A single lamb is born after a gestation period of approximately 180 days.

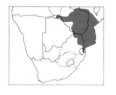

Sharpe's Grysbok *Raphicerus sharpei*
Shoulder height 50 cm; tail 6 cm; mass 7,5 kg.
Average horn length 6 cm; record horn length 10,48 cm (but 6,35 cm for subregion).
Identification pointers: Similar to Cape Grysbok but distribution ranges do not overlap (see map). The white freckling and buff underparts distinguish it from the Steenbok. Although larger and distinct in other ways, it could possibly be confused with Suni where ranges overlap.

Description: Small, stoutly built antelope with reddish-brown upperparts liberally flecked with white hairs. Incidence of white hairs diminishes down sides and legs. Underparts are buff-white, and area around mouth and eyes is off-white. Only the ram has the short, sharp, slightly back-angled horns. 'False hoofs' are normally absent (see Cape Grysbok).
Distribution: Restricted to the north-eastern parts of southern Africa, and then northwards into Malaŵi, Zambia, Tanzania and southern Zaïre.
Habitat: Sharpe's Grysbok requires good vegetation cover, preferring low thicket with adjacent open patches of grass. It is also found on vegetated rocky hills and in the scrub at their base.
Behaviour: Sharpe's Grysbok is almost entirely nocturnal but can be seen in the coolness of the early morning and late afternoon. Although usually seen singly it is possible that a pair may live in loose association within a home range. The rams are probably territorial. Because of its largely nocturnal activity and secretive nature very little is known about this small antelope.
Food: Mostly browse but also grass. It will take fruits, berries and pods.
Reproduction: Lambs may be dropped at any time of the year but more are probably born during the wet summer months than in any other season. A single lamb is born after a gestation period of approximately 200 days.

Cape Grysbok ewe

Cape Grysbok ram

Sharpe's Grysbok ram

Sharpe's Grysbok ewe

Red Duiker *Cephalophus natalensis*
Shoulder height 43 cm; tail 11 cm; mass 14 kg.
Average horn length 6 cm; record horn length 10,1 cm.
Identification pointers: Uniform rich reddish-brown coat; small size; black-and-white tipped tail and prominent crest on top of head. Lacks the white flecking of either Sharpe's Grysbok or Suni. Walks with 'hunch-back' gait.

Description: This is a small, thickset antelope with relatively short legs. The general colour is rich reddish-brown, with the underparts being slightly paler. The chin and throat are paler than the rest of the body. Although short, the tail is the same colour as the body at the base, with a well-developed tuft of mixed black and white hairs. A long crest is present on the top of the head and this sometimes obscures the short horns. Both sexes have horns which slope backwards at the same angle as the face.
Distribution: Occurs along the eastern coastal plain with an isolated population in the Soutpansberg Mountains of the northern Transvaal. It occurs as far north as southern Sudan and Somalia.
Habitat: Forest and dense woodland with permanent water.
Behaviour: Because of the dense habitat which it favours and its secretive nature little is known about this duiker's behaviour. It is usually solitary but it seems probable that a pair may live in loose association within the same home range. The dung pellets are deposited in specific areas and there are often many small piles of currant-sized pellets at these sites.
Food: They are browsers, taking leaves, shoots, fruits and berries.
Reproduction: Fawns are probably dropped at any time of the year but with a birth-peak during the summer months.

Blue Duiker *Philantomba monticola*
Shoulder height 35 cm; tail 8 cm; mass 4 kg.
Average horn length 3 cm; record horn length 5,72 cm.
Identification pointers: Smallest southern African antelope; grey to brown colouration with blue-grey sheen. Short horns in both sexes. Skulking nature.

Description: The Blue Duiker is the smallest antelope occurring in southern Africa. The upperparts vary from slate-grey to dark brown with a grey-blue sheen and the underparts are white or off-white. A constantly wagging tail is characteristic of this duiker. The tail is quite long, bushy and black, bordered with white. Short horns are present in both sexes but these are often hidden by the crest of hair on top of the head.
Distribution: Apart from a population in Mozambique and eastern Zimbabwe, the Blue Duiker is only found in the subregion in a narrow belt along the coast from George in the Cape Province to Zululand. It occurs widely in central and equatorial Africa and patchily in East Africa.
Habitat: Blue Duiker are confined to forests and dense stands of bush. They utilize open glades when feeding. Water is an essential habitat requirement.
Behaviour: It usually occurs singly, or in pairs during courtship. It is very timid and is rarely seen, its dung-pellet heaps usually being the only indication of its presence. The level of disturbance probably influences times of activity but it is known to feed both at night and during the day. It uses regular pathways to feeding- and drinking-sites.
Food: It is a browser and includes fruits and berries in its diet.
Reproduction: The young are born throughout the year with a possible peak in the summer months. A single lamb weighing approximately 400 g is born after a gestation period of about 165 days.

Red Duiker ewe

Blue Duiker ewe

Red Duiker ewe showing facial gland

Blue Duiker ram showing facial gland

Common Duiker *Sylvicapra grimmia*
Shoulder height 50 cm; tail 12 cm; mass 18 kg (ram), 21 kg (ewe).
Average horn length 11 cm; record horn length (Transvaal) 18,1 cm.
Identification pointers: Crest of long hair usually present on top of head;
uniform grey-brownish colouring of upperparts and paler underparts;
usually black blaze (vertical stripe) on face; fairly short tail – black above
and white below. Ears are long and somewhat narrow.

Description: Uniform grey-brown to reddish-yellow upperparts and paler
(sometimes white) underparts. Black blaze of variable length on face. Short
tail black above and white below. Front surfaces of slender forelegs are dark
brown or black. On top of head there is usually a crest of long hair. Ram has
well-ringed, sharp-pointed horns.
Distribution: Found throughout subregion.
Habitat: Wide range of habitats but prefers scrub and bush-covered country.
Behaviour: Usually single but sometimes pairs. Active in early morning and
late afternoon but also at night. Lies low when disturbed but on too-close
approach takes off at a fast zigzag run.
Food: Wide variety of browse species; also agricultural crops.
Reproduction: Single 1,6-kg lamb may be born in any month.

Deer Family Cervidae

European Fallow Deer *Cervus dama* (Introduced)
Shoulder height 90 cm; mass (male) 95 kg.
Identification pointers: Males carry branched antlers for much of the
year; distinctive white spotting. Restricted to enclosed farms.

Description: Variable in colour and patterning, with summer coat being rich
yellowish-fawn above, spotted boldly in white. White stripe along each flank.
Underside of tail and surrounding areas conspicuously white. Underparts and
inner leg areas are pale. Winter coat duller and hair longer. Males carry
antlers shed during midsummer months to make way for new set.
Distribution: Introduced from Europe to private farms in South Africa.
Habitat: Open woodland to scrub or grassland.
Behaviour: Adult buck establish territories during the rut and form harem
herds. Outside rut sexes are separate.
Food: Principally browse but also grass.
Reproduction: Usually single fawn born in summer, but sometimes twins.

Goats and Sheep Family Bovidae Subfamily Caprinae

Himalayan Tahr *Hemitragus jemlahicus* (Introduced)
Shoulder height 80–100 cm; mass 60–80 kg.
Identification pointers: Goat-like appearance; only found on Table
Mountain Range, Cape Town.

Description: Goat-like. It has a fairly long, shaggy coat, with a well-developed
mane in the case of adult males. The short, stout and back-curved horns are
present in both sexes, but better developed in the male.
Distribution: Table Mountain Range near Cape Town. Native to Himalayas.
Habitat: On Table Mountain it utilizes mountain fynbos.
Behaviour: Billies move in bachelor groups or singly, only joining the
nanny/young groups during the May rut.
Food: Browse and graze.
Reproduction: One kid is born in summer; gestation period 6 months.

Common Duiker ram

Common Duiker ewe

Common Duiker ewe showing crest

Fallow Deer doe

Fallow Deer buck with antlers 'in velvet'

Himalayan Tar nanny with young

WHALES AND DOLPHINS Order Cetacea

Baleen or whalebone whales Suborder Mysticeti

Eight species of baleen whales have been recorded off the coasts of southern Africa.

Rorquals or pleated whales Family Balaenopteridae

Long, slender, streamlined whales with flattened heads, pointed flippers and a small, back-curved dorsal fin set far back along body. Characterized by large number of grooves or pleats running longitudinally from throat and chest to upper abdomen.

Minke Whale *Balaenoptera acutorostrata*
Total length 9 m; mass 6–8 t.
Identification pointers: Smallest of the rorquals; white (but not always) on upper flipper surface – Humpback Whale flippers much longer and usually completely black above. Indistinct blow.

Description: This, the smallest of the rorquals, has one to three ridges running along top of head. Upperparts are dark blue-grey to almost black, with lighter-coloured whitish underparts. Flippers sometimes have a bright white patch on upper surface, and very occasionally are wholly white. Tail-flukes are rarely raised above the water. 52–60 throat grooves.
Distribution: World-wide. Infrequently off southern African coast.
Behaviour: Singly or in pairs but larger groups at feeding-grounds.
Food: Plankton and to a lesser extent fish and squid.
Reproduction: 3-m calf born after 10-month gestation period.

Bryde's Whale *Balaenoptera edeni*
Total length 12–14 m; mass 13 t.
Sei Whale *Balaenoptera borealis*
Total length 15–16 m; mass 14–16 t.
Identification pointers: Medium to large size; Bryde's Whale with three head ridges on top of head; only one in Sei Whale.

Description: Sei Whale is slender blue-black whale with white band from chin to abdomen, broadening dorsally. Throat grooves stretch back to flippers. Bryde's Whale similar but light-grey underparts. The main distinguishing character is that there are three ridges on head of Bryde's Whale from around the blow-holes to the tip of the snout, and only one (the median ridge common to most baleen whales) on the head of the Sei Whale. These whales submerge gently and their flukes and flippers do not show when they dive down from the surface. Bryde's Whale usually has around 45 throat grooves; the Sei Whale has 60 to 65.
Distribution: Sei Whale world-wide but Bryde's largely restricted to tropics and adjacent waters. Some Bryde's resident off southern African coast. Sei Whale is a deep-water species and rarely observed from land.
Behaviour: Both species are usually encountered in small pods of about five or six individuals but both may form groups numbering more than 100. Bryde's Whale is often seen close inshore.
Food: Both species feed on plankton and fish, with Bryde's Whale off the west coast, for example, taking shoaling fish such as pilchards.
Reproduction: Sei Whale calves are born around July and those of Bryde's Whale probably throughout the year. Sei Whale calves measure about 3,6 metres at birth and those of Bryde's Whale are slightly smaller.

Minke Whale: length 9 m

Bryde's Whale: length 12-14 m

Sei Whale: length 15-16 m

Fin Whale *Balaenoptera physalus*
Total length 25 m; mass 40–50 t.
Identification pointers: Large size; dark upperparts and light to white underparts with the right lower jaw being white, the left black. Rear end raised before diving but flukes not raised above water. Fin appears after the blow.

Description: Second largest living mammal. Unique colour pattern. Upperparts are dark grey and underparts lighter or white, but right lower jaw, right front baleen plates and undersides of flippers and flukes are white; left half of lower jaw is black and left-side baleen plates are bluish-grey. The asymmetrical colour pattern of the lower jaw gives it a somewhat twisted or lop-sided appearance. 50–60 throat grooves.
Distribution: World-wide. Not usually seen offshore.
Behaviour: Groups 6–15, but up to 100.
Food: Krill, fish and squid.
Reproduction: 6,5-m calf born in warmer waters during winter.

Blue Whale *Balaenoptera musculus*
Total length 25–33 m; mass 100–120 t.
Identification pointers: Massive size; blue-grey colour with lighter mottling. Diving – a smooth, even roll with no humping; the tail-flukes emerge shallowly and briefly. Fin only shows in dive.

Description: Largest mammal in world. Upperparts blue-grey mottled with light-grey spots; underparts of body and under-surface of flippers much lighter in colour. 88–94 throat grooves. Dorsal fin small and set very far back; not exposed whilst blowing but may be seen when whale dives. Flukes show briefly just above surface when diving. Blow may reach height of 12 m.
Distribution: World-wide.
Behaviour: Usually singly or in groups of 3 or 4 but up to 50 have been seen together. Southern Hemisphere populations migrate to Antarctic waters in summer to feed on krill, returning to warmer waters in the winter to breed.
Food: Various species of krill especially *Euphausia superba*.
Reproduction: 7-m, 2,5-t calf born during early winter.

Humpback Whale *Megaptera novaeangliae*
Total length 15 m; mass 35–45 t.
Identification pointers: Very long flippers – white below, and variable black or white or both above; body dark above, light to white below including flukes. Dorsal fin shows when blowing; when diving, flukes raised high above water. Often shows flippers and jumps clear of water.

Description: Humpback easily distinguishable from other rorquals because of less streamlined appearance, small dorsal fin situated further forward than in other members of this group, knobbly head and extremely long flippers which may measure up to one-third of body length. Leading edges of flippers are serrated and may be partly or entirely white. Upperparts of Humpback are dark-grey to black and underparts are usually dark although throat grooves are white. 30 or fewer throat grooves – considerably fewer than in other baleen whales.
Distribution: World-wide. Off the coast in midwinter and in spring.
Behaviour: In the Southern Hemisphere they migrate from the Antarctic feeding-grounds to overwinter and breed in tropical waters. Remain in warmer waters for a short period before moving southwards again.
Food: Although they are mainly plankton-feeders they also take fish.
Reproduction: Calves are born in tropical waters during the winter after a gestation period of almost one year. The calf at birth is about 4,5 m long and doubles in length in the first 10 months of life.

Fin Whale: length 25 m

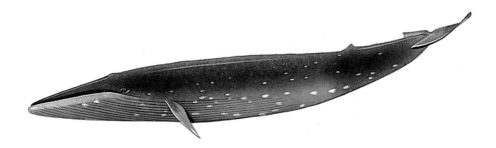

Blue Whale: length 25-33 m

Humpback Whale: length 15 m

Right whales Family Balaenidae

The right whales, of which two species occur in southern African waters, were so called because they are slow-moving and hence were easily caught by the early whalers; when killed they floated, allowing the whalers to tow carcasses to land. They were the 'right' whales to hunt. They are characterized by their large heads with arched jaw-line and smooth ungrooved throat.

Right Whale *Balaena glacialis*
Total length 14–18 m; mass 60 t.
Identification pointers: Large size; no dorsal fin; lumpy white growths on head; broad-tipped flippers; very large flukes; overall dark colour with occasional white patches on underparts; no throat grooves. Blows when much of back exposed, and when diving the flukes are clear of water. Flippers often seen. V-shaped blow. Frequently seen close inshore off south coast of Cape Province of South Africa.

Description: This is a relatively easy whale to identify and the only large whale regularly seen close inshore in southern Africa. There is no dorsal fin, there are no grooves or pleats on the throat, the flukes are large and pointed at the tips and the head is very large with a deeply arched jaw-line. The head and back are more or less on the same level. The flippers are broad-tipped. A distinguishing character is the presence of numerous white callosities on the head; the largest (the 'bonnet') is situated at the front of the snout. The overall body colour is dark grey-black with occasional white markings on the underparts.
Distribution: Circumpolar north and south of the tropics.
Behaviour: A typical pod usually consists of 6 or fewer individuals and this is usually a family unit. A regularly monitored and increasing population is frequently seen in sheltered bays off the southern and western coast of South Africa. Whales move north into southern African coastal waters from about May to October and spend the summer and autumn months in the Antarctic feeding-grounds. They will glide and roll on the surface, when the flippers and flukes are clearly visible, and not infrequently jump or 'breach' clear of the water – a sight once seen, never to be forgotten.
Food: Plankton.
Reproduction: Calves, some 6 m long, are born in southern African waters from about June to December with an August peak in sheltered bays.

Pygmy Right Whale *Caperea marginata*
Total length 6 m; mass 4–5 t.
Identification pointers: Small size and similar appearance to Right Whale but note possession of dorsal fin and absence of white head callosities. No throat grooves. When it rises to breathe, usually only the head breaks surface and then it sinks quietly back without exposing back.

Description: This is the smallest of all the baleen whales with an arch to the lower jaw like that of the Right Whale; the head, however, is comparatively small. Unlike the Right Whale, the Pygmy Right Whale possesses a dorsal fin. Again unlike the Right Whale, the flukes of this species are never raised above water; the fin is rarely seen. The overall colour is dark grey-blue, with a paler band around the neck. There are no callosities on the head.
Distribution: Circumpolar distribution south of the tropics. Rarely seen off the southern African coast.
Behaviour: Usually seen in pairs or small groups. It frequently associates with other whale species.
Food: Plankton.
Reproduction: Virtually unknown.

Right Whale: length 14-18 m

Pygmy Right Whale: length 6 m

Toothed whales and dolphins Suborder Odontoceti

Thirty species of toothed whales and dolphins have been recorded off the coasts of southern Africa.

Beaked whales Family Ziphiidae

Eight species of beaked whales have been recorded from southern African waters but most are known from very few specimens and sightings. For convenience the 8 species have been divided into two groups below.

Arnoux's Beaked Whale *Berardius arnuxii*
Total length 9 m; mass 7 t.
Southern Bottlenose Whale *Hyperoodon planifrons*
Total length 7 m; mass 3 t.
Cuvier's Beaked Whale *Ziphius cavirostris*
Total length 6 m; mass 3,5 t.
Identification pointers: Cuvier's Beaked Whale with white beak, head and back to just behind dorsal fin; head only slightly swollen. Southern Bottlenose Whale with very swollen head or 'melon'. Nothing distinctive about Arnoux's Beaked Whale, but if a stranded specimen should be encountered, note that it is our only beaked whale with two pairs of teeth in lower jaw and our only beaked whale in which the female has visible teeth.

Description: Arnoux's Beaked Whale is a medium-sized, dark-grey or black whale with paler underparts. The beak and forehead 'melon' are prominent. Both sexes have two pairs of teeth close to the tip of the lower jaw which protrudes beyond the tip of the upper jaw. The front teeth are about 8 cm long; the back ones are shorter. This species is known from a single record in southern African waters — a specimen stranded near Port Elizabeth. The Southern Bottlenose Whale is smaller than Arnoux's Beaked Whale and has a prominent beak; its bulging dome-like forehead rises vertically above the beak and is rounded on to the back. The dorsal fin is fairly prominent, situated well back and slightly curved at the tip. The colour of the upperparts is bluish-grey and the throat and belly are off-white or grey. Males have only one pair of teeth in the lower jaw; in the females the teeth do not erupt through the gums. Cuvier's Beaked Whale has a stubby beak and the domed head or 'melon' is poorly developed. This species may be separated from the other species by the fact that the snout, head and the back to just beyond the dorsal fin are white and the rest of the body is usually grey to black. The male has a single pair of teeth at the lower jaw tip, each about 7 cm long; the female's teeth do not erupt through the gums.
Distribution: Only Cuvier's Beaked Whale has a world-wide distribution, in temperate and tropical seas; it is absent from Arctic and Antarctic waters; the Southern Bottlenose Whale and Arnoux's Beaked Whale are only found in the Southern Hemisphere south of the Tropic of Capricorn.
Behaviour: Cuvier's Beaked Whale is an animal of deep waters and is usually seen alone or in small groups of 2 to 7. Also a deep-water whale, Arnoux's Beaked Whale is usually solitary although 2 to 3 individuals may on occasion be seen together.
Food: Arnoux's Beaked Whale and the Southern Bottlenose Whale feed predominantly on squid and cuttlefish but Cuvier's Beaked Whale also takes fish, crabs and starfish.
Reproduction: Calves of the Southern Bottlenose Whale and Cuvier's Beaked Whale are apparently born in the summer months.

Armoux's Beaked Whale: length 9 m

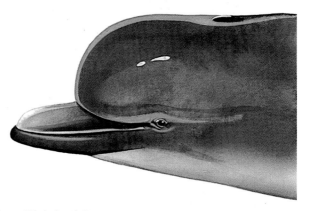

Southern Bottlenose Whale: length 7 m

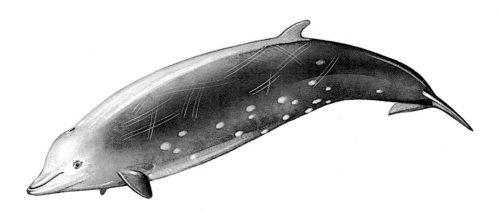

Cuvier's Beaked Whale: length 6 m

Blainville's Beaked Whale *Mesoplodon densirostris*
Total length 4,7 m; mass 1 t.
Gray's Beaked Whale *Mesoplodon grayi*
Total length 5,6 m; mass 1 t.
Hector's Beaked Whale *Mesoplodon hectori*
Total length 4 m; mass 1 t.
Layard's Beaked Whale *Mesoplodon layardii*
Total length 6 m; mass 1,5 t.
True's Beaked Whale *Mesoplodon mirus*
Total length 5 m; mass 1 t.
Identification pointers: See descriptions for specific pointers.

Description: All five southern African species in the genus *Mesoplodon* are very difficult to identify in the field. This is compounded by there being considerable variation in body colour within any one species. Only examination of the teeth of the males can ensure positive identification; like most beaked whales, female *Mesoplodon* whales lack visible teeth. The species most likely to be seen in southern African waters is Blainville's Beaked Whale; the male of this species can be identified by a massive upward extension of each side of the lower jaw. One tooth is situated about midway along each jaw, at the apex of the extended portion but although each tooth is about 10 cm long, only a small portion is visible above the jaw. Gray's Beaked Whale is usually dark grey above and whitish or light grey below; its head is almost flat on top and is not markedly swollen. Hector's Beaked Whale is only sketchily known from 6 or 7 skulls and incomplete specimens world-wide. Layard's Beaked Whale is blackish above but there is a grey area from the distinct (but not large) 'melon' to a point half-way along the back. The underparts are also black but the front half of the beak, the throat, and a patch around the genital area are white. The male is clearly identified by the two, 6-cm-broad, curved, tusk-like teeth, one to each lower jaw, which protrude from the jaw and curve over the top of the beak; these teeth apparently prevent the mouth from opening more than a few centimetres. True's Beaked Whale has a smallish but clearly bulbous 'melon' and its single pair of small teeth is situated at the tip of the lower jaw. It has a distinctive colour pattern, being blackish overall but white on the lower jaw, around the genital area and on the posterior section of both upperparts (including the dorsal fin) and underparts (including the underside of the tail-flukes). The edges of the jaw and throat are speckled with blackish on a light-grey background.
Distribution: Gray's and Layard's Beaked Whales are confined to the seas of the Southern Hemisphere south of the Tropic of Capricorn. Although little is known of Hector's Beaked Whale, it appears to have a circumpolar distribution in the colder waters of the Southern Hemisphere. True's and Blainville's Beaked Whales both occur in the Northern and the Southern Hemisphere, but Blainville's appears to prefer tropical waters while True's Beaked Whale is found in subtropical and temperate waters.
Behaviour: Although available information is scanty, True's Beaked Whale is thought to occur in pairs or as a cow with calf; Blainville's Beaked Whale is normally seen in groups of from 3 to 6 and Gray's Beaked Whale in groups of 6 or more. All species are usually associated with deeper waters.
Food: Squid appears to be the principal food but fish is included in the diet of at least Blainville's Beaked Whale.
Reproduction: Very little known.

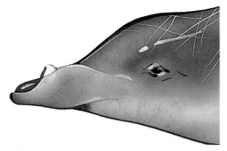

Blainville's Beaked Whale: length 4,7 m

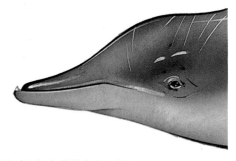

Hector's Beaked Whale: length 4 m

Gray's Beaked Whale: length 5,6 m

Layard's Beaked Whale: length 6 m

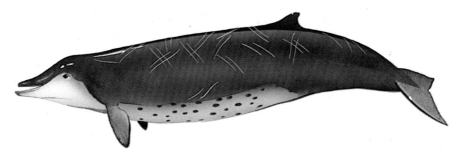

True's Beaked Whale: length 5 m

Sperm whales Family Physeteridae

All three members of this family have been recorded from southern African waters. Characterized by having square heads and by the possession of teeth on the lower, but not the upper jaw. They derive their name from the large spermaceti organ situated in a depression in the upper part of the front of the skull. Spermaceti wax is believed to assist in the regulation of buoyancy in deep diving and may also focus sound used in echolocation.

Pygmy Sperm Whale *Kogia breviceps*
Total length 4 m; mass 500 kg.
Dwarf Sperm Whale *Kogia simus*
Total length 2,6 m; mass 350 kg.
Identification pointers: Difficult to tell apart but head shape and body size should separate them from any other species. 'False gill' marking of Pygmy Sperm Whale is characteristic as is the mid-back placement of the larger dorsal fin of the Dwarf Sperm Whale.

Description: Species similar in appearance but differ considerably in size. Snout area swollen and projects beyond lower jaw, a feature which gives these two small whales a somewhat shark-like appearance. Dorsal fin of Dwarf Sperm Whale is large and situated half-way down the back, whereas that of the Pygmy Sperm Whale is smaller and situated further down the back. Both dark grey above and white to pinkish-white or light grey below. White 'false gill' marking is often present on head of Pygmy Sperm Whale.
Distribution: Both species have an extensive distribution within the tropics, but extend into the temperate seas of both N. and S. Hemispheres.
Behaviour: Both species may be seen singly or in small groups, the Dwarf Sperm Whale in schools of up to 10 individuals.
Food: Principally squid, fish and crabs.
Reproduction: Little known; gestation period may be 9–11 months.

Sperm Whale *Physeter macrocephalus*
Total length 15 m; mass (males) 40 t.
Identification pointers: Cannot be mistaken for any other species. Large size; high, blunt snout; dorsal hump instead of fin; forward blow.

Description: Unmistakable profile, with enormous square head, blunt snout and relatively small, undershot jaw. Head occupies nearly one third of total length and contains vast spermaceti organ. No true dorsal fin but there is a distinct dorsal hump about two-thirds of way along back and behind this in male is usually a line of four to five smaller humps. Flippers short and stubby; tail-flukes broad and powerful. Skin of body carries series of longitudinal corrugations and upperparts are dark grey-blue to black; underparts are paler. Skin around lips is usually white, with occasional white patches on the body. Blow-hole is at tip of front of head and is angled forward, giving a characteristic blow at an angle of approximately 45°. Sperm Whales may on occasion breach or leap from the water.
Distribution: World-wide.
Behaviour: Sperm Whales descend to great depths to feed and stay down for lengthy periods. Accurate sonar tracking has shown that they can certainly reach 1 200 m and long dives of between 1 and 2 hours are on record. Adult bulls hold harems, forming groups of 20 to 30 individuals. The species is not currently under threat of extinction: one estimate puts the Southern Hemisphere stocks of Sperm Whales at some 350 000.
Food: Mostly squid, but also fish.
Reproduction: Calves are born in subregion November-June with a peak in February and March. After a gestation period of almost 15 months a calf measuring about 4 metres and weighing some 800 kg is born.

Pygmy Sperm Whale: length 4 m

Dwarf Sperm Whale: length 2,6 m

Sperm Whale: length 15 m

Dolphins, pilot whales, killer and false killer whales
Family Delphinidae

This is a diverse group of small whales and dolphins, of which 19 species have been recorded in southern African waters.

They can be divided into four main groups on the basis of their general appearance, *viz.*:

1. no dorsal fin; beak present (1 species)
2. blunt or rounded heads; beak absent; dorsal fin present (7 species)
3. beak present, but very short; dorsal fin present (3 species)
4. long beak; dorsal fin present (8 species)

1. No dorsal fin; beak present

Southern Right Whale Dolphin *Lissodelphis peronii*
Total length 2 m; mass 60 kg.
Identification pointers: Small size; only dolphin with no dorsal fin; black above and white below; white beak, forehead, flippers and underside of tail-flukes.

Description: This small dolphin is unique in that it has no dorsal fin, and the back curves smoothly from the tip of the nose to the tail. It is further characterized by having a black dorsal surface and white underparts, with a clear dividing line between these colours along the side. The white colouration is continuous from the underside of the tail-flukes along the belly and flanks on to the flippers, throat and beak; it extends over the whole beak on to the forehead.
Distribution: Tropic of Capricorn south to about 50° S.
Behaviour: This is usually a deep-sea species but it occasionally comes close inshore. Normally school size varies from about 20 to 100 but over 1 000 have been observed together. Poorly known.
Food: Fish and squid.
Reproduction: Unknown.

2. Blunt or rounded heads; beak absent; dorsal fin present

Killer Whale *Orcinus orca*
Male: total length 7,5 m; mass (up to) 8 t. Female: total length 5,5 m; mass 3 t.
Identification pointers: Large size; very prominent fin; distinctive black and white markings; characteristic white oval patch behind eye; blunt, rounded head.

Description: This species is unmistakable with its large size, heavy build, blunt, rounded head, large paddle-like flippers, bold black-and-white colouration and very tall dorsal fin. The fin of the male may be up to 2 m in height and is erect and sometimes forward-pointing, while the female fin is smaller, and more shark-like in form. They are jet-black above, and white below from the chin to the vicinity of the anus and sometimes beyond. A short 'arm' of white extends from the ventral area on to the side in an angle towards but not reaching the tail. There is a characteristic oval white spot just above, and stretching a short way back from the eye. A greyish patch or 'saddle' is usually present on the back behind the fin.
Distribution: World-wide.
Behaviour: Usually encountered in pods of from 3 to 30 individuals; they hunt in packs, hence the name 'wolves of the sea'.
Food: Wide variety of vertebrate food, including fish, birds, seals, dolphins and even large whales. Only cetacean to prey on warm-blooded species.
Reproduction: Gestation period 12 months. At birth measure 2,1 m to 2,7 m.

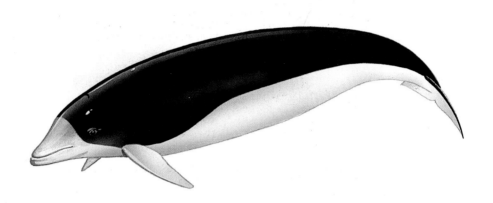

Southern Right Whale Dolphin: length 2 m

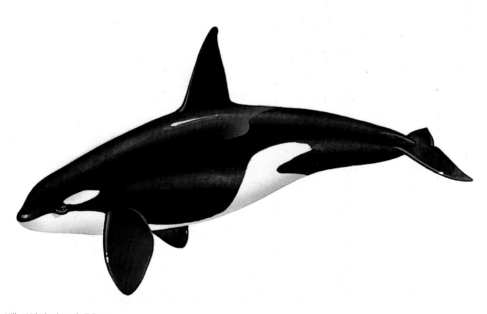

Killer Whale: length 7,5 m

False Killer Whale *Pseudorca crassidens*
Male: total length 5,8 m; mass 2 t. Female: total length 4,6 m;
mass 1,2 t.
Identification pointers: Dark and slender; dark grey to black with no
distinctive markings or white scars from interspecific fighting (see
Risso's Dolphin, page 242); prominent, centrally situated dorsal fin;
flippers pointed, narrow with 'elbow'. At distance could be mistaken for
Killer Whale, pilot whaleś, Pygmy Killer Whale or Melon-headed Whale –
but all of these have distinctive white or pale markings. For further
differences see species accounts. The False Killer Whale is the largest
species likely to be seen sporting in bow-waves of ships.

Description: This is a long and slender species with a slightly rounded head;
the upper jaw projects slightly over the mouth. The flippers are pointed and
narrow with a distinct bend or 'elbow'. The dorsal fin is situated at about
mid-back and is prominent, narrow and strongly curved; it is never as
strongly developed as in the Killer Whale. The overall colour is dark grey to
black with a narrow grey blaze ventrally. The common name is presumably
derived from the fact that these whales have a wide gape and well-developed
teeth.
Distribution: False Killer Whales are found world-wide in all tropical and
temperate seas.
Behaviour: They usually travel in small family pods but several such pods
may come together to form larger groups. This species appears to be prone
to stranding; the first recorded stranding in southern Africa was of 108
individuals on the beach at Kommetjie near Cape Town in 1928. Amongst
other strandings, 58 died at St. Helena Bay north of Cape Town in 1936 and
a further 65 stranded and died on *exactly* the same 1 500-metre stretch of
beach in 1981.
Food: Squid or fish.
Reproduction: Apparently young can be born at any time of the year but this
aspect of their biology is poorly known.

Pygmy Killer Whale *Feresa attenuata*
Total length 2,4 m; mass 170 kg.
Identification pointers: Much smaller than either the Killer or False Killer
Whale; rounded head with white lips and chin patch; could be confused
with Melon-headed Whale but the latter species has its head curved into
'parrot beak' and the white of its lips does not extend on to chin.

Description: The Pygmy Killer Whale has a slender tapered body, with a
compressed, narrow and rounded head. The dorsal fin is long, pointed and
the tip is curved towards the tail. The flippers are relatively short and rounded
at the tip. Much of the body is black, although the sides may have a greyish
tinge, and a pale-grey anchor-shaped blaze is situated between the flippers.
There is a large white anal patch and this may stretch almost back to the tail.
They have white lips and a white patch at the tip of the chin as an extension
of the white on the lips.
Distribution: Found in warmer waters world-wide.
Behaviour: This species hunts in groups of from about 10 to 50 individuals. It
rarely moves close inshore and is essentially a species of the open sea.
Food: Fish and squid.
Reproduction: Poorly known.

False Killer Whale: length 5,8 m

Pygmy Killer Whale: length 2,4 m

Short-finned Pilot Whale *Globicephala macrorhynchus*
Total length 6 m; mass 1,5–3 t.
Long-finned Pilot Whale *Globicephala melaena*
Total length 5 m; mass 2–4 t.
Identification pointers: Prominent fin, slightly forward of mid-body; rounded head with prominent 'melon'; dark or black dorsal surface and sides with grey patch behind dorsal fin of Long-finned Pilot Whale. White anchor-shaped blaze along belly of Long-finned; dark-grey anchor-shaped blaze in Short-finned. Distinguished from False Killer Whale by that species' more tapered head, narrow, more pointed fin and all-black back. The False Killer Whale frequently sports in bow- and stern-waves of boats but this is extremely rare in the case of the pilot whales. Short-finned Pilot Whale is most likely to be seen off the east coast of subregion; Long-finned Pilot Whale off the west coast.

Description: Difficult to tell apart. They are long, thin and rather cylindrical with blunt, rounded and bulbous heads; this 'melon' is usually better developed in old males. Head of Short-finned more prominent and rounded than that of Long-finned. Flipper form is characteristic: in Long-finned they are long (18–27% of body length) and pointed with distinct bend or 'elbow'; in Short-finned they are short (15–18% of body length) and lack 'elbow'. Prominent and back-curved dorsal fin of both is set slightly forward of body midpoint. Upperparts of both dark grey or black but there is distinct pale-grey patch situated behind dorsal fin in Long-finned. White anchor-shaped blaze runs from throat to belly in Long-finned; Short-finned dark-grey anchor-shaped blaze is only on belly, from between flippers to anal region.
Distribution: Short-finned world-wide in warmer waters. Long-finned has two populations, one south of Tropic of Capricorn and other in North Atlantic.
Behaviour: Both species come together in large schools, but groups may vary in size from fewer than ten to several hundreds. In the case of the Long-finned Pilot Whale several thousands have been observed together.
Food: Predominantly squid, but also fish.
Reproduction: Gestation lasts about 16 months in both species.

Melon-headed Whale *Peponocephala electra*
Total length 2,7 m; mass 180 kg.
Identification pointers: Fairly slender with prominent centrally situated fin; overall dark uppersides and flanks without markings; rounded head; white lips but no white chin patch as found in the fairly similar Pygmy Killer Whale. Presumably very rare in southern African waters.

Description: This is a fairly long and slender whale which superficially resembles the Long-finned Pilot Whale; despite the implication of its common name, however, the swelling on the head is not as pronounced as that of the pilot whales, the head more closely resembling that of the False Killer Whale. The front of the head has a 'parrot-beak' appearance. The fin is prominent, about 25 cm high, and strongly curved and set more or less in mid-back. The overall body colour is dark grey to black, with a white or pale grey ventral anchor-shaped patch between the flippers and throat and a lighter coloured patch around the anal and genital area. The lips are white but there is no white chin patch as in the Pygmy Killer Whale.
Distribution: World-wide in warm waters. Only once stranded on South African coast.
Behaviour: Very little is known but schools of from 20 to several hundred have been recorded.
Food: Probably squid and fish.
Reproduction: Calves in the Southern Hemisphere are born between August and December after a gestation period of about 12 months.

Short-finned Pilot Whale: length 6 m

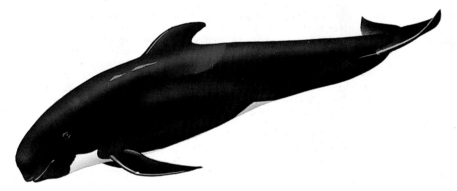

Long-finned Pilot Whale: length 5 m

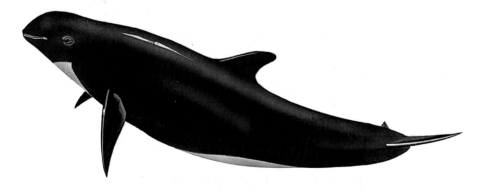

Melon-headed Whale: length 2,7 m

Risso's Dolphin *Grampus griseus*
Total length 4 m; mass 400 kg.
Identification pointers: Usually overall grey with darker appendages; numerous fine white scratch-marks – thus differs from False Killer Whale which never has these scratches, and from the pilot whales which rarely carry obvious scratch-marks. Prominent crease running from blow-hole to upper lip. Teeth only on lower jaw – only member of the dolphin family Delphinidae without teeth on upper jaw.

Description: Risso's Dolphin is similar in appearance to the pilot whales. It is robustly built in front of the tall, thin, back-pointing fin situated in mid-back, but behind the fin the body tapers and narrows rapidly towards the tail. There is no beak and the head bulges slightly. This species can be easily identified at close range as it is the only species with a deep crease down the centre of the head from the blow-hole to the upper lip. The flippers are fairly long (but shorter than in the pilot whales) and pointed and the flukes are broad and deeply notched. This dolphin is dark grey above and pale grey below, with dark-grey flippers, dorsal fin and tail-flukes. With increasing age the body may become paler, to become almost white on the belly, face and anterior portion of the back. The fin, flukes and flippers retain their dark colour with age. There is, however, considerable variation in overall colour. Risso's Dolphin is usually criss-crossed with numerous fine white lines produced by the teeth of other members of this species during fights, and perhaps also by squids.
Distribution: This species is found world-wide but avoids colder waters.
Behaviour: Between 3 and 30 individuals make up the normal school but larger groups have been observed.
Food: Squid.
Reproduction: Calves are apparently born during the summer months after a gestation period of about 12 months. They have a length at birth of 1,5 m.

3. Beak present, but very short; dorsal fin present

Three species occurring in southern African waters have short but clearly visible beaks: they are Heaviside's Dolphin, the Dusky Dolphin and Fraser's Dolphin.

Heaviside's Dolphin *Cephalorhynchus heavisidii*
Total length 1,3 m; mass 40 kg.
Identification pointers: Small size; distinctive black-and-white markings; flattened, broad head; stocky body. Only likely to be seen off the west coast of southern Africa. Should not be confused with any other species.

Description: Heaviside's Dolphin is easily distinguishable from the other two dolphins with short beaks because of its small size and stocky appearance. In addition it has black upperparts which contrast with white areas on the lower throat, chest and abdomen, with white extending from the throat towards the eye, and from above the flipper towards the eye. Another broad white band extends from the abdomen in a shallow sweep across the flank back towards the tail to a round-ended point just beyond the back line of the fin. The fin is broad-based and triangular. The head is broad and flat, without a real beak, although from a distance the flattened head could appear to have such an extension.
Distribution: Apparently restricted to the cold waters of the Benguela Current off the west coast of southern Africa.
Behaviour: Little known, but it is said to form small schools only.
Food: Squid and bottom-dwelling fish.
Reproduction: Unknown.

Risso's Dolphin: length 4 m

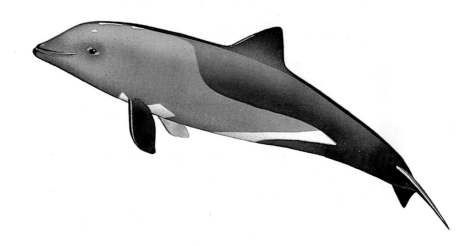

Heaviside's Dolphin: length 1,3 m

Fraser's Dolphin *Lagenodelphis hosei*
Total length 2,6 m; mass 90 kg.
Dusky Dolphin *Lagenorhynchus obscurus*
Total length 2,1 m; mass 115 kg.
Identification pointers: Fraser's Dolphin – dark above, white below and both separated by two stripes, a lighter upper stripe broadening over upper hindquarters and a darker lower stripe from corner of mouth and through eye to anus. Dusky Dolphin – dark above, whitish below and grey along flanks with two dark blazes from black upperparts extending into the grey in broad backward and downward-pointing sweeps. Fin has pale concave edge behind. Both species have short beaks. Both species rare in southern African waters.

Description: Both species have definite but very short beaks. They have a typically dolphin appearance but the flippers and fin of Fraser's Dolphin are shorter than those of the Dusky Dolphin. Fraser's Dolphin is dark grey-blue above (from head to three-quarters along the back beyond the fin) and pinkish-white below, with two parallel stripes along the length of the body creating a boundary between the dark upper- and light underparts. The upper stripe is pale grey to cream and runs from above and in front of the eye along the side to below the fin where it widens over the upperparts behind the fin as a light-grey area extending to the tail. The more prominent lower stripe is black or dark grey and runs from the beak through the eye along the flank to the anus. The throat, chin and the rest of the underparts are white. The edge and tip of the lower jaw are usually black. The Dusky Dolphin has dark-grey to black upperparts, flippers and flukes, the fin having a light-grey to white margin to its trailing edge. The underparts are white and between the upper- and underparts there is a broad band of light grey along the flanks. Intruding into the grey of the flanks are two backward-pointing blazes of blackish colouration extending downwards from the blackish upperparts. No other species should be confused with the Dusky Dolphin.
Distribution: The Dusky Dolphin has a circumpolar distribution south of the Tropic of Capricorn. Fraser's Dolphin is apparently restricted to tropical waters on both sides of the equator.
Behaviour: Both species are usually observed in small groups but Fraser's Dolphin has been recorded in schools of up to 500 and the Dusky Dolphin as many as 300. It is probable that these large groups are temporary. The Dusky Dolphin is more coastal than Fraser's Dolphin and often accompanies ships and rides the bow waves.
Food: Both species feed on squid and fish.
Reproduction: The calves of the Dusky Dolphin are apparently unusually small and are born after a gestation period of about 9 months. Other than this nothing is on record for the two species.

4. Long-beaked dolphins; dorsal fin present

Humpback Dolphin *Sousa plumbea*
Total length 2,8 m; mass 280 kg.
Identification pointers: Long dorsal hump supporting prominent fin.

Description: Easily distinguished from other long-beaked dolphins by long thickened ridge along middle of back, supporting long, pointed dorsal fin. Dark-grey to black upperparts fade gradually to off-white underparts.
Distribution: Largely restricted to coastal areas of Indian Ocean and extreme western Pacific Ocean. Unlikely to be seen west of Gouritz River in southern Cape.
Behaviour: School size 1–30 (average 7); shallow coastal waters.
Food: Fish, mostly from reefs near rocky coastlines.
Reproduction: Calves at any time of year but peak in summer.

Fraser's Dolphin: length 2,6 m

Dusky Dolphin: length 2,1 m

Humpback Dolphin: length 2,8 m

Spotted Dolphin *Stenella attenuata*
Total length 2,3 m; mass 100 kg.
Identification pointers: Long dark beak with white lips; dark-grey body spotted with white.

Description: Robust, prominent, curved dorsal fin, prominent long flippers, and marked ventral keel towards end of tail-stock. Dark slate-grey above, paler to pinkish below; fin, flippers and flukes are dark. Blackish circle around eye connected to blackish line around beak base, extending further as dark band from jaw to flipper. Beak black with pink or white lips. Numerous white spots on body, particularly on sides and underparts posterior to genital aperture. Young animals have few or no spots.
Distribution: World-wide in the tropics; in subregion only likely to be seen off east coast from Natal northwards.
Behaviour: Large schools (100 +). Surface-feeder.
Food: Squid and fish.
Reproduction: 11-month gestation period. One new-born calf stranded in Natal in November.

Striped Dolphin *Stenella coeruleoalba*
Total length 2,3 m; mass 130 kg.
Identification pointers: Distinctive light and dark longitudinal striping. Stripes appear to commence around eye and diverge from each other posteriorly.

Description: Upperparts usually dark greyish-blue, with or without a brownish tinge; on death darkens to deep blue. White underparts. Black stripe from eye along side to anus and another dark stripe from eye to flipper. V-shaped lighter band runs above main side stripe, its shorter upper arm running towards fin and longer lower arm extending to tail.
Distribution: World-wide from southern continental tips northwards to Northern Hemisphere. Most likely to be encountered off the southern and eastern coastal areas of southern Africa although generally in deeper waters and not considered to be a coastal dolphin.
Behaviour: Large schools (100 +). Surface-feeder.
Food: Squid, fish and crustaceans (crabs, lobsters and shrimps).
Reproduction: Gestation period around 12 months. Cows calve at 3-year intervals.

Long-snouted Dolphin *Stenella longirostris*
Total length 2,1 m; mass 75 kg.
Identification pointers: Habit of 'spinning' while jumping out of water.

Description: Very long rostrum or beak and long, pointed flippers. Upperparts dark grey-brown with pale-grey to white underparts, spotted with small darker areas. Difficult to identify on appearance but its striking behaviour is diagnostic: individuals from its large schools periodically hurl themselves into air, twisting and spinning their bodies along longitudinal axis – thus often called 'Spinner Dolphin'.
Distribution: World-wide in tropical waters. Very few records off southern Africa.
Behaviour: Schools of 30 to several hundreds. Deep-water feeder.
Food: Predominantly squid.
Reproduction: New-born calves less than 1 m long. Calving interval just over 2 years.

Spotted Dolphin: length 2,3 m

Striped Dolphin: length 2,3 m

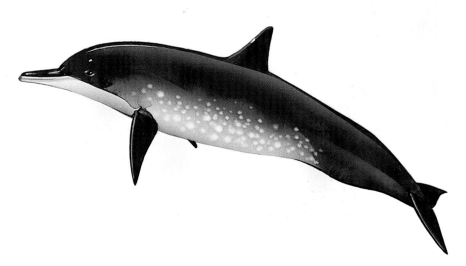

Long-snouted Dolphin: length 2,1 m

Indian Ocean Bottlenosed Dolphin *Tursiops aduncus*
Total length 2,4 m; mass 120–190 kg.
Identification pointers: Dark grey and plain coloured. No distinctive
identifying features.

Description: Robust with tall, curved fin and medium-length beak wide and
rounded at tip. Lower jaw projects slightly beyond upper jaw. Usually
dark-grey back with paler grey sides and ventral area. Thin pale line usually
runs from eye to flipper.
Distribution: Coastal waters of Indian Ocean to China and Australia.
Behaviour: Large schools of several hundreds. Inshore and deep sea.
Food: Fish and squid.
Reproduction: Gestation 12 months; new-born calves about 1 m long.
Note: Some scientists believe Indian Ocean and Atlantic Ocean Bottlenosed
Dolphins are the same species.

Atlantic Ocean Bottlenosed Dolphin *Tursiops truncatus*
Total length 3,2 m; mass 200 kg.
Identification pointers: Dark grey and plain coloured. No distinctive
identifying features.

Description: As for Indian Ocean Bottlenosed Dolphin above.
Distribution: North Sea, Mediterranean Sea, North and South Atlantic.
Behaviour: Large schools of several hundreds. Inshore and deep sea.
Food: Fish and squid.
Reproduction: Gestation period 12 months; calving interval perhaps 2 years.

Common Dolphin *Delphinus delphis*
Total length 2,5 m; mass 150 kg.
Identification pointers: Clear 'figure-of-eight' or 'hour-glass' pattern
along flanks.

Description: Sleek and streamlined; pointed flippers and a prominent
back-curved fin. Rostrum or beak is long. Dark grey to brown-black above
and pale grey below. Characterized by having elongated 'figure-of-eight' or
'hour-glass' pattern on each side, from eye to tail-flukes. Colouring of
'hour-glass' variable but section from eye to mid-body is commonly
brown-grey (occasionally tinged yellow), while hind section usually pale grey.
Thin black line from corner of mouth to flipper.
Distribution: World-wide in tropical and warm temperate waters. In subregion
most frequently seen off south and east coasts.
Behaviour: Usually in schools of about 20 but can be several hundreds or
even thousands. Usually feed in deeper waters.
Food: Squid; cuttlefish; small schooling fish.
Reproduction: New-born calves around 85 cm long.

Rough-toothed Dolphin *Steno bredanensis*
Total length 2,4 m; mass 140 kg.
Identification pointers: Dark above; white throat and belly; flanks
blotched with pinkish-white.

Description: Centrally placed sickle-shaped fin. Dark purplish-grey above with
white throat and belly as far as genital area. Dark flanks blotched with
pinkish-white.
Distribution: Only one record from southern Africa. Found world-wide in the
deep waters of tropical, subtropical and warm temperate seas.

Bottlenosed Dolphin (both species): length 2,4-3,2 m

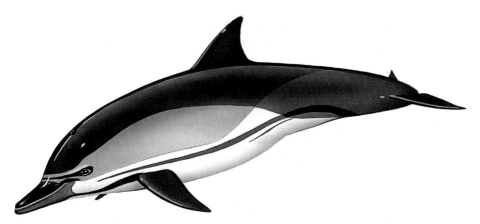

Common Dolphin: length 2,5 m

Rough-toothed Dolphin: length 2,4 m

DUGONG Order Sirenia Family Dugongidae

Dugong *Dugong dugon*
Total length 2,5–3 m; mass 350–500 kg.
Identification pointers: Cigar-shaped body; possesses flippers and tail flukes. Completely aquatic; found only in shallow waters.

Description: Entirely aquatic, never coming on land. Forelimbs are paddle-like flippers; no hindlimbs. Large, fleshy, boneless tail flattened horizontally like tail-flukes of dolphin. Skin greyish-brown with sparsely scattered bristles; upperparts slightly darker than underparts. Front of mouth and lower lip covered with short, thick bristles.
Distribution: In subregion restricted to sheltered areas along southern Mozambique coast but stragglers occasionally seen in northern Natal.
Habitat: Shallow, sheltered waters close to the coastline. (See 'Food').
Behaviour: Although they are usually seen singly, in pairs or in family parties, groups of up to 30 have been recorded in southern Africa. They are slow swimmers (2 knots) but can achieve speeds of up to 5 knots to escape danger; they are able to remain submerged for over 5 minutes although the average dive lasts for just over a minute.
Food: Several species of sea-grass in sheltered shallow bays and lagoons.
Reproduction: Single young (rarely twins) born November – January.

SEALS Order Pinnipedia

Fur seals Family Otariidae

Only two species of fur seal have been recorded from southern African waters, one as a permanent resident and the other as a rare vagrant. A third species, the Antarctic Fur Seal (*Arctocephalus gazella*), is recorded from islands that fall under South African jurisdiction (*viz.* the Prince Edward Islands) but has never been recorded from coastal waters off the mainland.

Cape Fur Seal *Arctocephalus pusillus*
Male: Length 2,2 m; mass 190 kg. Female: length 1,6 m; mass 75 kg.
Identification pointers: Large size; only seal likely to be encountered in southern African waters, along west coast and about as far east along south coast as East London. Males lack crest on top of head found in Sub-Antarctic Fur Seal.

Description: Males much larger than females (up to 300 kg in summer), with powerfully developed necks. When moving on land hindlimbs are brought forward to support some of body mass and forelimbs bend out and slightly backwards. Dark brown to golden brown but tend to be darker. Coarse outer hair of bulls may be greyish-black with a tinge of brown. Females tend to be more brownish-grey. New-born pups have black velvety coat.
Distribution: Offshore islands and along parts of the mainland of the western and southern coastline to Port Elizabeth but rarely as far as East London.
Behaviour and Reproduction: Within southern African waters there are estimated to be over one million fur seals in some 23 breeding colonies. In mid-October mature bulls move to the breeding sites to establish territories and these are actively defended against rival bulls. The cows arrive several weeks later to give birth. A territorial bull establishes a harem of several cows. Mating takes place about 5 or 6 days after the cow has given birth. The territories and harems break up before the end of December.
Food: Shoaling fish such as pilchards; other fish, squid and crustaceans.

Dugong rising for air: note open nostrils

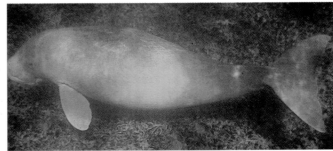

Dugong

Cape Fur Seal bull

The Cape Fur Seal has small, pointed ears

Cape Fur Seal colony

Sub-Antarctic Fur Seal *Arctocephalus tropicalis*
Male: total length 1,8 m; mass 120–165 kg. Female: total length 1,4 m; mass 50 kg.
Identification pointers: Yellow-brown face and chest lighter than rest of body and contrast with brown upperparts. Males have crest and cape of long hair on top of head – a feature not found in the Cape Fur Seal.

Description: Similar in form to the Cape Fur Seal but differs in colouring. The upperparts are variable grey-brown to brown, with the head, shoulders and flippers being darker and the face and chest being yellow-brown or creamy brown. Mature bulls have a crest and cape of long hair on the head and shoulders.
Distribution: They occur in sub-Antarctic waters and haul out on small oceanic islands such as Gough Island and the Prince Edward Islands. Vagrants occasionally haul out on the coastline of southern Africa.
Behaviour and Reproduction: This species does not breed within southern African waters. Behaviour, however, is similar to that of the Cape Fur Seal. Most pups are born in mid-December.
Food: Squid and fish seem to be equally important but crustaceans are occasionally taken.

True seals Family Phocidae

Three species of true seals have been recorded along the coastline of southern Africa, but all as rare vagrants. The Leopard Seal has only been recorded twice on the southern African mainland.

Southern Elephant Seal *Mirounga leonina*
Male: total length 4,5–6,5 m; mass 3 500 kg. Female: total length 3,0–4,0 m; mass 350–800 kg.
Identification pointers: Massive size, particularly in the case of bulls; bulls also have swollen, prominent snout.

Description: This is the largest of all living seals. The massive bulls have a short, prominent, bulbous proboscis which projects from just below the eye and hangs over the mouth. This organ can be inflated during threat displays. Fur colour is usually greyish-brown to brown but in mature males and before the moult, the fur takes on a yellowish-brown colour. Old bulls are usually heavily scarred on the head and shoulders from territorial fighting.
Distribution: This seal has a circumpolar distribution and is largely restricted to a belt of sub-Antarctic waters as far north as the southern tip of South America. Vagrants occasionally beach on the southern African coastline.
Behaviour and Reproduction: The elephant seal moults on land, remaining there throughout the duration of the moult. Adult bulls spend much of the winter at sea. In spring they haul out on island beaches for mating. Mature bulls arrive first to establish the territories in which they will keep their harems of cows. The pregnant cows haul out shortly after the bulls and the pups conceived the year before are born within about one week of their arrival. The females come on heat two to three weeks after the pups are born and are mated by their harem bull.
Food: Southern Elephant Seals feed mostly on squid and fish but some crustaceans are also taken.

Sub-Antarctic Fur Seal

Southern Elephant Seal showing proboscis

Southern Elephant Seal

Crabeater Seal *Lobodon carcinophagus*
Total length 2,3–2,7 m; mass 250 kg.
Identification pointers: Sleek, long body; usually silvery-grey but no prominent markings; distinctly serrated edge to each cheek-tooth. Rare vagrant to southern African waters.

Description: This slender and agile seal has a general body colour of silvery grey-fawn with paler underparts. Numerous brown markings are scattered on the shoulders and sides of younger animals. The flippers are darker than the rest of the body. The fur becomes creamy-white towards the moult and older animals become paler with age. The cheek-teeth have up to six cusps each and have a distinctive saw-like profile. When the jaws are closed the teeth interlock neatly and are used to sieve out the small crustaceans upon which this seal feeds.

Distribution: The Crabeater Seal is by far the most abundant seal in the world and is confined to the pack-ice zone around Antarctica. Hauls out rarely on the southern African coast.

Behaviour and Reproduction: It is estimated that there are between 30 and 50 million Crabeater Seals in Antarctica. Despite their abundance, the harsh environment in which they live makes them extremely difficult to study and therefore little is known about them. In contrast to the fur seals and elephant seals, Crabeater Seals during the breeding season associate in family pairs of mother and new-born pup, with an attendant bull waiting nearby for her to come into oestrus. The pup is born on an ice-floe between September and November. Outside the breeding season Crabeater Seals form large and small groups of both sexes.

Food: Despite their name, Crabeater Seals do not eat crabs but feed almost exclusively on krill, a small crustacean which abounds in Antarctic waters. A Crabeater Seal will swim into a krill shoal with open mouth and then close its jaws; it then forces the water out between the closely fitting teeth and the krill remain in the mouth to be swallowed.

Leopard Seal *Hydrurga leptonyx*
Male: total length 3,5 m; mass 300 kg. Female: total length 4,0 m; mass 450 kg.
Identification pointers: Sleek; silvery-grey above, white below; numerous dark spots especially on throat, shoulders and sides; only two records from the coast of southern Africa.

Description: These are slender, agile seals, with silvery-grey fur on the upperparts and (usually) white fur on the underparts. There is a liberal scattering of darker grey to black spots, particularly on the sides, throat and shoulders. The head is long and slender and it has a large 'gape'.

Distribution: It is a species of the pack-ice of Antarctica but in winter and spring it moves towards the sub-Antarctic islands.

Behaviour and Reproduction: The Leopard Seal is a solitary species which spends summer and autumn around the pack-ice and which tends to disperse towards the small mid-oceanic islands of the sub-Antarctic in winter and spring. Little is known about its reproduction.

Food: The Leopard Seal takes a wide variety of food items – predominantly penguins but also fish, the young of other seals (and possibly adults), as well as squid and krill.

Crabeater Seals

Crabeater Seals on ice-floe

Leopard Seal

Leopard Seal

Spoor drawings

Reproduced by kind permission of the University of Pretoria from *The Mammals of the Southern African Subregion* by R.H.N. Smithers. In each case the forefoot spoor is shown above, the hindfoot spoor below.

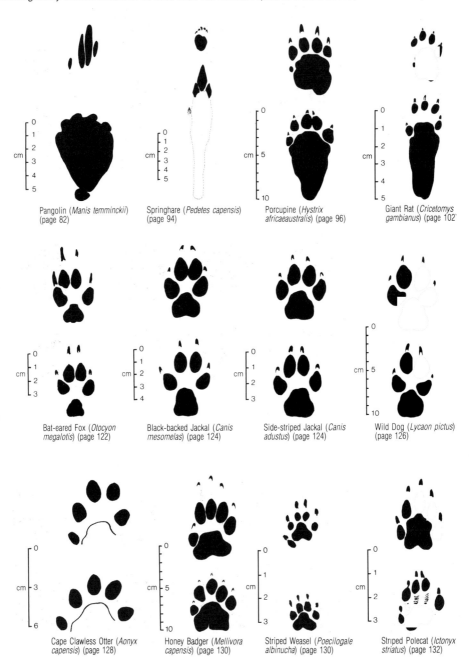

Pangolin (*Manis temminckii*) (page 82)

Springhare (*Pedetes capensis*) (page 94)

Porcupine (*Hystrix africaeaustralis*) (page 96)

Giant Rat (*Cricetomys gambianus*) (page 102)

Bat-eared Fox (*Otocyon megalotis*) (page 122)

Black-backed Jackal (*Canis mesomelas*) (page 124)

Side-striped Jackal (*Canis adustus*) (page 124)

Wild Dog (*Lycaon pictus*) (page 126)

Cape Clawless Otter (*Aonyx capensis*) (page 128)

Honey Badger (*Mellivora capensis*) (page 130)

Striped Weasel (*Poecilogale albinucha*) (page 130)

Striped Polecat (*Ictonyx striatus*) (page 132)

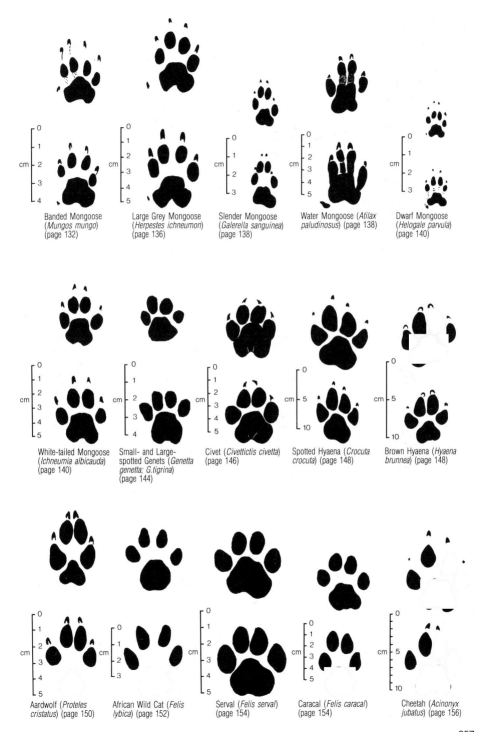

Banded Mongoose (*Mungos mungo*) (page 132)

Large Grey Mongoose (*Herpestes ichneumon*) (page 136)

Slender Mongoose (*Galerella sanguinea*) (page 138)

Water Mongoose (*Atilax paludinosus*) (page 138)

Dwarf Mongoose (*Helogale parvula*) (page 140)

White-tailed Mongoose (*Ichneumia albicauda*) (page 140)

Small- and Large-spotted Genets (*Genetta genetta; G.tigrina*) (page 144)

Civet (*Civettictis civetta*) (page 146)

Spotted Hyaena (*Crocuta crocuta*) (page 148)

Brown Hyaena (*Hyaena brunnea*) (page 148)

Aardwolf (*Proteles cristatus*) (page 150)

African Wild Cat (*Felis lybica*) (page 152)

Serval (*Felis serval*) (page 154)

Caracal (*Felis caracal*) (page 154)

Cheetah (*Acinonyx jubatus*) (page 156)

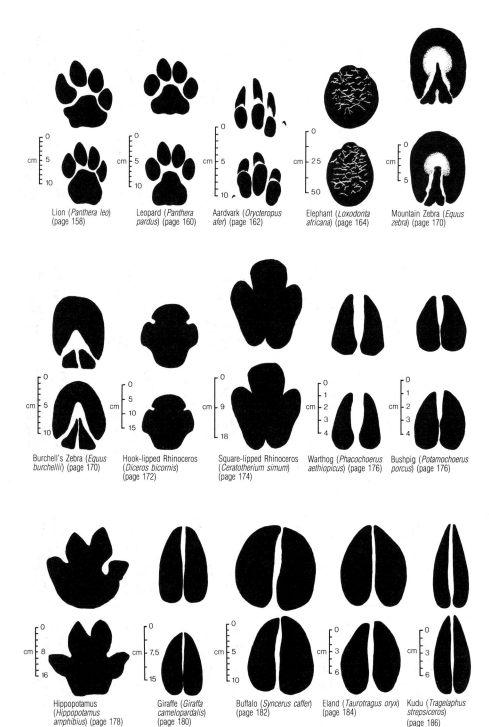

Lion (*Panthera leo*) (page 158)

Leopard (*Panthera pardus*) (page 160)

Aardvark (*Orycteropus afer*) (page 162)

Elephant (*Loxodonta africana*) (page 164)

Mountain Zebra (*Equus zebra*) (page 170)

Burchell's Zebra (*Equus burchellii*) (page 170)

Hook-lipped Rhinoceros (*Diceros bicornis*) (page 172)

Square-lipped Rhinoceros (*Ceratotherium simum*) (page 174)

Warthog (*Phacochoerus aethiopicus*) (page 176)

Bushpig (*Potamochoerus porcus*) (page 176)

Hippopotamus (*Hippopotamus amphibius*) (page 178)

Giraffe (*Giraffa camelopardalis*) (page 180)

Buffalo (*Syncerus caffer*) (page 182)

Eland (*Taurotragus oryx*) (page 184)

Kudu (*Tragelaphus strepsiceros*) (page 186)

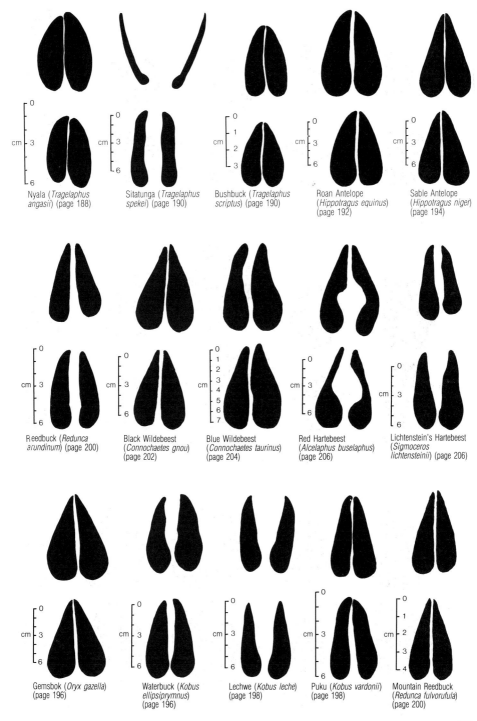

Nyala (*Tragelaphus angasii*) (page 188)

Sitatunga (*Tragelaphus spekei*) (page 190)

Bushbuck (*Tragelaphus scriptus*) (page 190)

Roan Antelope (*Hippotragus equinus*) (page 192)

Sable Antelope (*Hippotragus niger*) (page 194)

Reedbuck (*Redunca arundinum*) (page 200)

Black Wildebeest (*Connochaetes gnou*) (page 202)

Blue Wildebeest (*Connochaetes taurinus*) (page 204)

Red Hartebeest (*Alcelaphus buselaphus*) (page 206)

Lichtenstein's Hartebeest (*Sigmoceros lichtensteinii*) (page 206)

Gemsbok (*Oryx gazella*) (page 196)

Waterbuck (*Kobus ellipsiprymnus*) (page 196)

Lechwe (*Kobus leche*) (page 198)

Puku (*Kobus vardonii*) (page 198)

Mountain Reedbuck (*Redunca fulvorufula*) (page 200)

259

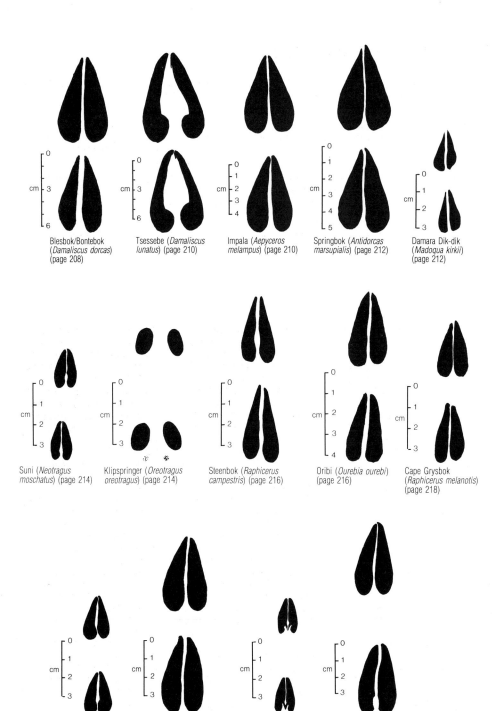

Blesbok/Bontebok (*Damaliscus dorcas*) (page 208)

Tsessebe (*Damaliscus lunatus*) (page 210)

Impala (*Aepyceros melampus*) (page 210)

Springbok (*Antidorcas marsupialis*) (page 212)

Damara Dik-dik (*Madoqua kirkii*) (page 212)

Suni (*Neotragus moschatus*) (page 214)

Klipspringer (*Oreotragus oreotragus*) (page 214)

Steenbok (*Raphicerus campestris*) (page 216)

Oribi (*Ourebia ourebi*) (page 216)

Cape Grysbok (*Raphicerus melanotis*) (page 218)

Sharpe's Grysbok (*Raphicerus sharpei*) (page 218)

Red Duiker (*Cephalophus natalensis*) (page 220)

Blue Duiker (*Philantomba monticola*) (page 220)

Common Duiker (*Sylvicapra grimmia*) (page 222)

Suggested further reading

Dorst, J. & Dandelot, P. 1983. *A field guide to the larger mammals of Africa.* Macmillan, Johannesburg.

Haltenorth, T. & Diller, H. 1984. *A field guide to the mammals of Africa including Madagascar.* Collins, London.

Smithers, R.H.N. & Wilson, V.J. 1979. Check list and atlas of Zimbabwe Rhodesia. *Museum memoir* 9:1 (Trustees of the National museums and Monuments of Zimbabwe, Harare).

Skinner, J.D. & Smithers, R.H.N. 1990. *The mammals of the Southern African subregion.* University of Pretoria, Pretoria.

Stuart, C. & Stuart, T. 1992. *Southern, Central and East African mammals: a photographic guide.* Struik Publishers, Cape Town.

Stuart, C. & Stuart, T. 1994. *A field guide to the tracks and signs of southern and East African wildlife.* Southern Book Publishers, Halfway House.

Stuart, C. & Stuart, T. 1995. *Africa: a natural history.* Southern Book Publishers, Halfway House.

Stuart, C. & Stuart, T. 1996. *Africa's vanishing wildlife.* Southern Book Publishers, Halfway House.

Glossary

Aquatic. Living in or near water.

Arboreal. Adapted for life in trees.

Baleen. Comb-like structures in the mouths of baleen whales, used for filtering plankton from the water.

Cheek-teeth. Molar and premolar teeth lying behind the canines or incisors.

Crepuscular. Active during the twilight hours of dawn and dusk.

Diurnal. Active during the daylight hours.

Drey. A domed nest of leaves and twigs constructed by some species of tree squirrels.

Endemic. Native to a particular country, region or restricted area.

Exotic. Not native to a country or region but introduced from other countries or areas. Also 'alien'.

Foraging. Searching for or seeking out food.

Fossorial. Adapted for burrowing underground and for life in burrows.

Gestation period. The period between conception and birth in which offspring are carried in the uterus.

Gregarious. Living together in groups, herds or colonies.

Guano. Accumulations of droppings, usually used of bird and bat colonies.

Herbivore. Any organism that feeds principally on plants. Large mammalian herbivores may be classed as 'grazers' (subsisting largely on grasses) or 'browsers' (subsisting largely on woody or herbaceous plants).

Home range. The area covered by an animal in the course of its day-to-day activities.

Incisors. Sharp-edged front teeth, usually in both the upper and lower jaws.

Insectivore. A mammal that subsists largely on insects.

Interfemoral membrane. The thin membrane situated between the hindlegs of bats.

Moult. The process in which old hair is shed to make way for new hair.

Nuchal patch. A contrasting patch of hair on the nape (between and behind the ears).

Omnivore. An animal which feeds on both plant and animal food.

Pelage. Hair covering or coat.

Plankton. Mainly microscopic organisms, both plant and animal, that drift or float in the surface layers of the sea or fresh water.

Predator. An animal that preys on other animals for its food.

Riparian. In close association with rivers and river-bank habitats.

Scrotum. The pouch that contains the testes in most mammals.

Species. A group of interbreeding individuals of common ancestry, reproductively isolated from all other groups.

Subterranean. Living underground.

Terrestrial. Living on land.

Territory. A restricted area inhabited by an animal, usually for breeding purposes, and actively defended against other individuals of the same species.

Tragus. A small cartilaginous process situated in the external ear opening of most species of bat.

Vibrissae (sing. 'vibrissa'). Prominent coarse hairs or whiskers, usually on the face.

Index to common names

Index to scientific names

268

Index to Afrikaans common names